HOPE FOR ZIMBABWE ORPHANS

A BOOK OF INSPIRING STORIES

THE JOURNEY OF RALPH & ROBERTA PIPPITT

BY ROBERTA PIPPITT

Trilogy Christian Publishers

A Wholly Owned Subsidiary of Trinity Broadcasting Network

2442 Michelle Drive

Tustin, CA 92780

Copyright © 2024 by Roberta Pippitt

Scripture quotations marked ESV are taken from the ESV® Bible (The Holy Bible, English Standard Version®), copyright © 2001 by Crossway Bibles, a publishing ministry of Good News Publishers. Used by permission. All rights reserved. Scripture quotations marked (RSV) are taken from the Revised Standard Version of the Bible, copyright © 1946,1952, and 1971 National Council of the Churches of Christ in the United States of America. Used by permission. All rights reserved worldwide.

All rights reserved, including the right to reproduce this book or portions thereof in any form whatsoever.

For information, address Trilogy Christian Publishing

Rights Department, 2442 Michelle Drive, Tustin, Ca 92780.

Trilogy Christian Publishing/TBN and colophon are trademarks of Trinity Broadcasting Network.

For information about special discounts for bulk purchases, please contact Trilogy Christian Publishing.

Cover design by:

The cover design was inspired by a sketch provided by an African child.

Trilogy Disclaimer: The views and content expressed in this book are those of the author and may not necessarily reflect the views and doctrine of Trilogy Christian Publishing or the Trinity Broadcasting Network.

10 9 8 7 6 5 4 3 2 1

Library of Congress Cataloging-in-Publication Data is available.

ISBN 979-8-89333-541-5

ISBN 979-8-89333-542-2 (ebook)

ENDORSEMENTS

What do you think about collecting old schoolbooks to send to Zimbabwe?

The question came from Ralph and Roberta Pippitt, a retired couple who recently returned from a trip to South Africa. During their travels, a chance conversation led them to consider the needs of a school in Zimbabwe. It planted a seed of possibility. Though they could not initially explain it, Ralph and Roberta sensed an unmistakable "yes" from within. Now, they wanted to know if their church would join them.

Having recently arrived as their pastor, the first thing I remember thinking was, "I'm sure glad there are people here like Ralph and Roberta!" I said, "Sure, let's do it!" The second thing I remember thinking was, "I need to find Zimbabwe on the map!" So it began. Small.

Yet, like the proverbial mustard seed, something that started small eventually grew into something extraordinary. A few boxes of books soon transformed into containers filled with desks. School supplies expanded into school buildings. Concern for education blossomed into initiatives for food, health, orphans, bridges, and economic sustainability. One congregation's project grew into partnerships with many congregations, organizations, and groups.

This book is about how a seed of possibility took hold in one couple and what happened when they said, "Yes." Like a mustard seed (Mark 4:30–32), it started small, but it didn't stay that way! It is an amazing story and I am grateful to be one of the many who witnessed and became part of it. Their "yes" made ours possible, and we are all better because of it!

> *And he said, "With what can we compare the kingdom of God, or what parable shall we use for it? It is like a grain of mustard seed, which, when sown on the ground, is the smallest of all the seeds on earth, yet when it is sown it grows up and becomes larger than all the*

garden plants and puts out large branches, so that the birds of the air can make nests in its shade."

Mark 4:30–32 (ESV)

Russ Kane,
Retired Pastor—New Hope Presbyterian Church

"Therefore, my beloved brothers, be steadfast, immovable, always abounding in the work of the Lord, knowing that in the Lord your labor is not in vain" (1 Corinthians 15:58, ESV).

This book stands as a testament to the extraordinary dedication, compassion, and selflessness of my dear friend, Roberta Pippitt, and her late husband, Ralph. Guided by their faith and a deep sense of purpose, they embarked on a remarkable journey during their retirement years.

Roberta's unwavering commitment to improving and saving the lives of children in Zimbabwe is profoundly inspiring. Through her steadfast belief in God's call to serve others in need, she has become a beacon of hope in a world often overshadowed by hardship and adversity.

Meeting Ralph and Roberta—and the years of work and friendship that followed—continues to be one of the greatest blessings of my life. As a new grandma, I now more fully understand the sacrifices that Ralph, Roberta, and their family made to care for these dear children on the other side of the world.

During my first visit to Zimbabwe in 2010, I stayed with Ralph and Roberta in their very humble abode, then situated on school property. I was deeply touched to witness how basic and simple their existence was when they visited for long stretches of time in rural Zimbabwe, and how they were fully immersed in their single focus: helping children in a community in need. The Pippitts accomplished so much with so little, always putting their own needs last. Every day, seeing firsthand how the children adored the Pippitts and then debriefing each night in the dim light of their small kitchen table, we were always amazed at where and how God showed up in the day. These moments are forever imprinted on my heart.

Despite Ralph's passing a number of years ago, Roberta, with unwavering determination and resilience, continued to carry on in his footsteps, undeterred by her grief, with God at her side every step of the way.

Roberta's decision to immerse herself fully in this work, supporting orphans and vulnerable children in rural Zimbabwe amidst the challenges of poverty and the devastating effects of HIV/AIDS, is a true testament to her compassionate heart and unwavering faith. Through her provision of essential necessities such as food, clothing, education, and medical care, she has not only transformed the lives of countless children but has also sown the seeds of hope and opportunity for a brighter future.

This book is dedicated to Roberta, with deepest gratitude and admiration, for her extraordinary dedication to following God's call and making a profound difference in the lives of others. Her legacy of love, faith, strength, and resilience will continue to inspire us all and those who will come after. With heartfelt appreciation.

Deanna Heyn,
Moderator—Zimbabwe Mission Partnership

Roberta and I met at our church when she gave an update about her ministry to orphans in Zimbabwe—the country that used to be called Rhodesia—a place I had known since I wrote letters to my boyfriend there, who was a foreign exchange student in high school. A God wink.

I wrote a book about my life stories called "From Minnesota with Manna: God's Provision and Protection in My Life." (A–Z stories of the persons, places, and things most impacting my life). The "Z" chapter was in Zimbabwe, so I told Roberta I would also help her write "her story," so we started meeting weekly for her to tell me her stories and write them down. What a privilege it has been. Roberta and her husband dedicated all their retirement years to serving the Lord in Zimbabwe—"not on their bucket list"—but certainly God's plan for them. Roberta was married the year I was born, yet God connected our lives in a special way. She is now over ninety years old, and I hope this book—the Ralph & Roberta legacy—will inspire many to listen to the Lord and offer their time, talents, and treasures in such a selfless way in their lives.

Kathy Kramer,
Published author
And, more importantly, a mom who has adopted
children from foster care

It is with great honor and privilege that I lift up this book written by Roberta Pippitt, our dear friend and fellow Christian, to worship together with her and those who look up to her as the model to carry out God's command, "You shall love your neighbor as yourself" (Mark 12:31, ESV).

This ministry was started by Roberta and Ralph Pippitt and is described in this book. It will spread the adventure and results of obeying the call of God that this couple heard and then carried out over several decades. The call involved traveling to a remote rural area of Zimbabwe. Initially, the call was to do some building renovations at a rural school. After much prayer and research, Ralph, who was an engineer's engineer, and his wife Roberta decided to go and see for themselves what needed to be done.

The enormity of the situation demanded their time, their treasures, and their love for both the children and the adults of the community. The need for safe drinking water was a top priority.

My wife and I met Roberta and Ralph at church. We were most pleased to be asked to join the board of the fund-raising organization they designed and named Renewed Hope Charitable Foundation. They would travel back to Zimbabwe yearly and spend four to six months there. Roberta's blogs kept the church informed on what was happening.

Ralph, the engineer, wrote back with a very detailed listing of every piece of the pump mechanics that needed to be repaired or replaced and the cost of each one. So, we knew exactly what was needed and quickly sent the desired amount. When they returned, Ralph said, "I have something to show you," and presented a slide presentation of the repair and final results.

He related a story of an elderly widow who had to walk miles to fetch water from an unsafe source. When the well was repaired and the flushing complete, this woman, who had walked miles for water, was wide-eyed when the water came out clean and clear.

The orphanage today has buildings, running water, vehicles, and student uniforms made by local women trained by Roberta. They have a trained nurse as well as much, much more that would not have been available without this brave couple. We lost Ralph a few years ago, but Roberta still flies the flag of love and concern for the orphanage. She has a board of admirers that help her to keep the call from God to love our neighbor. We know now who our neighbor is through their adventure.

Roy Koerner,
Retired Executive—Texaco Inc.

TABLE OF CONTENTS

Endorsements.. 3

About Zimbabwe (Formerly Rhodesia)............................. 13

Not on My Bucket List.. 15

HIV, AIDS 19

Why Rural Zimbabwe... 23

Initial Visit 25

Writing in the Sand: Rural School in Zimbabwe 29

Safe Water to Drink 31

Random Experiences... 37

Mr. Bondeponde's Story 39

Welcome Back... 45

Teacher Housing 47

Madamombe Clinic 51

School Gardens 57

Brick Molding... 61

Repairs 65

Sweaters for Children 67

Sewing Generates Income.. 69

Girls Surviving with No Parents 81

Sick Child 85

Parents Died.. 87

A Bridge Is Needed... 89

Ralph—the Loved One 93

Beginning of Orphan Care 97

Pippitt House.. 105

Ralph's Helpers... 107

Dedication Celebration 109

Bible Study.. 113

Ralph's Accident 117

Treating for Ringworm 121

Boys without Parents.. 123

Madanha Family Story 127

Bilharzia, a Parasite... 131

Oswald: A Teen Story about AIDS 135

Knitting Co-op 141

Preschool & Clinic Building... 145

Expanding Support for Orphans in Ward 1 147

Feeding Children... 149

Loading Sea Containers... 151

Shipments 157

Blanket Distribution 165

Stories of Appreciation 167

Wheelchair for a Crippled Child 171

God's Children 173

Needing to Be in School 175

First Aid 177

Ashley—a Granddaughter's Impressions 179

Leg Wound Heals: "Miracle Workers" 185

Visit to Orphans 187

Inyagui Primary School 189

Guzha Primary School 193

Electricity (2006) 195

Truck for HCOC 199

Four Mothers with Infants 201

Roof Damage 203

Orphan Caregivers Are Trained 205

Nyamashato Secondary School 207

Orphan Stories 211

God's Protection 219

Signs of Desperation 221

Tirivanhu—Stone Sculptor 225

Injured Hand 227

Orphan Care Program Relocates 229

Moringa 233

Albert and Beauty Join the Team 239

Rethatching Rondavels 241

Training Secondary Girls to Sew.................................... 245

Community Well Repair 247

Amanda—a Granddaughter's Story 251

Challenges.. 255

A Son's Visit 259

Pastor Eric's Visit... 261

Rotary Visits Water Projects 265

Poultry 267

U.S. Visitors... 271

Organizing the Community... 275

Girls with a Dream... 279

Street Children... 281

Orphans Living Alone 283

Religious Training for the Children 287

New Clinic... 291

Epilogue.. 293

Afterword.. 297

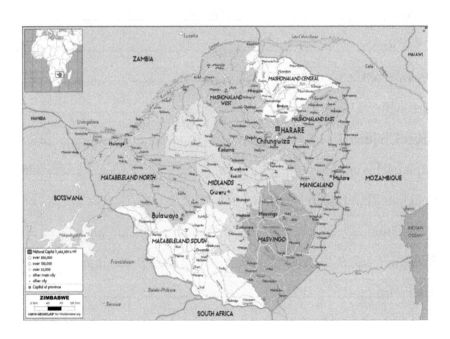

ABOUT ZIMBABWE (FORMERLY RHODESIA)

And this gospel of the kingdom will be proclaimed throughout the whole world as a testimony to all nations, and then the end will come.

Matthew 24:14 (ESV)

According to Wikipedia, Cecil John Rhodes (5 July 1853—26 March 1902) was a British mining magnate and politician in southern Africa who served as prime minister of the Cape Colony from 1890 to 1896. He and his British South Africa Company founded the southern African territory of Rhodesia (now Zimbabwe and Zambia), which the company named after him in 1895.

Harare is the capital of Zimbabwe. The city was named Salisbury, Rhodesia, during the time of British control. In 1980, an apartheid took place, and the indigenous people took over the white British rule. Robert Mugabe served as prime minister from 1980 to 1987. He then became president and continued to rule until 2017, when he passed away. The once beautiful country and city went into decline starting in the 1980s due to political corruption and the stealing of resources. It is now 2024, and the country has continued to decline, especially so since the white farms were taken over in 1999 and 2000.

In April 2003 the cost of diesel doubled in price and petrol tripled overnight. Immediately, bus fares went up. It was reported that it cost 3,000 Zimbabwe dollars to go from Nyamashato to Harare one way. In addition, there is a charge for each bag or bucket of produce the local people take with them to sell at the open market in Harare, the capital city. It was simply a lost cause. The decline has continued since 2003.

NOT ON MY BUCKET LIST

And then he told them, "Go into all the world and proclaim the
gospel to the whole creation."

Mark 16:15 (ESV)

Retirement. For Ralph and me, this meant leaving Texas, building
a new home in Colorado, and then traveling around the world to enjoy
adventures together. But God. The dream home on five acres in Parker,
Colorado, with a view of Pikes Peak, was completed in the summer of
1993. So, the goal was to take one major trip a year. Nineteen ninety-four
found us traveling through England and Scotland.

Early in 1995, we traveled to Ecuador and the Galapagos Islands off
the coast of South America for a total of four weeks. This was the trip
of a lifetime! There was so much to do and nature to see. Swimming
and snorkeling with fish that you only see in aquariums and interacting
with huge turtles was a new experience. This was an extension of our
adventurous spirit. We camped and backpacked with our boys in Idaho
during the time the boys were growing up. However, when we retired,
I thought I had graduated from camping. Little did I know what God
had planned for our retirement.

As members of an International Travel Club, we were asked to join a
planned trip to South Africa late in 1995. This adventure lasted about a
month—from Cape Town to Pretoria, staying with club members along
the way. A ten-day bus trip to Durban, visiting various game reserves
along the way, was an exciting experience.

A member of the group, named Pat, joined us when the group landed in Cape Town. Pat had a home near Evergreen, Colorado, and was
a member of the same travel group that Ralph and I were members of.
She spent most of the year living in Cape Town, South Africa, where she

had founded a retreat for hurting pastors. She told Ralph and me about a school in rural Zimbabwe that she had recently visited. It was in a serious state of disrepair. The school was in danger of being condemned, and more than 600 children would have no place to attend school. She talked to both of us about the skills we each had that would be so useful to that school. She described the area like the American Indian Reservations in the U.S. In the late 1800s, native people in Zimbabwe had been forced from the area white farmers wanted and were sent to a lesser quality environment. Pat knew Ralph was a retired engineer and had many skills that would be so useful to the school. She talked about all the ways Ralph could help in Zimbabwe. This planted some seeds in our minds. As we traveled home, we discussed the possibility of going and seeing the place for ourselves. Little did Ralph and I know that our lives were about to make a drastic change.

When we returned home from that trip, Christmas decorations and music greeted us at the airport. We were quickly caught up in the festivities of the season. After the holidays, we began talking about our trip and what we had learned. We debated the issue of whether to go to Zimbabwe to see the situation for ourselves. At that time, we barely knew where Zimbabwe was located. We had no idea where we would live.

The area we had been told about was very poor, and there were few, if any, jobs available. Pat explained that the location was very rural and there was no accommodation anywhere around. It quickly became apparent that we would have to be prepared to camp. Camping was not foreign to us as we had camped with our boys as they grew up. I remember telling Ralph, as we were going through our equipment, that I thought this stage of my life was history. He just laughed at me.

Fundraising for the work ahead was a concern. Ralph and I were reluctant to ask people for money to enable us to drill a well in Zimbabwe, etc. A few individuals had the idea we were just going on a vacation. One morning in early February, just one month before our planned departure, we received a quote for drilling a well. It was more money than we had raised to that point. Our airfare was more money than we had been able to raise for projects once we were at our destination. We felt defeated. We didn't know what to do. I remember saying, "God, it is in Your hands. We are willing to go and do the work, but You must provide the funds.

We just aren't fundraisers." That afternoon, a check appeared in the mail for $500. It was from friends of my parents, who were deceased. The following afternoon another $500 came in the mail from other friends of my parents. Additional checks came in the mail for the next several days as well. We were puzzled. How did these people know about our planned trip and our goals? God, I am certain, had provided the additional money that was needed to drill the well.

When our church congregation learned of our plans, some individuals from the church gave us financial support. We left on our trip with not a lot of money, but we had *enough*. A deep well was drilled, and a hand pump was installed. Materials for four toilet structures were purchased. The remaining funds facilitated the purchase of materials to re-roof a classroom building. The roof had blown off in a windstorm just prior to our arrival. The roof had not been budgeted, but God provided.

When we arrived in Zimbabwe in March of 1997, we discovered how far this money could go given the exchange rate with the U.S. dollar. One U.S. dollar would buy five or six Zimbabwe dollars. This increased our available funds to over 60,000 Zimbabwe dollars! This was a lot of money at that time. We paid all our own expenses and continued to do that for all the years we worked in Zimbabwe. The donated funds were invested in the local projects.

We knew that when we arrived in Harare, the capital of Zimbabwe, we would be on our own and would have to find accommodations for the night. It was a pleasant surprise to see Pat when we cleared customs. She had a driver and a van to pick us up with all our luggage. What a relief! It didn't take long to discover the van had some issues. At the first stop light, the van stopped running. Our driver struggled to get it restarted. Was our transportation a blessing or a sign of things to come? The van quit running at every stop light. Finally, we arrived at the home of the president of CCOSA College (Christian College of Southern Africa). We were treated to a lovely lunch served in their beautiful garden.

After lunch, the driver took us to a house in the city that was owned by the college as a dormitory for girls who attended the college from rural areas. At that time, there were no girls staying in the house. We had the house to ourselves. Sleep at last! God had planned for our temporary housing. Pat stayed at the house as well. It gave us an opportunity to make some tentative plans. She indicated she needed to find mosquito netting to sleep under. We had our pop-up tent, and it would give us needed protection. So shopping was on our agenda for the following day.

Harare was a large city of about two million people. It was important that we register our presence in the country at the U.S. Embassy in the event of any political uprising. This took longer to accomplish than we had planned. It was only the beginning of everything taking longer than one planned for. It was also necessary to pick up food supplies before heading to the rural area. We knew there would be no groceries available where we were going. We had to stock up with at least a week's supply. All the food that was purchased needed to be canned or dried because there would be no refrigeration in the rural area. There was no electricity and so no refrigeration and no ice, no running water, no telephones and certainly no cell phones, and no internet. The situation reminded me of growing up on a farm in Illinois in the 1930s.

We needed to locate some white gas for the one-burner backpack stove that was in our luggage. If there was no white gas, it would be necessary to resort to cooking over a wood campfire. Campfires were fun when we had two young boys, but I preferred not to have to resort to such at this point. We soon learned the local people cooked over an open fire. We decided we might have to resort to doing that as well!

Ralph and I knew we would have challenges and that we would have to adapt to situations that arose. We tried to be *flexible* and take things in stride. If we had not, we never would have continued this "missionary journey." We thought this was a "one-time trip—maybe two years, and then someone else would have to pick up the ball from us." As I write this, it has turned into twenty-five years. I no longer have the energy required to travel and work in Zimbabwe. Leadership has been turned over to others who have a real interest in the work we started.

Many of our friends thought we were crazy. I knew that if I was with Ralph, things would work out. Ralph believed strongly that God would provide, and He did. His interventions were not always what was expected, but things always worked out.

HIV, AIDS

According to the Centers for Disease Control (CDC), the definition of HIV (human immunodeficiency virus) is a virus that attacks the body's immune system. If HIV is not treated, it can lead to AIDS (acquired immunodeficiency syndrome), which was considered a death sentence when first discovered in 1981. Within the United States, urgent research began to find a treatment for this disease. However, once a treatment was found, it did not make it to the rural areas of Africa for many years. The transmission of AIDS was primarily attributed to sexual transmission, especially among the gay population and prostitution. It was thought of almost as leprosy, and if one got the disease, this "label" was often hidden. This "killer disease" was a mystery but also something many were afraid of...

When I first traveled to sub-Saharan Africa (Zimbabwe) in 1997 with my husband, Ralph, our travel immunizations and medications were more focused on things like malaria, smallpox, and typhoid. There was no immunization for AIDS, and we were careful when we encountered anyone who needed medical attention. We carried rubber gloves in a zip lock bag in the glove box of our vehicle and always on our person as we went about our work. It was necessary to protect ourselves in case we needed to give aid to anyone who was ill or injured and might need assistance. Rubber gloves would protect from contaminated body fluids entering any open break in the skin we might have. We always assumed a person was HIV positive until we knew otherwise.

Early in our time in Zimbabwe, we learned that rural men often traveled to the big city (Harare) looking for work. If they became sexually infected by this strange disease, they would unknowingly (at that time) carry it home to their wives in the rural area whenever they would return from the city for a visit. Frequently, the wife would become infected by the husband, and sometimes she would become pregnant as well. When the mother delivered, the baby would become infected as it passed through the birth canal. The mother frequently became ill, sometimes before she delivered the baby, but usually, she would become ill later and would eventually die. No one at that time knew why she died, and if they did know, it was never verbalized. I have seen women die a day or so after childbirth, and I also knew of women who lived a length of time before passing away.

When the husband became ill and eventually died, nobody knew about the cause of death. It was never discussed nor questioned, especially in our presence. Little or no information was available to the rural population. The length of time that these individuals lived after becoming infected depended largely on the general health of the person. The healthier they were, the longer they perhaps would live. But they would die at some point.

A child infected at birth had a limited life expectancy. The length of time the child lived depended largely on the nutrition available to the child. These children, however, never seemed to ever live beyond five years of age. Finally, the child would become ill and eventually die. No one ever knew what was wrong with the child or why the child died. In July of 2001, I recall that the population growth rate for the country fell to zero due to the high death rate attributed to AIDS.

The death of pre-school children was always so very sad. These children obviously had not been infected during childbirth because they had lived beyond the age of five years. The only conclusion was that the child was being sexually abused. Situations like this really were difficult to cope with. We could only imagine what those children had gone through. Children who had been abused were sometimes obvious. They had a look that seemed spaced out. The experience had to be traumatizing for such children.

After several years, more women began going to the government clinic to deliver their babies rather than delivering at home. By that time, the clinics had medication to give the pregnant woman during labor. This medication prevented the infant from contracting the disease when passing through the birth canal. The mother often died later, but the infants lived a normal life if they had access to food as they grew. The mission received many requests for formula and bottles after the death of the mother of a newborn. These items were not always readily available in Harare. Bottles, nipples, and formula were items added to our shipments. Our bookkeeper kept an inventory of the supplies on hand and contacted us when more were needed.

When we became aware of the sick children in school, it was heartbreaking to realize that some of the children probably had AIDS. Usually, a child that is born with AIDS does not live beyond about five years of age, as was previously mentioned. The one thing we did know was that there were a lot of funerals! When people died, all work stopped, and everyone attended the funeral. There were times when several funerals were held in one day in the rural community where we served poor families and orphans. There was no embalming done, so funerals had to be held within twenty-four hours of a death. We could hear the "wailing" in the night when people died. It was very sad but also a frustrating situation, especially for Ralph, because work was only done one or two days a week at best. People were dying like flies—predominantly men who were the breadwinners. This went on for several years.

The number of deaths began to decline when people became educated about the disease and had access to medicines. They called it "ARV" (antiretroviral) medicine to help prevent the development of the virus in the body. As such, the number of parents dying decreased, so the number of orphans declined. At the height of our ministry, we served over 1200 orphans. By 2022, the number had dropped to just under 700 children who needed assistance because of the death of one or both parents. This number has varied little since then. The need to serve orphans will never go away. The government's stability is not good, so money for drugs has diminished. Many of the drugs in the HCOC Clinic are provided by UNICEF. However, UNICEF does not supply medication for AIDS. The AIDS medication continues to be supplied by the government. Deaths often occur because of a lack of food and nutrition in a country with drought and government mismanagement.

I have previously touched on the fact that, at one point, Zimbabwe was a wealthy country. The decline came about when the white farmers were driven off their farms or moved out of the country. The country has not been able to recover since that point in time. It has continued to decline.

WHY RURAL ZIMBABWE

In all your ways acknowledge him, and he will make straight your paths.

Proverbs 3:6 (ESV)

Ralph and I had never considered doing mission work. We certainly were not Bible scholars. Our plan for retirement was to build our retirement home in Colorado and travel the world. In 1995, we completed our retirement home and had done some traveling. An opportunity arose for us to make a trip to South Africa with friends from Friendship Force International. Ralph and I thought this might be our only opportunity to ever visit Africa. Little did we know that this trip would change our lives in a significant way.

As previously stated, a Colorado woman who lived most of the year in South Africa joined the group when we landed in Cape Town. Ralph and I knew who Pat was but did not have much contact with her. Some of the time in Africa, the group traveled by bus from different points of interest. During our time traveling on the bus, Pat would seek out Ralph and me and engage us in conversation. She talked to us about a trip she had taken recently to Zimbabwe with an acquaintance. Pat explained that during her time in Zimbabwe, she and the woman she was traveling with chose to go to the rural area to visit an uncle. They traveled by way of the big green bus. While there, Pat explained that she saw what appeared to be a school way in the distance. So, she and Heather, the woman she was traveling with, walked a long distance to visit the school.

Pat described to us the deplorable condition of the school. She told of livestock roaming in the classrooms because there were no doors in the rooms. Or if there were doors, they had no way of being secured. Pat explained that she felt called to do something to make a difference.

However, she didn't know where or how to begin. Pat had learned that the school was going to be condemned because it was unsafe for children to be in some of the buildings.

Pat pointed out that Ralph had many skills that could be so helpful at the rural school she had visited. I have no idea how she had knowledge of Ralph's skills. She kept saying she felt called to do something, but she didn't have the skills that she knew would be needed to put the school in any kind of condition for children. Little did Ralph and I know that our lives were about to make a drastic change.

We talked some about what we had learned about a school in rural Zimbabwe on the very long flight back to the U.S. from Africa. Christmas was in the air when we arrived back in the U.S. However, in the new year, the school in Zimbabwe would come up again and again in our conversations. Finally, in August of 1996 we decided to make plans to go to Zimbabwe and see for ourselves what could be done for the children in the rural area that needed a school. We set March 1997 as our departure date. This was to be a fact-finding trip. Little did we know how many trips we would make to Africa in the coming years.

We knew in the beginning that the school needed a well. Pat had told us that there was no water source near the school. We also knew that the staff had no sanitary facilities near staff housing. Those projects would be our initial goals.

It was sometime later that we learned that the headmaster had walked up to the school in August 1996 to begin his new assignment at the school. Was this a coincidence or God working? He told Ralph and me he didn't know where to begin to put things right. He didn't know how he could ask his family to live in such deplorable conditions. Then, one day, he received a letter from us telling of our plans to come to Zimbabwe in March. He said he started making a list of urgent renovations that were most needed. Priority one was a well for safe drinking water.

INITIAL VISIT

It is the Lord who goes before you. He will be with you; he will not leave you or forsake you. Do not fear or be dismayed.

Deuteronomy 31:8 (ESV)

We were delivered to the school, Nyamashato Primary, by the same vehicle that had picked us up at the airport. The sliding door was held closed by a piece of barbed wire. It was a long, slow trip. Dust from the rough roads drifted up through the holes in the floorboards of the van. We were dust-covered by the time we arrived.

Children were on the playground and came running when they saw the vehicle. There were no cars or trucks in the area at that time. Many of the children had probably never seen a vehicle except the big green bus that traveled the road between their community and Murewa a couple of times a day.

When we stepped out of the van, the children quickly backed away. I wasn't sure if it was because they had never seen a white person or if it was because we were covered in dust.

A teacher stepped forward and asked me how we had found out about them from so far away and how we had found the school way out here. The teachers thought no one knew they existed. My reply was that God had sent us. She did not say anything after that.

Ralph and I had brought a backpack tent, sleeping bags, and a one-burner backpack stove. Pat had only a mosquito netting and a sleeping bag. Ralph had brought a supply of rope that he hooked over a rafter to tie the mosquito netting to for Pat. Initially, we were taken to a teacher's house that had a vacant room on the backside. It was so small that Ralph was doubtful we could even set up our pop-up tent in the small space. If we could set up our tent, there would be no room to move about. There was absolutely no space for Pat and no place to hang her mosquito netting. The tent was necessary to protect us from insects and varmints. Plans changed, and we were allowed to stay in an empty classroom with a roof that leaked when it rained. The windowpanes were mostly missing, allowing bats to pay a visit at night. Thank goodness for the tent and Pat's mosquito netting. After the fact, I learned that Mrs. Bondeponde had moved her class out of the room so we could have a place to stay. She moved her class to a building that was in extremely poor condition.

Mr. and Mrs. Bondeponde were very helpful but skeptical of us, from Colorado. Their experience with white people had not always been good. Could they trust these white people? Could these people really make a difference in their world with so many needs. The "community talk" (gossip) was suspicious of these white Americans. They must want something.

Men soon arrived to continue working on the pit toilets that were being built. The well and the toilets were the two projects that we were prepared to fund when we arrived. Once Mr. Bondeponde learned of our plans, he organized the community to make and fire the brick for the toilet buildings, men to dig the pits for the toilets, and others to haul sand and pebbles for the concrete that would have to be mixed and poured. We would supply the cement and the roofing material when we arrived.

Our first morning at the school was full of new experiences. The sunrise was the most beautiful experience we had ever seen. I have seen many sunrises in my life, but nothing like that African sunrise. We were up before dawn and witnessed women with a bucket on their heads going to a well for the day's supply of water. Some of the women had to walk long distances. Soon after this sight, masses of children began to appear from every direction out of the hills. We learned that some of these children walked as much as five to eight kilometers (three to five miles) to get to school. No big yellow school buses here. In most of these cases, there are no roads for the buses to travel to the homes.

We were surprised to see the well we planned to drill already being drilled the day we arrived at the school. School had been dismissed so the children could observe the work taking place. This was an experience they might never see again. Some of the teachers joined the children who were watching the drilling process.

Shortly before our arrival, a windstorm had passed through the area. It had severely damaged one of the classroom buildings. Most of the roof had blown off. I observed children sitting in class with the sun beating down on them. I had no idea how they could concentrate.

When the planned projects were complete and all the bills paid, there was some extra money remaining. Ralph and Mr. Bondeponde worked together to see if it would be enough to replace the roof for a five-classroom building. The result was that the money would buy the necessary materials, but there would be no money for labor. Mr. B was certain that if Ralph could provide the materials, he would provide the labor to get the roof put on. We later learned that Mr. Bondeponde used the men who could not pay school fees for their own children to provide the labor in exchange for the unpaid fees. The roof was completed after we returned to the U.S. Ralph and Mr. B. formed a good team.

The children gathered at the assembly area at the beginning of the day. There were announcements and a time of prayer before the children were dismissed to go to their classrooms. I noted how quiet and well-behaved the children were. I learned as the weeks went by that it wasn't usually like that. They had been intimidated by those white people. They warmed up to us in a short time and became accustomed to seeing us around.

Initial Visit

27

WRITING IN THE SAND:
RURAL SCHOOL IN ZIMBABWE

Train up a child in the way he should go; even when he is old he will not depart from it.

Proverbs 22:6 (ESV)

Do you remember learning to write in elementary school on paper with bold and thin lines? This is a luxury in Africa. One of our earliest memories was seeing children writing in the sand. This sight was totally unexpected. We soon learned that there were no pencils or paper available for children to practice with. They practiced in the sand using a small stick or just their finger, and when the teacher felt they were ready, they went into the classroom and wrote their letters or numbers on paper, a coveted school supply.

When we entered the classrooms, we found no furniture. Some classrooms had no door or only a piece of a door hanging from broken hinges. The floor was in poor condition. Huge chunks of concrete had broken out. We later learned that the floors were not concrete but cow dung that had been soaked in water, mixed, and then poured out on the floor, smoothed out, and allowed to dry. Windowpanes were missing in most of the windows. When it rained, water often blew in the windows.

There were no student desks or tables in most of the rooms. There were no teacher desks or chairs anywhere. Occasionally, we found one table in a classroom in questionable condition.

Often, there were few or no benches for the children to sit on. If there was a bench, usually the legs were broken off, and the seat was held up by a stack of bricks.

Most children sat on the floor. Chalkboards were painted on the wall in the front of the room, and the condition of the chalkboard varied from room to room. There was no chalk available in most of the classrooms. The teachers kept it in their possession until it was needed. There wasn't a single classroom that had a roof in good condition. They all leaked to some degree when it rained.

There was no sign of a textbook, dictionary, or notebook anywhere. They didn't exist. Even pencils were few and far between. The teachers kept the pencils in her possession until needed, and then they were passed out to the class. There were no pencil sharpeners. There were no brightly colored maps or pictures on the walls. How could children learn in such circumstances? Where to begin to put things right was the question. Writing in the sand might be the least of these children's challenges.

I rarely saw a child with a pair of shoes on their feet; most were bare-footed. If a child wore a pair of shoes, they might not match, and they rarely had shoelaces. Needs were everywhere. Ralph and I could see the needs, but the question was where to begin. It was overwhelming.

Despite the needs everywhere one looked, the children, for the most part, seemed happy. I am certain they had no idea how poor their lives were. Our dilemma was where to begin to put things right.

Ralph began to wonder what happened to school furnishings in the U.S. when they began to show significant wear. Where did these items go when the classrooms were refurbished? Ralph began to make plans to visit local schools when we returned to the U.S. He also wondered what it would cost to ship discarded furnishings to Zimbabwe.

SAFE WATER TO DRINK

And whoever gives one of these little ones even a cup of cold water because he is a disciple, truly, I say to you, he will by no means lose his reward.

Matthew 10:42 (ESV)

Water is the key. We knew one of the greatest needs of Nyamashato Primary School was water. The school had no access to water. We later learned that this was not just a Nyamashato problem. It was a problem for all rural schools in all of Ward 1 where we went to work. We quickly learned that this is true throughout Zimbabwe. Children carried to school various plastic bottles or containers of water. The water was usually cloudy. I often wondered if the water came from the river or if the container was dirty. Why the children were not all sick puzzled me.

While we were still planning our trip, Ralph, with the help of the internet, contacted a well driller in Zimbabwe. They talked a couple of times on the phone. Ralph explained what was needed. A plan was made, and Ralph gave the well driller a date that we expected to arrive in Zimbabwe. Ralph told the gentleman he would contact him when we arrived in Harare and when our money reached the bank.

When Ralph and I arrived at Nyamashato on that first trip, the well driller was already on site, and work was in progress. School had been dismissed, and a large group of children were standing around watching the well driller. Teachers were as excited as the children to see what was happening. This was a totally new experience for the children as well as the teachers. The well was deep, so a very long handle was needed to pump the water. Small children were unable to even reach the handle to pump the water.

Ralph and I learned later that there was probably no other rural school in all of Zimbabwe that had its own drilled well. Wells in the rural area were hand dug and many only produced water during the rainy season and for a limited time after the rains stopped.

One day, Mr. Bondeponde came to the classroom where we were staying. He had a big smile on his face. He had come to tell us that the children had emptied the water bottles they carried to school and had washed them out. The children had filled their bottles at the new pump. When he inquired about what they were doing, the children explained that they were taking water home to show their parents the water they now had at school. It was clear water, not muddy water like at home. Mr. Bondeponde got a real laugh out of that. The children no longer had to carry water to school. It is difficult for Westerners to understand how such a simple thing can bring joy to people in a third-world country.

This well was only used for a few years when Mr. Bondeponde called to tell us the water was very muddy and not usable. There had been an extremely rainy season that year. Further investigation indicated that the well had not been drilled deep enough. We eventually learned that well drillers try to get water without drilling into granite. However, it only produces surface water. In such cases, the water eventually gives out during the dry season. It had also been an extremely rainy season, and wells often became cloudy after an extreme year of rain. Lesson learned: be careful who you have drilling a well. It is necessary in Zimbabwe to drill deep enough to get into the granite layer. Hydrologists usually recommend drilling seventy-plus meters or at least 200 to 225 feet. Well drillers, of course, resist drilling into the granite. It takes time, and it is difficult to drill in granite and produces a lot of wear on their equipment. Drillers are anxious to get water before hitting granite. They are not concerned about the water not drying up in the dry season. Water at such a stage will not hold out in a dry period because it is just surface water.

When we arrived in Zimbabwe on a succeeding trip, Ralph was anxious to see if he could get any help from the U.S. Embassy on getting a new well drilled and a windmill installed. Ralph was not happy with the wells that had been drilled previously. He engaged a hydrologist to do a well-site at Nyamashato Primary School. That was to take place the following week. We were optimistic that this time, we would get good water. Ralph had worked through the U.S. Embassy to get a grant for a windmill to pump the water from the new well that was to be drilled. Things move slowly, and of course, they must come and inspect the site.

The embassy told us that they would make their visit the following week. They did not come, and they had no way to contact us at the school. There was no phone at the school, and cell phones were not a thing yet. We were out of food supplies since we had not gone to Harare the previous week waiting on the embassy to make their visit.

Early in the morning on Monday, we left to go to Harare so Ralph could check with the embassy and we could get groceries. It never fails—when we returned from Harare, you guessed it, the embassy people had come in our absence. This turned out to be a serious mistake on our part. Unfortunately, Mr. Bondeponde was not on site either. The deputy head met with the embassy representatives and apparently did not paint a very encouraging picture of our efforts. As a result, our project was turned down by the embassy and we had to purchase the windmill and install it. This cost money that could have gone to other projects. I have never seen Ralph so discouraged.

Ralph contacted a hydrologist. He learned a great deal about drilling wells in Zimbabwe from the hydrologist. It is necessary to drill deep enough to get into the granite layer to avoid the muddy water the previous well produced after heavy rains. Ralph learned that it is advisable to have a hydrologist site a location before drilling anywhere in Zimbabwe. That proved to be good advice.

Ralph hired a well driller, identified by a hydrologist, to drill a well at the new site. The well exceeded all our hopes. It was tested and proved to be an excellent source of water. A windmill was installed to pump the water. Two 20,000-liter tanks were installed on stands that stood about twelve to fifteen feet in the air. The tanks were located a distance from the well but near the classrooms and teacher houses. There was a celebration when the tanks were full for the first time. Two 20,000-liter tanks hold a lot of water!

There are no backhoes or trenchers near the area of the school. All work is done by hand labor. To contract someone in Harare to come out where we were working was not likely to happen. Most contractors did not want to venture out of the city. The cost would have been prohibitive, and the machine would probably have broken down in the process of doing the work.

A local man was hired to dig the trench from the windmill to the tanks on stands. This man also dug trenches for piping water from the storage tanks to each teacher's house and the school garden, where standpipes and spigots were installed. The women could not thank Ralph enough for the convenience of water at their door. This eliminated the time-consuming job each day of carrying water from a distant hand-dug well to their homes. The teachers were singing and dancing when they realized that they no longer had to walk a long distance and bring water home for their families. The well is still producing an abundance of water more than twenty years later. The joy shown by the school staff and surrounding community was like a Christmas celebration.

A week or so after the water project was completed and there was piped water to each teacher's house, I received a visitor. One of the teachers came to my house with a stack of five-gallon buckets. She told me she was selling buckets. She very seriously asked me if I needed to buy a water bucket. This was not uncommon to have people peddling things to make a bit of money. There I was, trying to figure out how to get out of buying her buckets and not hurt her feelings, when she began to laugh. She was playing a joke on me. She explained that she no longer needed the buckets because she now had running water at her house. We had a good laugh!

Having water come from a tap was new to not only children but many of the local adults as well. Mr. Bondeponde told Ralph and me that most of the children had never seen water coming from a faucet. He had observed one child filling a bucket for watering plants in the garden. In attempting to turn off the faucet, he had accidentally turned it on more. He was so frightened that he dropped his bucket and ran.

On our next trip to Harare, Mr. Bondeponde requested that we bring onion sets and tomato plants back with us when we returned to school. The following day everyone was busy in the garden planting onions and tomatoes. We were only able to locate 200 tomato plants. Mr. Bondeponde was disappointed, he had wanted as many as 600 plants. So, the next trip to Harare would require looking for more plants. Tomatoes are in high demand all the time in Zimbabwe and sell very well. Tomatoes are an item in nearly every dish that is prepared. With water easily available, the school is counting on the garden for income to fund some of their needs.

Ralph had made plans with the well driller he liked to use before we left the country in 2010 to drill more wells the following year when we returned. Little did we know that he would never be returning. At the beginning of 2011, Ralph's health began to deteriorate. It took time for the doctors to diagnose the problem. By the time we knew what was wrong, the progression of the cancer was out of control. He passed away in early May 2011.

Ralph had no idea that I would continue on. He suggested I return and tell the people, our friends by that time, goodbye. I felt it was necessary to finish with planned work. So, I returned to make certain the planned wells were drilled. Safe water is such an issue for the rural people. That led me to make many more trips back to Zimbabwe. Many buildings were constructed at the new site, including an office building, staff housing, poultry buildings, etc.

A surprise occurred when we attempted to drill a well at Guzha that year. That school had never had a source of water. It was the last well to be drilled for the schools in Ward 1. The hydrologist said that it would be a miracle if we got water. The drillers worked very hard and saw no signs of encouragement. They were preparing to pull the drill and return to Harare, and then it happened. The water erupted from the drill site and was coming in so fast that the driller couldn't blow out the borehole to install the casing. The casing that they were attempting to install kept breaking from the force of the water. It was necessary for them to call Harare for a heavier casing. The final results were 2,000 liters per hour.

This was far beyond our wildest expectations. When we left for the evening, the people who had gathered were dancing and celebrating. God provided where water was so desperately needed.

Since there is no electricity in that area and no electricity in the foreseeable future, it was necessary to install a solar pump. We had learned by this time not to rely on electricity. It is not a reliable source of power. A special celebration was held by the community. Water is coveted in an area that has little water. The well is so strong that the school cannot use all of the water that is pumped. Sometimes, it is necessary to turn the pump off to keep the storage tanks from overflowing.

A trench was dug by men in the community from the site of the well to the tank stand that was erected between the classroom buildings and teacher housing. Teachers would no longer need to carry a five-gallon bucket of water on their heads from the distant community well to their homes.

When electricity was brought to Nyamashato Primary and Secondary Schools, the windmill was replaced with electric pumps. Over the years, electric pumps were installed when new wells were drilled. After much infrastructure was in place, electricity could not be relied upon. The poultry project could not operate on a large scale without power. It was at this point that we began to replace all existing electric pumps with solar pumps and solar panels. This was a costly experience, but we needed to have a constant source of power. We do not use batteries to pump water at night. The well sites are fitted with storage tanks on stands that provide gravity-fed water twenty-four-seven. This system is working well.

RANDOM EXPERIENCES

Several things happened in our early experiences that raised questions in our minds. The most concerning for me was noticing all the children on the playground during class time. Didn't the teachers require the children's attendance? On one occasion, I thought the teacher had dismissed some children during a test so that she could space the children apart. I quickly became aware that this happened daily. I began to ask questions and was told that the classes were too large (sometimes sixty-plus children) and the teachers would divide their classes in half. Some of the children were sent to the playground while others were in class. Later, the groups would be switched, and the playground group would go in for class while the others went to the playground. I decided the teachers did what was necessary to be able to give the children the best learning experience possible under the circumstances.

As the years went on, we were able to provide more classroom furniture. Eventually, Mr. Bondeponde was able to get more teachers assigned to the school. This meant that we needed a house to live in. The school needed the classroom that we had been occupying for several years. It wasn't until during our fourth visit that there was a house renovated for our use. What happened to our plans to go for two years, and someone else would take over? We believe that God had a hand in what was ahead of us. Little then did we know what lay ahead.

Another observation! During every week, it seemed there would be days that the builders did not show up for work. This was frustrating because we had limited time and much work planned. We did not like to leave with many things to be completed in our absence. Construction moves slowly when builders are only present one or two days during the week. Finally, one of the evenings that Mr. and Mrs. Bondeponde came to visit, Ralph brought up the issue of the builders' irregular work schedule. He explained why he felt it important to keep the momentum moving.

Mr. Bondeponde explained the reason. In their culture, especially in rural areas, when an individual dies, the body is not embalmed because there are no facilities available, and besides, rural people cannot afford the service. Usually, the burial takes place within twenty-four hours of the death, if possible. It was explained to us that when a person dies, it is necessary that the entire community attend. People fear that if they do not attend, no one will attend their funeral when they die. So, no matter what is going on, everything stops for a funeral. This explains the work stoppage on school construction projects.

The reader may be wondering why there were so many funerals. This was happening in the late 1990s. AIDS was running wild throughout Africa. There was no medication for AIDS. Many people were dying of AIDS. The cause of a person's death was never mentioned or spoken of. Most often, the cause was never known. However, Ralph and I were aware of the pandemic of AIDS in the world, especially in Africa. This was frequently the cause of work stoppage. Not all deaths were related to AIDS, but unfortunately, too many were related. It was all these deaths that were responsible for all the orphans in the community.

We even found families of children living alone because both parents had died from AIDS. During this period, not much was known about AIDS. Many people did not know what caused AIDS or how to prevent it. They feared AIDS enough that if a member of the family became ill, they would evacuate and leave the person to die alone. Ralph and I encountered this on many occasions.

As we were preparing to leave at the end of our first year in Zimbabwe, the community gathered under the shade of the mango trees on the school grounds to thank us for our time with them and the work that had been accomplished. One of the gentlemen in the community stood and spoke to Ralph. He thanked him for all that had been accomplished during our stay. He said that Ralph had not had time to speak to them at one of their worship services, but what Ralph had accomplished was far more than the words of most men. He indicated he didn't know enough words to thank us for coming and helping their community.

MR. BONDEPONDE'S STORY

(Also known as Mr. B)

And my God will supply every need of yours according to his riches in glory in Christ Jesus.

Philippians 4:19 (ESV)

Mr. Bondeponde told us, soon after we arrived on our first trip, that when he walked up to the school in August of 1996 to begin his assignment, he was devastated by the condition of the school. It had deteriorated terribly since he had taught there in 1985. He said that he didn't know where to begin to put the school back together. It was going to take a miracle, for sure. He also said he didn't know how he could bring his family there and ask them to live in such dilapidated conditions. Upon receipt of our letter in November of that year, he knew his prayers had been answered. God works in miraculous ways to accomplish His purposes.

Ralph and I had learned about the school in late 1995 while on a sightseeing trip to South Africa. It wasn't until August of 1996, the very time Mr. Bondeponde was starting his assignment at Nyamashato, that

Ralph and I finally decided that we would make the trip to Zimbabwe to a school named Nyamashato in the rural area of the country. We would go and see for ourselves what the conditions were and what we might be able to do to help. The decision to go was made about the same time Mr. Bondeponde arrived to start his new assignment. It is interesting how God brings people together from halfway around the world. This is the beginning of a very long story.

***

Mr. Bondeponde had moved his family into a dilapidated house when he began his new assignment. The house had only three very small rooms. His family consisted of him and his wife and three children. It was the best that was available. One could almost put a hand through the cracks in the door. The roof rafters were so termite-eaten that they appeared to be ready to collapse. Ralph and I could hardly believe our eyes when we first saw the conditions. We did not have enough money to begin to rebuild staff housing at that point.

When we returned to the U.S., one of our goals was to raise funds for building additional staff housing and renovating housing that could be salvaged. The timeline had to be speeded up after Mr. Bondeponde called Ralph one day after we had returned home to report that he had moved out of the house his family was occupying because the roof had collapsed.

There was no vacant housing available. It was necessary to move the six members of his family into a house that already had two other families living in it. Ralph told Mr. Bondeponde to begin making plans to build a new teacher's house. It was unfortunate that we were not in Zimbabwe at the time. When we arrived on our next trip, a new house was nearing completion.

In mid-April, during school term break, the house for the Bondeponde family was finally finished and ready for occupancy. Earlier in the day, some of the teachers had helped Mrs. Bondeponde clean and wax the new floors. Once the floors were dry, the house was ready to be moved into.

Ralph was busy doing numerous things and checking on new house construction in progress. He stopped what he was doing to help Mrs. Bondeponde move their furniture. When Mr. B returned from his meeting, he was able to finally enter his new living quarters. His family were all so excited.

Ralph had built a work counter in the kitchen of the house we were using. A sink had been put in one end of the counter, and water was piped from the tank outside on a stand into the house. This was certainly a step up in our living situation. We no longer had to carry water from the well, a distance away, to our house. It wasn't long until Mrs. Bondeponde requested the same setup for her kitchen. So Ralph diverted his attention to that project. Mrs. B. thought life couldn't get much better.

During the many years that followed our initial visit, Mr. and Mrs. Bondeponde spent nearly every evening coming to wherever we were staying to visit. First, that was in a classroom, and finally, nearly three years later, in a renovated house very near the Bondepondes' new house. We learned a lot about each other through these visits. We knew that Mr. Bondeponde had practice taught at the school from 1986 to 1988. He was pleased to receive the assignment to be the headmaster at Nyamashato but was shocked to see the deterioration of the buildings.

One evening, he explained that when he returned to begin the new assignment he discovered that some school fees money had been embezzled. As a result, it was a struggle to gain the community's confidence. He explained that he still was working with a divided faculty but things were beginning to turn around.

Mrs. B told of her struggle for acceptance when she finally joined Mr. B. She even considered leaving this place and finding a teaching position elsewhere because of the way she was treated. Mr. B persuaded her to remain there and weather the storm.

Mr. B shared with us a dream he had in August 1996. He since believes it was God talking to him. The dream happened just before his promotion to this school. He said there was a very bright light, and he was walking down a long corridor. At the end of the corridor was a gathering of people waiting for him. He believes that the corridor in the new administration building is the place and the group of people was the community. The administration building had not yet been built. God must have been at work in us because it was that same August that Ralph and I made the decision to go to Zimbabwe on our first of many trips.

Mr. Bondeponde's Story

One evening, after we had been traveling to Zimbabwe for several years, the Bondepondes came to visit, as was their habit. Mr. B brought a tape recorder he had found in a box from a recent shipment. There had been some story tapes in the box as well. Ralph spent time showing him how to play the tapes and also how to record. The look on his face when Ralph played back a recording of the two of them talking was priceless. He suddenly had all kinds of ideas of how he could use the piece of equipment.

Mr. Bondeponde is a special person. Over many years, we learned that he was kind but he was very strict. Seventh-grade students had been told to come during term break for extra lessons in preparation for the end-of-year exams. These exams would determine if they were eligible to attend secondary school the following year. Some students did not come for the lessons. When school resumed after term break, Mr. B decided that there was some discipline needed. He found small jobs for them to do during recess time.

Mr. Bondeponde assigned work for the girls who had skipped the extra study time during school break. They had to carry buckets of water to fill the barrels for the men who would be pouring foundation footings for the Orphan Feeding Center. He would not let them carry the water from the new taps but made them carry it from the well a distance away that was used before piped water was installed. The boys were working in the garden, digging up new ground. The ground is as hard as rock. I think they decided that it would be easier to come for review lessons.

Mr. Bondeponde even gave me assignments. He requested that I spend some time teaching English to the sixth- and seventh-grade classes. Most of the children could read English and understand what they read, but they had difficulty carrying on a conversation. I was happy to do this, but my experience was that I got started and then someone came to the door of the class needing me for one reason or another. When teaching conversation, consistency is necessary and practice. Often, I got called away and then didn't have a chance to return.

Mr. Bondeponde reported to Ralph and me one evening, when he and Mrs. Bondeponde came for their evening visit, that the school enrollment was increasing steadily. He told Ralph that the total enrollment stood at 676 pupils, excluding preschoolers. That was an increase of about a hundred children in one year. When school opened in May for the second term, he requested one additional teacher from the district offices. The staff would then be seventeen teachers in total, not counting preschool teachers. Dictated class size was forty students per class. The school was out of classroom space. Classes would obviously exceed the dictated size as more children enrolled. The sewing women would need to vacate the old classroom they had been using.

Building more classrooms was not possible because, at that moment, cement was unavailable. More teacher housing was also needed, but that required cement as well. Teachers were once again required to share housing. In my mind, that was never a good plan, but at that moment, there was no other option.

WELCOME BACK

In every way and everywhere we accept this with all gratitude.

Acts 24:3 (ESV)

On one of our early trips to Zimbabwe a whole new scene greeted us on our arrival. The little church at the far end of the grounds was open, and singing was coming from the building. As we drove closer to the school, we noted that it was surrounded by a six-foot-high cyclone fence. There was a gate at the entrance that could be locked. The school grounds had been cleaned, and shrubs and flowers had been planted. What a change from the previous year!

We heard singing, and when we looked to see where it was coming from, we noticed people walking from the church to the school. They had come to welcome our return. We were invited to the church for a proper welcome. At the church, the people sang the first verse of "Amazing Grace." They had been practicing so they would be able to sing to us in English. That was a real effort on their part. I suspect Mr. Bondeponde had been their coach, as none of them would have known very much English at that point.

After the welcome "home," we went back to the school for a welcome by many parents who had gathered. During that time, some of the contents of a recent shipment were brought from the new library building out to the assembly grounds for the parents to see. Everything had been stored in the new library until we returned to witness the unpacking.

Ralph demonstrated how to open the tables so that they could be used. The local people had never seen tables like this. So, Ralph assisted some of the men in moving the tables from the library where they had been stored to some of the classrooms. They were opened for use. I doubt that there was ever a need to fold the tables up. The teachers were so excited.

Two of the cafeteria tables were put in each classroom as far as they would go. Student desks and chairs had also been shipped and were put in the classrooms that housed the older children. When the task was finished, all the classrooms had adequate furniture. The first year there had been no furniture at all in most of the classrooms. There were even enough office desks for each teacher to have one in their classroom. There are no words to describe the joy the teachers experienced.

When we arrived on the next trip, we noticed that the roofs of the newly renovated buildings had been painted with oxide paint. Mr. Bondeponde explained that they had been told that the paint would extend the life of the roof. Paint was expensive but if it extended the life of the roof, it was well worth the extra expense.

The first time we sent money, $3,000, and were not there to supervise its expenditure, we had to trust that the relationship we had built could be relied upon. When we returned the following year, Ralph was given receipts for the $3,000 Ralph had wired to Mr. Bondeponde. They had completely reconditioned the house that had collapsed on Mr. Bondeponde and his family. The only remaining thing needed was to paint the outside of that house. They painted inside and out of the new administration building that they had broken ground for on our previous trip. The two new roofs that had been put on were painted with red oxide paint. Two hundred fifty-nine broken windowpanes had been replaced. The area was beginning to finally look like a school where learning could take place.

TEACHER HOUSING

God is our refuge and strength, a very present help in trouble.

Psalm 46:1 (ESV)

Ralph received a call from Mr. Bondeponde after we returned to the U.S. from our first of many trips, indicating that the roof on the house they had occupied while we were there had collapsed. His family had been living in a house with two other smaller families. The house was wall-to-wall people. He was pleading for a new house to be built. Ralph gave Mr. Bondeponde permission to begin the construction of a new house and told him he would wire some money. Ralph cautioned him to keep receipts for every purchase he made.

When we arrived on our next trip, there was still some finishing-up on the inside of the new house that needed to be completed. The new house was small, but the plan was dictated by the government. It certainly gave them more space than they had since their arrival at Nyamashato. The house was ready for occupancy near the end of our stay that year. I helped Mrs. Bondeponde move some of their things and get a bit organized. What an exciting time when the family all gathered that evening. Ralph had built a work counter along the window wall in the kitchen. He installed a sink at one end with a drain that went to a dry sump outside the house. Water was carried to the home from a well in the community. Later, water was piped to all houses from the storage tanks that were installed. A small storage tank on a stand was installed outside each house near the kitchen. Water was gravity-fed into the house at the kitchen sink. Mrs. Bondeponde thought this was as good as it could get.

Ralph toured the house that the Bondeponde family had occupied prior to the roof collapsing. He decided that the foundation and basic structure were sound. The house just needed a new roof and doors. Some of the windows needed repair as well. It was also necessary to replaster the inside and outside of the house. When the repairs had been completed and the house painted inside and out, it looked like a new house. A family with fewer members than Bondeponde's soon moved in. This provided relief for the house that had more than one family living in it.

Teacher housing in the rural area is specified by the government. We had to use their plans when adding new teacher housing at Nyamashato. For families with several children, the houses were a bit crowded. It still was better than one family living in a three-room structure or sharing a house with another family.

Mr. Bondeponde and Ralph had a meeting nearly every day. Ralph was anxious to get some new teacher houses under construction. On the far side of the school, there was an area that would accommodate three teacher houses. Work began! By the time we left to return to the States, there were three five-room houses at different stages of construction. The teachers were so excited. They were anxious to know who would get assigned one of the new houses when they were completed.

A new teacher, who is living in the only remaining old house, woke Mr. Bondeponde during the night after we had returned to the U.S. The house was infested with termites, and they were dropping from the beams in the house. Termites were everywhere, and the family was unable to sleep. So, the following morning everyone around was helping to clean another house for the teacher and his family to move into. Two families needed to occupy one house until the new houses were completed.

The house infested with termites was torn down the next day. Ralph was anxious to get the remains of the house hauled away. The ground was treated for termites before a new structure was erected. A new teacher's house was built immediately on that same site. Housing for teachers was a problem at all the schools. There never seemed to be enough housing. Providing adequate housing became one of our goals.

Soon after this event, new teacher housing was needed at Inyagui. Three new houses were built at Inyagui. Parents were involved in hauling sand and pebbles for mixing with the cement. They hauled brick from Nyamashato while more brick was being molded in their community. Everyone turned out to help.

Over the years, additional housing was needed at Nyamashato for additional teachers. The school was growing with children. Eight new houses were constructed for staff members over a period of many years. Additional staff housing was built over time at the secondary school next door to Nyamashato Primary School, Nyamashato Secondary School, and Inyagui Primary School.

MADAMOMBE CLINIC

So those who were engaged in the work labored, and the repairing went forward in their hands, and they restored the house of God to its proper condition and strengthened it.

2 Chronicles 24:13 (ESV)

Our initial introduction to this mission was at Nyamashato Primary School. During our first three trips we worked at the primary school and at the government clinic about three kilometers from the school. Our interest in the clinic was because it was the only source of medical care in the immediate area. The only transportation to Murewa was by bus, and that cost money that many in the local community did not have. These people had to rely on the local clinic for medical needs. I learned of cases that were more than the local clinic could handle. Often, the bus driver would not assume responsibility for transferring a patient to the hospital. The clinic did not have an ambulance or any kind of transportation.

On our first visit to the local government clinic known as Madamombe Clinic, we had the opportunity to meet both Albert and Beauty Mukondwa. Albert was stationed at the clinic as an environmental health technician. He was responsible for environmental issues for several clinics in the area. We learned that he was provided with no form of transportation to facilitate his visits to the outlying clinics. Beauty, Albert's wife, was a nurse at the clinic. Our first contact with Albert was regarding the pit toilet buildings that were being constructed at Nyamashato Primary School. We had to obtain clearance at the various stages of construction from Albert.

Our initial visit to the clinic was an eye-opening experience. The patient rooms had no furnishings, not even a single mattress. The windows of the clinic were cracked or broken out. Exterior doors were in very poor condition. This clinic was the only source of medical help the local people had without traveling to Murewa. Some of the people did not even have the bus fare necessary to make the trip. It quickly became apparent that it was not just schools that needed help but the local clinic as well. They had flush toilets in the clinic, but none of them worked. There was no electricity, but a power pole stood at the corner of the property where the clinic was located. Running water was no longer available because the pipe from the water tower to the clinic was rusted out. How does a clinic operate under such circumstances? And this clinic was a government clinic.

The only equipment available for sterilizing instruments was a container that looked like a pressure cooker. It had not been usable for the previous two weeks and so, the nurses were unable to properly sterilize the instruments. An autoclave had been donated. Tom Staab (a church member) was bringing it with him as he came for a visit. The nurses were so appreciative to know that they would have a way to properly sterilize their instruments.

Madamombe Clinic was under Albert's supervision and the hospital administrator in Murewa. Ralph went to meet with the hospital administrator and to describe the circumstances that the clinic had to operate under. The administrator gave the excuse he had no money for repairs. We quickly learned that was the standard answer to everything. Ralph asked for the names of some reputable electricians to do the electrical work and he would finance it. The administrator indicated he had to hire the electrician, and he asked for the money. He said the money had to go through their books. Reluctantly, the money was left with the administrator.

The following week, a gentleman came to Ralph, explaining he had come to do the electrical work at the clinic and needed the supplies. At that time, there was no phone service, so Ralph made yet another trip to Murewa. The roads were so bad that a thirty-five-kilometer or about twenty-plus miles would take an hour plus, depending on the weather at that time. It was certainly not a trip that a person looked forward to. Our truck took a beating but served us well.

A promise was made to have the supplies delivered. That did not happen, and several weeks passed, and more requests were made for supplies to be delivered. Our departure was approaching, and nothing had been done. Ralph made one more visit and, this time, requested the funds be returned to him since it appeared they had no plans to use the money for electrifying the clinic. Very quickly, Ralph saw some action. He witnessed the signing of the contract with the electrician. The electrician rode from Murewa with Ralph as he returned to where we were staying. Rarely did Ralph return from town without a truckload of people. Electrification of the clinic was almost complete by the time we left to return to the U.S.

The water lines were rusted and so, the clinic did not have access to water without the nurses having to carry it some distance in a bucket. This is no way to run a clinic. So, Ralph hired a gentleman from the community to repair the water lines. When he was finished, Ralph drove to the clinic to check the work. It was difficult for Ralph to believe his eyes when he saw the break in the pipe repaired by using a piece of old innertube tied around the break in the pipe. How long would that last?

During the time we were waiting for the electrical work to begin, Ralph had gone ahead and purchased plumbing supplies and repaired the water lines himself, so the clinic had water. The nurses were so grateful to have the flush toilets working again. Money was also provided to the clinic to get the broken windows repaired and new doors and locks installed. Albert oversaw that work. The last step was painting the inside and out of the clinic. This was done after we returned to the U.S. Albert did not want to paint until the electrician and plumber had done their work.

Soon after our arrival the following year, we paid a visit to the clinic to check on the work that was to be done after our departure the previous year. We had brought a suitcase of infant clothing with us, and some had come on a recent shipment. This we delivered during our visit. We found the electricity was working. The nurses did not have to carry water in a bucket. They were all smiling. The broken windows had all been replaced, and the painting was complete. New doors replaced the old ones that were falling apart. The facility looked so welcoming.

A shipment that arrived before our return included hospital beds, donated by C. U. R. E. Several of the beds were put in patient rooms at Madamombe Clinic that had never had beds. The rest was donated to the hospital in Murewa. The hospital had just completed the construction of a female wing to their complex. They needed furnishings for the rooms. It was perfect timing.

Bedding and blankets were also given to the clinic. Some boxes included infant-sized and toddler clothing. Infants in our country outgrow small sizes before they get a chance to wear them. Babies in Zimbabwe are much smaller at birth than babies in the U.S. The donated clothing would last these mothers for a while.

While we were at the clinic, Albert arrived from making visits to homes in the community. He was very discouraged. His comment was that people were dying like flies due to the AIDS pandemic. There were three deaths that week in the immediate community. Albert felt limited in what he could do; he had responsibility for three clinics serving over 30,000 people each, covering an enormous area. The government did not provide a vehicle to facilitate employees getting to the outlying clinics. He said he had no money to support a vehicle of his own.

Early in our stay in the third year, there was a celebration and opening ceremony for the newly renovated clinic for the purpose of showing the community all the work that had been accomplished. The entire community turned out. The media from Harare even came to see the celebration. Many dignitaries were in attendance for the festivities. The media took their pictures for sure. I had hoped that after the dignitaries had traveled over the rough road, we would see some improvements made to the road. But that did not happen.

A huge meal was served for the hundreds of people in attendance. I never learned how the food was funded for such a meal for hundreds of people. Speeches were made, and Ralph was asked to say a few words. He first enumerated all that had been accomplished at the clinic and school. The money that had been invested, plus the estimated value of all the shipments, was revealed. During his speech he informed all in attendance, and particularly the officials from Harare, that he would not repair things again. It was their responsibility to care for all the improvements that had been put in place. Ralph stuck to his word over the years.

Ralph asked the dignitaries to give him some support by delivering electricity to the school. He promised to electrify both the primary and secondary schools if the main power line was brought three kilometers from the clinic to an area between the primary and secondary schools. During his speech, he emphasized the fact that we were here because God had led the way. Ralph said he would return the following year if it were possible to get over these roads. Any improvements to the road over the years were only token improvements on rare occasions.

After all the speeches, tours were given through all the clinic's facilities. This included the housing for the staff. Ralph pointed out to the dignitaries that painting was needed inside and outside of all the housing and other buildings. The electricity that was installed in the staff housing was a hazard. There was no way it would pass inspection. Ralph recommended that the housing should be wired properly but he had no money for this project. He requested the deputy minister of transportation and energy to have the nurses' housing electrified so that it would be safe and up to standard.

Along with all the speeches there was also entertainment as well. Each act was an effort to thank us for all the work done. Even the sewing co-op was represented. The women were all dressed alike in black skirts and white blouses. They wore homemade buttons that said S. E. W. (Sewing Enables Women), the name they had selected for themselves. At the end of the entertainment, Ralph was presented with a hand carved walking stick. We were told that this distinguished him as an elder.

The nurses have difficulty making certain that all newborn infants get the shots necessary. The clothing for infants was an enticement to get mothers to bring their children to the clinic for new clothing. Even mothers whose religion did not believe in medical care came to the clinic for the clothing available. The nurses used this time to teach the mothers such things as sanitation and eating habits for the young baby. They took advantage of their presence to also administer the vaccines. The nurses said that the clothing we had shipped was working miracles and made a special request that we ship more infant clothing.

One request the nurses had: they needed to be able to weigh infants. They had a spring scale but nothing to put the babies in to weigh them. I told them I would find something. I did find some heavy fabric to make a sling. I put buttonholes in each corner that would allow the nurses to put a cord through. The cords connected to the hook on the scales. The hook was connected to a fixture on the ceiling. The infants could be placed in the sling. Problem solved!

Just when one thinks a project has been completed, there is an unexpected event. During the night, a patient with a mental illness was able to gain access to the clinic property. He ripped out of the ground the new water line that had recently been replaced. The line was bent and twisted to the point it had to be replaced with new piping. When Ralph saw what had happened, he told Albert to get quotes on what it would cost to repair the damage and to bring the quotes to him. Life in Zimbabwe is such a struggle. There is never enough money to cover the needs and certainly no money for repairs. Ralph did make certain that the water line was put back in good condition.

The following evening, after the festivities at the clinic, we were invited to Mr. and Mrs. Bondeponde's house. They had a tiny TV. They wanted us to see the news coverage of the celebration at the clinic the previous day. Ralph appeared on the news giving his speech. The newly renovated clinic was shown with Dr. Parirenyatwa flipping the switch to turn on the electricity. That made him a celebrity in the community.

Early one morning, soon after the opening of the newly renovated clinic, a messenger arrived at our door, needing Ralph to come quickly to the Madamombe Clinic. They had an expectant mother and refused to admit her to the clinic. It was the mother's first baby, and there appeared to be complications. They wanted Ralph to take the woman to the hospital in Murewa. So, even before breakfast, the day had begun. Ralph and the truck quickly became an ambulance. A mattress was put in the back end of our truck for the expectant mother, and a nurse climbed in to care for the woman.

On another occasion and a different year, Ralph had just returned from Murewa when a messenger from the clinic sent word that they needed Ralph to take newborn twins to the hospital in Murewa. The twins were three months premature. The clinic wanted to get the babies to the hospital as quickly as possible. Off Ralph went in a cloud of dust for his second trip that day over incredibly rough roads. One twin died, probably en route, and the other twin was put in intensive care. Ralph returned with the grandmother and the deceased twin.

Ralph struggled with that experience for days. He was so sad that he was unable to get to the hospital any sooner. So much of the world lives so far away from any modern medical facilities. Even in the situation just described, there is little to no support available for expectant mothers or newborns.

SCHOOL GARDENS

For as the earth brings forth its sprouts, and as a garden causes what is sown in it to sprout up, so the Lord God will cause righteousness and praise to sprout up before all the nations.

Isaiah 61:11 (ESV)

On our initial visit to the communal lands of Zimbabwe, the last thing on our minds was a school garden. We had initially gone to this area to see what we could do to help a school in need of some support. The buildings were in various stages of collapse. Initially, one classroom building was totally renovated, and the roof that was damaged by a storm was replaced in another classroom building. Four toilet buildings were constructed for the teachers. These buildings were long overdue. Initially, the only toilet building was for the students.

The following year, when we returned, we saw the school buildings and grounds immediately around the buildings had been fenced with six-foot high cyclone fencing. A gate had also been installed. The gate was locked at night. Ralph and I were puzzled and wondered how they were able to financially accomplish this work. Mr. Bondeponde told us the work had been accomplished with funds raised by selling old roof sheeting that had been removed when a classroom building had been renovated the previous year. Nothing in Zimbabwe is thrown away. There is always a use to be found.

While the school had fenced the classroom buildings, Mr. Bondeponde wanted the entire property fenced. He had plans for a school garden to help generate income for the maintenance of the facilities. However, that was not possible until cattle could be eliminated from the school grounds. Eventually, the entire school property was fenced with a barbed wire fence. Cattle guards were put in place so vehicles could enter and exit.

One day, Ralph and Dale Buss, who had joined us for another visit, helped Mr. B by staking out a very large garden. Mr. Bondeponde had shared with us the previous evening his plans for the garden. He planned to give each teacher and their class a designated section for a garden. The responsibility of the students was to plant, weed, and water their section. The income realized when the produce was sold would be used to maintain the renovated school facilities. It was a huge undertaking and it required only a few children each day with designated tasks to accomplish. It worked well if the teachers were in the garden at the same time as the children. It turned into a learning experience for the children and, I think, for the teachers as well.

The garden served another purpose. Each teacher who requested a plot of ground for their family was given an assigned area. They were able to raise a few vegetables for their own family's use. Later, when the windmill and the storage tanks were installed, water no longer had to be carried from a distant well to the garden. Water was piped to the garden from the storage tanks. This allowed the teachers to run a hose from the standpipe to their individual garden plots. Over the years we traveled to Zimbabwe, I never saw another school do this except the schools in Ward 1, where we were helping.

When the school garden was initially staked out, Mr. Bondeponde expressed a desire that the garden be fenced with a six-foot high cyclone fence. He was afraid produce would be stolen if the garden was not fenced. The passage gate was locked at night, and he was the keeper of the key. There was also a large gate at the front end of the garden to enable a team of oxen or a tractor to enter to plow the garden. This gate was kept locked when it was not needed. The first time a tractor came to plow the garden, it promptly took out two posts. The man left with his tractor and never did plow the garden. As I recall, we ended up getting a community member to plow it with oxen. This was a tough job because that piece of land had never been plowed before, or at least not for a very long time. The oxen could only work for a short while. They aren't like tractors; they get tired and will refuse to work. So, plowing the garden took more than one day.

The cyclone fencing required metal posts because of the weight of the fencing. Wood posts would attract the termites. Ralph knew it would require many steel posts to support that fence. He retrieved one of the metal posts that had been removed from the roof overhang on one of the old classroom buildings to use in making a post-driver. He took it to the welder, near Madamombe Clinic, at the Madamombe town center. Since there was no sheet stock available to weld to one end of the pipe, Ralph had bought a sledgehammer head. The welder had a difficult time understanding what Ralph wanted him to do. However, when Ralph was finally able to make him understand, the job was accomplished. Ralph demonstrated how the post-driver worked. The man was so excited to learn something new that he bought some round stock and made some of the post-drivers to sell.

When HCOC (Heather Chimhoga Orphan Care) was established, and the operation moved to the new site, a garden was put in as one of the first projects. The garden supplied vegetables to the feeding program. Sometimes, if someone was going to Harare, a load of extra produce from the garden would be taken to the market there. Produce was sold locally as well if anyone had the funds to make a purchase.

It was common to see marigolds blooming in the garden. The workers planted the marigolds among the tomato plants because they warded off aphids that could destroy an entire crop.

In the beginning, community members helped to plant and weed the garden beds. Now, it requires constant attention. A staff of workers was hired to weed, water, and pick the produce for the feeding center. Gradually, the garden idea spread, and Inyagui and Guzha each had their own feeding centers and their own gardens. Any excess produce was sold to local community members or taken to Murewa or Harare, depending on where a truck was going.

Recently, one of our orphans who received support from HCOC to go to the university to study agriculture has now returned and is donating her time in the gardens as a thank-you for all that HCOC did to help with her education. This has been welcomed by the staff and it is hoped other students will follow her example.

BRICK MOLDING

Therefore thus says the Lord God, "Behold, I am the one who has laid as a foundation in Zion, a stone, a tested stone, a precious cornerstone, of a sure foundation: 'Whoever believes will not be in haste.'"

Isaiah 28:16 (ESV)

Termites are a problem in the area of Zimbabwe where Ralph and I went to work. Upon our arrival at Nyamashato the first year, we noticed mud trails running up the inside of the walls in the classrooms. We soon learned that the trails were mud tunnels built by the termites. These trails ran all the way from the floor to the rafters. The termites would start the tunnel underground and enter the building where the cement floor joined the cement-plastered brick wall. They would build a tunnel on the wall all the way to the wood rafters. Once the insects were in the rafters, the roof had a limited life expectancy. The floor had been poured after the brick wall had been plastered with cement. How the insects got through is a mystery to me. This explained why the roof rafters were weak and the wind was able to blow off the roof. Stopping this destruction was Ralph's first priority.

Ralph's first stop was the lumber yard in Murewa. They told him what product he needed to get, but they had none. So the first trip to Harare, Ralph checked with lumber yards until he found some of the poison. It was expensive, but somehow, the termite damage had to be stopped. He was afraid to use it around the children. Mr. Bondeponde explained that school would be on spring break in a couple of weeks. So Ralph waited until there were no children in the buildings. This would allow three weeks for the buildings to air out before children returned to school.

Ralph mixed the concentrate with water and poured a thin stream of the poison at the joint where the wall and floor joined. He also dug a small trench around the outside of each building. More poison was mixed and poured into the trench. Since most of the windows were broken out at that point, the rooms were able to air out. This was a big project as it was slow work digging the trenches. Some of the local fathers saw what Ralph was doing and came to help him. Ralph worked until all of the buildings had been treated.

The cost of the poison was expensive but replacing roof rafters was also expensive. The members of the community had little money. They were subsistent farmers and had little or no cash. The school survived on the money collected from school fees. Some parents couldn't even afford to pay school fees, and the children were not allowed to attend school if their fees were not paid. The school couldn't afford to purchase the treatment for termites. Ralph and I decided we had to find a way to raise funds for school fees for the children who could not afford them.

When we began to talk about building new buildings, such as the administration/library building, Ralph said that the budget had to include treatment for termites. He had the workmen treat the ground where the floor would be poured. Then, black plastic was laid down before the floor was poured. Those buildings have survived at least twenty years without termite infestation.

Where to get bricks was an important question. Would it be necessary to have them trucked from Harare? Mr. Bondeponde said that the community would make the bricks. This would be the way the community would have ownership of the project. One day, when Mr. B had gone to Harare with us, he asked Ralph to take him to the high density area of Harare. He wanted to purchase a number of brick molds so that the bricks the local people made would all be the same size. In the past, when the local people made their own molds, they varied a bit in size. This made laying the bricks by the bricklayer very difficult. It required less mortar in laying the brick if the bricks were all the same size.

Ralph saw for the first time how much of the business was conducted in that country. The high-density area was a chaotic place near the downtown area of Harare. Mobs of people were each selling their wares out of little one-room shanties. Some just staked a claim on a section of

62   Hope for Zimbabwe Orphans

REPAIRS

But all things should be done decently and in order.

1 Corinthians 14:40 (ESV)

It was the end of the school term, and parents had gathered for the end-of-term celebration. Easter was just around the corner. Excitement reigned! After the ceremony, the parents gathered in the new library to welcome our return. Ralph had an opportunity to tell those gathered of the plans for the community this year.

He also expressed disappointment when he saw some repairs needing to be done at the newly renovated school. The purpose of establishing the garden was to generate income for the maintenance of the school buildings. Ralph explained that he had renovated all the buildings and had built new buildings. He emphasized it was their responsibility to take care of the property and that he would not come and repair things that he had already repaired once. Ralph pointed out that parents must teach their children to respect the school property.

It was emphasized that the purpose of establishing the garden was to provide vegetables for the kitchens where food was prepared for the orphans. The garden also generated income for maintaining the school. The children could help with caring for the school by spending time weeding and watering the garden under teacher supervision. Ralph emphasized the necessity of teaching the children to respect the property of others and, most especially, the school property that belonged to the entire community. He encouraged the school to provide waste containers for the children to throw wrappings and other paper into. Their effort would help to keep the school grounds clean and tidy.

Breaking old habits is never easy. This was a new concept for not only the children but for the entire community. It took many years of our returning to the issue. Over time, our persistence did bring improvement to the appearance of the school.

SWEATERS FOR CHILDREN

And he answered them, "Whoever has two tunics is to share with
him who has none, and whoever has food is to do likewise."

Luke 3:11 (ESV)

Our trips grew longer and longer. We always had so much to get
accomplished. Frequently, we ended up staying there during their winter
season. While it isn't cold like Colorado, it is cold enough to need warm
clothing, especially at night. The children's homes have no source of heat
other than a very small cooking fire. I often observed children coming
to school without shoes because they had none. Some didn't even have a
sweater or jacket. It makes me cold just to think about the children having no way to be warm. Some would even need to wade across a stream,
so their feet and lower legs would be wet. It is a wonder they didn't die
from pneumonia.

On one trip, we didn't arrive in Zimbabwe until late June. Our
trip had to be postponed due to a granddaughter graduating from high
school. June is the beginning of their winter. I had been given a large
amount of yarn. The yarn was not all the same, and there were varying
amounts. Someone was cleaning out odds and ends and had given it to
me. It wasn't enough to hold for a container going to Zimbabwe. So, the
yarn was packed in a suitcase and taken with us as extra luggage. One
can pack a lot of yarn into a suitcase by vacuum sealing it.

When Ralph and I arrived in Zimbabwe, I gave the yarn to some
of the teachers. It wasn't long before they came back to see me. All were
knitting sweaters for the children who had nothing to wear when it was
cold. Mrs. Bondeponde suggested that we hold onto the finished product
until the children needed them. The sweaters were varying sizes depending
on how much yarn the teacher had been given. One teacher ran out of

yarn, so she just continued knitting with another color. Things like that don't matter when one is cold. Mr. Bondeponde stored the sweaters in his office until the weather was cold enough to need a sweater.

Later, Mr. Bondeponde stopped by where we were staying one morning on his way to the office. He said he thought we should distribute the sweaters that the teachers had knit to children who had nothing. Overnight, the weather had made a significant change. We agreed that the children needed something to help them stay warm. Mr. Bondeponde sent messages to some of the teachers to send certain children in their class to his office. He handed out the sweaters according to the size of the child. The children were so appreciative. It hurt to think how miserable these children had to be.

Not only were the children cold, but the mosquitoes also became intolerable. I guess the insects were cold as well. Bug spray was a waste of effort. Ralph and I had to escape into our tent in the evenings to get away from the insects.

SEWING GENERATES INCOME

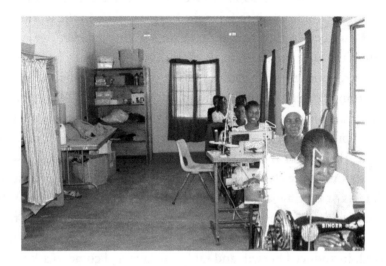

In all toil there is profit, but mere talk tends only to poverty.

Proverbs 14:23 (ESV)

When I was a teenager, I was required to take a first aid course in high school, and that training stuck for many years. I would use these skills in raising two sons and then in providing care for many orphaned children and their families in Zimbabwe. Who knew? God.

I received a degree in home economics with a minor in science from the University of Illinois and spent twenty years as a teacher of home economics and science. I took time out to be a stay-at-home mom for our two sons. Once our youngest son joined the high school marching band, I was up early to take him to marching practice. I needed something else to do to fill my days. I was approached by an elementary school principal to consider substitute teaching. I did this for a couple of years, and then I was asked to take a full-time position as a fourth-grade teacher. This required that I go back to the university and get an elementary certification. Ralph and our sons helped with all those many projects that were assigned! I have always stretched myself to meet the needs around me. Those skills would come in handy in Africa.

When Ralph retired, I also retired from my teaching position. Since one of our sons and family lived in Colorado, we decided to retire in Colorado. We wanted to get back to the mountains. We had lived in Idaho for ten years and came to love the mountains and outdoor areas to explore. I couldn't wait to leave the buggiest place in the world, Texas.

As described in the chapter "Not on My Bucket List," we were not thinking about doing mission work in our retirement. But God. Our hearts were touched by the stories of the people of Zimbabwe and their needs from the very beginning. Ralph originally said, "We can do this for two years, but then someone else can step in and carry on the work." God had other plans. We listened. Our hearts were opened for the Lord.

Near the end of the second year in Zimbabwe, a group of women gathered outside the classroom where Ralph and I were living. Most could speak little or no English. I knew only a few words of Shona. I wondered why they had come and what they wanted. Had they come just to visit me, or did they have a need and had come for help? One woman stepped forward, introduced herself, and said that they had come to ask for help.

It didn't take long to learn that they had been raising chickens and selling them to raise money. In fact, they had brought a dressed chicken for me to cook for Ralph. They wanted to start a sewing co-op to make school uniforms to sell to raise a bit of money. They wanted help from me to get started. I have taught sewing at different times during my teaching career. I thought this would be a piece of cake.

As the meeting progressed, I quickly learned that I should have been more cautious. Before the meeting ended, I learned that most women had never sewn before. That wasn't all I learned. When I asked them to sign their names on a piece of notebook paper so I could learn who they were, it became apparent they didn't know how to write. After some questioning, it was obvious that most of the women had never been to school. At the time they were growing up, girls did not attend school, only boys. The girls had not had the opportunity to develop fine motor coordination. What a revelation! This was going to be an uphill climb.

70   Hope for Zimbabwe Orphans

I couldn't let that fact interfere because I had already made a commitment. I explained to the women that I would go home and do all that I could to raise money to buy sewing machines. If I was successful, when I returned, I would plan to teach them to sew. It was necessary for me to investigate if and where treadle sewing machines were available in Zimbabwe. There was no electricity anywhere near our location at that time. Before Ralph and I left the country, we did check to see if treadle machines were available in the country and what the cost would be. That gave me an idea of the amount of money I would need to raise to buy the sewing machines.

So, when we returned to the States, the fundraising began. Several people donated funds to purchase one machine each. I returned the following year and was able to purchase six machines. It wasn't one for each woman in the group, but they could make it work by rotating their tasks. Some of the women could cut out a uniform while others were sewing at the machines. The women also made a schedule so that all twenty women did not come on the same day. The women could get their housework done on the days they did not come to sew. It was apparent that was not what they had in mind. Obviously, they wanted the time to be as much social as work. It made perfect sense to me, but I insisted that only the number of women should come as there were machines to use. That way, I could closely observe their progress.

One objective on one of our first trips to Harare after our arrival back in the country was to purchase as many sewing machines as the money donated would buy. The shop we needed to make the purchase from was in a less-than-desirable part of town. It was not possible to park in front of the shop, so Ralph drove around the corner and parked. You guessed it! We were robbed. The camera was stolen from under the driver's seat. This required at least two hours of our time at the police station, and we knew full well that nothing would come of it. And it didn't!

We returned to Nyamashato with two new sewing machines. That was all that would fit in the truck at one time. We always returned from Harare with a full load. It was necessary for Ralph to go all the way to Harare to obtain supplies. There are no words to describe the joy the women exhibited when they saw the machines for the first time. Two more machines were picked up on our next trip to Harare, and later, two more were obtained. This time, we parked right in front of the store so we could keep an eye on our truck.

Now, the work was about to begin. It was first necessary for the women to learn to control the machines before they could begin making uniforms. The new sewing machines were kept in the classroom that Ralph and I were still living in. The first group of women arrived, and the work began. The needles had been removed from the machines until it was determined the women's level of skill. They began with just learning to treadle the machines. Easy, right? Not so much! Most of them would have the machine sewing backward. They practiced and practiced treadling and making certain that the needle would sew forward. I quickly learned this was going to be a long, slow process. This was only the first day, and only six women out of about twenty had an opportunity to practice on the machines. When I found one woman who could make the treadle do what she wanted, I had her become the teacher. The women spoke the same language and I was new and didn't want them to feel intimidated.

Later that afternoon, after the women had left for home, I heard singing coming from the stream the women needed to cross to go home. They had gathered under a tree and were singing and dancing because they were learning to sew. When Ralph came in, he asked what all the singing was about. I told him I assumed the women were so happy with the new sewing machines that they were celebrating. It was almost totally dark before they broke up, and each went her own way.

Mr. Bondeponde informed me after the women had gone that the treadle machine is believed to be the man's machine in this culture and that women use the hand crank machine. I feared that the women might never learn, and no one had told me. He assured me that it was okay. He was pleased to know that some were doing well.

The procedure of just learning to treadle the machine correctly lasted for many weeks. Just getting to the point that the women could make the machine sew like they wanted was an achievement worth celebrating. When they achieved this, they would move around the room, dancing and singing. They finally graduated to sewing with the needle on lined notebook paper. The lined paper was an attempt to learn to control the machine and to guide fabric so it was sewn properly. The next step was sewing with thread on scraps of material. Some struggled to keep the machine from sewing backward because that caused the thread to jam up the machine. I must admit this was a true test of my patience. Some people are naturally more coordinated than others, but education also plays an enormous role. I began to wonder what I had gotten myself into.

During the time I was teaching the women to use the machine, I was searching for patterns for the uniforms, only to discover there are no pattern books in Zimbabwe, at least ones that would have patterns for uniforms. Businesses that made uniforms were not going to share their patterns with me. *So*, what to do? I had made patterns when I was at the university but that had been many years ago. Reluctantly, I purchased an exceptionally large roll of heavy brown wrapping paper. I knew the tissue paper that patterns are made from in the U.S. would never survive, with many women using the patterns on a regular basis. I borrowed a girl's uniform from one of the teachers and used it as a guide to get started. It was necessary to use the initial pattern and construct a garment to make certain the pieces would fit together as intended. It took a considerable amount of time to get the pattern pieces adjusted so that they would fit together properly. The next step was making patterns for all sizes, from preschoolers to secondary school sizes. The pattern edges of each piece were taped with masking tape to reduce the nicks from the scissors. Eventually, the patterns were constructed from lightweight cardboard. These would serve as a template when the paper patterns needed replacing.

Another problem was finding buttons for the uniforms. Fabric stores had limited supplies. One store owner told me where the buttons were made. This was a blessing. I was able to buy in bulk, which reduced the cost considerably. The wife of a member of parliament was very helpful in assisting me in finding fabric in bulk. Uniform fabric was not available in regular fabric shops. This woman was knowledgeable of the city and helped me locate other sewing supplies in bulk. We traveled many miles back and forth through the city, trying to locate the necessary supplies. While I was working on finding and making patterns and trying to locate supplies in bulk, the women were learning to use the machines properly.

When two or three sizes of patterns were ready for use, I demonstrated how to lay out a pattern and cut the fabric pieces. Next, the women were allowed to do the same. Oh my, what a struggle! The women did not understand the straight grain of the fabric, and I knew we had an uphill climb ahead. Some women caught on, and they moved on with the work. Others required more close supervision. I would go back to the house at night, completely exhausted. I felt that this plan was never going to work. The machines had been paid for; the only thing to do was to push forward.

One of the sewing women had been absent. I knew that she was expecting a new baby. It was a surprise to see her two weeks later coming to continue learning to sew. The tiny baby was tied to her back as she sewed. She had to take breaks to change a diaper or to nurse the baby. Where there is a will, there is a way. I could hardly get her to go home at the end of the day. She was determined to catch up with the rest of the women.

The women used the same size pattern and continued cutting out uniforms and sewing the pieces together. I never left the room; I monitored every step the women made. Initially, there was much ripping out and restitching. A few of the women learned very quickly, but others required undivided attention. Along with observing the women laying the pattern on fabric and others sewing at the machine, I was attempting to make the uniform pattern in other sizes. It was finally necessary for me to go to the sewing lab early in the morning to make patterns before the women arrived to begin work. Unfortunately for me, when the women learned I was in the sewing room early, they began coming as early as I did. So much for having quiet time to make patterns.

When the women came early to sew, I had to watch closely what the women were doing and tried to catch mistakes before they happened. I would explain to the women what the problem was so they could learn to avoid making such an error in the future. It is best to stop a mistake before it happens. Little by little, I was finally able to get the patterns made.

Progress was slow, and I wondered what would happen when Ralph and I returned to the U.S. As things turned out, Ralph was still in a back brace from the broken vertebrae and was not allowed to travel for several months. I capitalized on the extra time and pressed forward with the sewing co-op, teaching them to make girls' uniforms. All the time, I was praying that the women would catch on before my departure.

One day, the group that was to come was the group that had the most difficulty controlling the machine. Only four of the six women who were scheduled to come showed up. I assumed that they were discouraged. I decided to try an experiment. I had one hand crank for a sewing machine and asked Ralph to put it on one of the machines. I had resisted up to that point, hoping the women would learn to treadle the machines. This frees both hands to guide the fabric. One of the women took right off with the hand crank. Whatever works!

I always insisted that the women do neat work. Pressing seams was a must. One day, I walked into the sewing room, and the women were all laughing. I couldn't figure out what they were laughing about. It turned out they had decided on a new name for me. They called me Mrs. Perfect! I laughed; it was funny and perhaps even appropriate. I had been insistent that they do good work. I didn't let up because I knew when I left to return home, they would probably slack off.

***

I have mentioned before that nothing in Zimbabwe goes to waste. A use can be found for everything. When one sews, there are always fabric scraps that are discarded. One day, I walked into the sewing room and discovered one of the women, who was less skilled at sewing, sitting with a cement sack in her lap. She had a pile of fabric scraps at her feet. I was curious about what she was doing. She showed me how she was making a door mat by using a crochet hook to pull scraps of fabric through the plastic weave of empty cement sacks that had been laundered. I thanked her for doing this. The mats were to be sold for twelve to fifteen Zimbabwe dollars each. This was all profit because the materials were waste, as were the cement bags.

Late November arrived, and it was time for our return to the U.S. We had been in Zimbabwe since early March. I encouraged the women to continue the work and follow the instructions I had given. The women were paired with a woman who had shown ability. I had hoped this would give the women the courage to move forward.

When the women had sold many uniforms, they would bring the money to Ralph. They only trusted him to make a deposit for them. One year, when the economy was reasonably stable and fabric was available, the women worked steadily. Ralph made several large deposits for the women at the bank. The last deposit brought the total at that point to 33,000 ZD. They were so proud of themselves.

On my last day before our return to the States, the sewing women came with pumpkins, dressed chicken, sugar cane, etc., to show their appreciation for the support that I had given them. They thought I should take all this home with me on the plane. They had been trying the entire time to teach me how to carry things on my head as they do. Without success, I might add.

The following year, it was exciting to see the storeroom at the feeding center full of school uniforms that the sewing women had made. However, when I began to examine the construction, I sadly realized most uniforms were not usable. I was devastated when I realized the amount of fabric that had been wasted and that the uniforms were not acceptable. It was obvious upon examination that the patterns had not been placed on the straight grain of the fabric as I had taught. The cutting out of the pattern had been done by individuals who did not or could not hold the scissors properly. I was heartbroken. I knelt right in the storeroom and asked God to help me do what had to be done.

A meeting was called for the women in the sewing co-op. I showed them what I had discovered. I talked about the uniforms that had been made that were sewn together with huge basting stitches. I asked how long they thought those uniforms would hold together when one of their children put them on. The women got the picture very quickly. It just wasn't going to work for some of them to continue to sew.

I explained to the women that it was nothing against them, but not everyone is good at everything. I said that I was not good at crocheting. I had noticed some of the women crocheting as they walked to and from the school. I pointed out that some of them could sew better than others. Perhaps some of them were better at other things than sewing. I recommended that those who were not doing well sewing should find another way to generate income for their families. One suggestion made was to knit sweaters for the school uniform. I had observed women knitting baby layettes. All the orphans needed sweaters during the colder season.

A list of names of those who were to continue to sew was read to the group. The others were asked to find another way to generate income for their families. Dismissing the women was the most difficult thing I had ever had to do.

The women who remained were shown the uniforms that were not wearable. It appeared the patterns had not even been laid on the fabric as they had been taught. The uniforms had obviously been cut out by people who did not know how to hold a pair of scissors properly. Many looked like they had been chewed out rather than cut with scissors. I asked the women who remained in the co-op to take the uniforms that were not wearable and to pull them apart. The women were to decide if these uniforms could be re-cut to a smaller size and some of them salvaged. This took the five remaining women many weeks. The work had to be completed before more fabric could be purchased.

When the women were ready to start cutting and making uniforms of varied sizes, they asked about a label for the uniforms so that people would know who made the garment. The women chose a name. It was S. E. W. This stood for "Sewing Enables Women." The label went in all the garments that they produced.

Soon after I purchased the labels for the uniforms, the women began to spend long hours in the sewing room. There was a big celebration the day two of the women were able to make a complete uniform in one day. That was a true accomplishment. Others began trying to meet the same level of accomplishment. A real competition developed among the women who had finally mastered the sewing machines.

One day, the sewing ladies came to me and asked me to make patterns for the secondary school uniform. That was a new challenge. I needed to make patterns for both the girls' and the boys' uniforms. This would also require the women to learn to set in a zipper. I was skeptical but they did succeed with patience on my part. The patterns needed to all be made in assorted sizes. That was going to be a time-consuming effort. Gradually, the task was accomplished.

***

Several years after the sewing women were well established, I began working with two orphan girls who had completed secondary school. I taught them to sew, and eventually, my plan was that they would become part of the sewing co-op. It was amazing how quickly they caught on. I found it much easier to teach them than to teach the women I began with in 1999. Some of the women I began with have quit, and others still don't do a good job. I have suggested that they find something else to do to make money. We can't afford for them to mess up expensive materials anymore. Some of these women were the cause of some of the machines being broken down. Perhaps this is the beginning of our vision of a skills training center for the orphans who complete their "O" levels satisfactorily. I began with only two girls and waited to see how it might work out and where it might lead.

Just before we left to return to the U.S., I had one last meeting with the sewing women. Mr. Bondeponde came to pay the women for the uniforms he was preparing to distribute to the orphans. He also planned to pay the knitting co-op for the sweaters they had made to go with the school uniform.

The orphan girls that were new to the group were to receive their first pay. I was anxious to see their reaction. There were no words to express their joy.

I encouraged the sewing women to consider taking on some more orphan girls who have graduated from secondary school to train as soon as they move into the new facility where they will have more space. That never happened. Apparently, the older women were jealous and felt the young girls would take over. Later, I learned that all the young girls left after Ralph and I returned home. Obviously, more was going on behind the scenes than I was aware of.

At about this same time, other groups of women came to speak with us. All of them were seeking help in starting a co-op of one kind or another. I had to listen to each group, and I spent hours attempting to help them understand all that would be involved. I did not have the heart to turn them away without at least listening to their plans. Usually, there were no plans. They were grasping at straws and had no idea what they were asking for. Most people in the U.S. do not have any idea what a struggle it is to just exist in some countries!

One day, Ralph and I were called to Inyagui School. When we arrived, there was a group of about sixty women waiting to talk with us. They wanted to start a sewing co-op. I had to explain that it was not wise to start another sewing group in the same community. I tried to explain why.

It was also necessary for them to understand that their group was too large. I could not teach so many women to sew at one time. There were no machines and no funds to purchase machines. It was exceedingly difficult for me to turn them down. I physically just could not take on another job. There was not even a facility at Inyagui for them to operate from. Ralph and I did not have the funds to build another structure. Saying no is so draining. I felt they really did not understand.

Getting fabric for the existing sewing group was a challenge. While we were in the country, the women would go to town with us to make the purchase, and we would deliver it in our truck. To transport the huge rolls of fabric by bus was a complicated issue. The rolls of fabric were sixty inches long and heavy and cumbersome. There were no large vehicles in the area at that time. If they tried to transport it on the public bus, they had to pay a charge to an individual driving the bus to load the fabric on top of the bus. So, the women tried to stock up on fabric before we left the country. Another consideration for the women was that it cost 600 ZD each round trip to go to Harare by bus to purchase supplies. They just couldn't afford that amount of money.

When the sewing women began doing well by themselves, I thought I could give my attention to other issues. However, I discovered that even though the women no longer needed my help, they seemed to think that if I was around, I should spend my time with them. It has become a job of weaning gradually.

One year, Ralph and I were asked to be present when new uniforms were given to the orphans at Guzha Primary School. More than 400 uniforms for both girls and boys were distributed on that occasion. The uniforms had been made by the S. E. W (Sewing Enables Women).

Sewing Generates Income

There are no words to describe the joy it brought to the children; they could not keep from smiling after they put on the new uniforms. Often, the new uniform was the first new clothing they had ever owned. Teachers told of finding some of the children's clothes that they had worn to school in the trash after they put on the new uniform.

Over the years, the women gained confidence and skill. One year, when I returned, I found some women making shirts for men and dresses for women to sell in the community. The group also made uniforms for schools surrounding their area. At about this same time, electricity was brought to the area. Gradually, as money became available, electric machines were purchased. This turned out to be a disappointment because the power was inconsistent. Now, power has become prohibitive in price and is not always reliable. They ended up having to continue to use the treadle machines. Now, the treadle machines are worn out, and the electricity is more unreliable than ever.

The power plant on the Zambezi River, at one time, did not operate because the river was not flowing due to drought. I was heartbroken for the women who worked so hard to get ahead, and now it isn't even profitable. The entire country was nearly at a standstill. There is no way to generate income because the cost of supplies is more than the product can be sold for if the supplies are available. Without power, the electric sewing machines are of no use. The treadle machines are worn out by now, I am sure. I pray that the skills that were taught to these women may continue to give them direction that will offer them hope for their future. I also pray that the women will train some of the young girls who want to learn to sew.

GIRLS SURVIVING WITH NO PARENTS

But a Samaritan, as he journeyed, came to where he was, and when he saw him, he had compassion.

Luke 10:33 (ESV)

Ralph and I had our first encounter with orphans when Dianna came to Nyamashato looking for us. She had come to see Ralph and plead for help for her and her sisters. She explained to Ralph that her parents had both died and that the girls had been divided up among extended family members.

She told Ralph that life was very difficult for some of the girls. One of the girls was being sexually abused. Some of them were starving because there was not enough food to go around. One of her sisters was not allowed to attend school and was used as slave labor. Her reason for coming to Ralph was to plead for help in getting her sisters back together so they could live at their parents' homestead.

Ralph took Dianna in our truck to where her parents had lived. When Ralph examined the homestead, he quickly realized that the rondavel was not habitable. He showed Dianna the termite infestation and explained that it was not a safe structure to live in. It was apparent that the bricks had not been fired adequately and so the termites had done their damage.

Ralph discovered that the property had a deep, hand-dug well on site. The well was bricked up and had a secure cover. Dianna explained to Ralph that the family used this source of water and that it was good water. She also showed Ralph the area the family had used to plant a garden. However, Dianna was concerned that she had no blankets, cooking utensils, or any other household items. Those items had been taken by extended family members when the last adult passed away. They left nothing for the girls as is the tradition for that culture. Ralph assured her that he would see what he could do.

When Ralph returned to our house, he proceeded to Mr. Bondeponde's office. They had a long discussion about how to deal with the situation. The two discussed possible options. They both knew that they had to come up with a plan for the safety of this group of girls.

The following day, a man came to Nyamashato looking for Ralph. This individual lived near the girls' homestead and had learned what Ralph had discovered when he examined the rondavel. He told Ralph that he would mold and fire the bricks. He also offered to build a two-room structure for the girls, providing Ralph would purchase the cement, rafters, roofing, door, and windows. Just before we left, Ralph planned with the lumber yard in Murewa to purchase the list of supplies needed. The owner of the lumber yard agreed to deliver the supplies to the site when Mr. B. indicated they were needed. The money for everything was left with Mr. Bondeponde to pay the bills and oversee the work as it progressed.

The neighbor to the girls molded and fired the bricks for their new home. This gentleman also built the two-room structure. When we returned the following year, the house was complete, and the family of girls was living in the house. The house consisted of two rooms, one for gathering in and eating their meals, and the second room served as the sleeping room. There are no words to express the joy they exhibited.

Helping one another was a totally new idea for the community. It was not a custom in that culture to help someone outside the immediate family. We were determined to help the community change. I often used the story of the Good Samaritan as an example for the community to work together. Each time I told the story, I would ask them if they were a Levite or a Samaritan.

When the house was completed, the community came together and brought items to the girls that would be needed to live in the house. Most people in the community have nothing to spare, so we ended up supplying some of the larger items, such as blankets, large cooking pots, etc.

As the girls grew older, they left the home one by one to find work where they could. Dianna became a police officer in the Mazoe Valley, where our friends lived. The next oldest girl, at one point, became a secretary for Nyamashato and staffed the reception office at the primary school for several years. Each girl found employment after she finished school at Nyamashato Secondary School.

The youngest girl was the last child at home, and I know she was lonely. She was often ill and missed school much of the time. When she was the only child left at the homestead, some extended family came and took her a long distance away to live with them outside our area of operation. Later, we learned the family discontinued giving her the medicine that Beauty was supplying. They told her she did not need the medication. We learned that she passed away in a short time after the medicine was stopped.

The Orphan Care Program is the outgrowth of this experience, along with other similar situations that we encountered. Looking back, I believe God gradually exposed us to these situations as we were ready to handle them.

SICK CHILD

And the King will answer them, 'Truly I say to you, as you did it to one of the least of these my brothers, you did it to me.'

Matthew 25:40 (ESV)

I was called to a homestead to visit a child who was very ill. The grandmother explained that she had stopped eating and would not talk to anyone. She feared the child would not survive. The grandmother guided me to the rondavel where the child was located. A knock on the door brought no response. I entered and began talking to the child. The girl was curled up in a fetal position on the floor in a corner of the room. Her arm covered her face, and she did not respond to me or anyone. The floor was not clean, and there were no furnishings or bedding in the room. Flies were everywhere. The flies were crawling all over the child. She needed some loose clothing to keep the flies off her sores.

After trying for some time to get the child to talk to me, I went out and talked with the grandmother and told her they must take the child to the clinic. The grandmother said they had been there more than once, and the clinic did nothing. She was afraid the child was not going to live. The family pleaded with me to do something.

I returned to the room where the child was on the floor. I again attempted to get the little girl to talk. I asked the child, "If you could have anything you wanted, what would you like to eat?" After much coaxing, she said she would like an egg. I promised to return with some bread and some eggs that her grandmother could cook for her.

The raw area under her arm went three-quarters the way around her chest. She had herpes, which is AIDS-related. The flies were an issue because they were all over the sores around her middle. I planned to make her a loose-fitting shift from sheeting material. I had hoped this would not stick to her skin and would keep the flies away.

The clinic had said they were unable to do anything for the child. This was a disease that the health workers knew little about. The grandparents were very fearful they would lose her as well. I had recently spent 700 ZD in Harare on medicine for this child. Both the child's parents and all her siblings, except a twin sister, had recently died from AIDS. I felt helpless to do much for the child.

Finally, I left in the truck with the intention of collecting some bananas, eggs, tea, and bread, returning to the child, and feeding something to her. When I arrived back at the school, I learned that Ralph had fallen off a ladder when a step broke. He was inspecting the progress of the work taking place on one of the houses that were being torn down to make way for the new feeding center. He had landed on a broken brick on his back. My plans quickly changed. Ralph had to get to a hospital as soon as possible. I gathered food items and gave them to a teacher to take to the family. My focus was on Ralph and what lay ahead for him.

One afternoon, after Ralph was out of the hospital and back at our house at Nyamashato, Mrs. Bondeponde and another teacher went with me to visit the little girl I was caring for when Ralph had his accident. I had medicine for her that I had gotten in Harare. The open wounds were showing some signs of improvement. She seemed to be in less pain and in better spirits. The teachers that were with me felt encouraged.

Through much care and medication, the girl did survive, but being so sick left an impact. Her attitude was that she would soon die, so why work at school? Before we left to return to the U.S., the grandmother brought the young girl who had been so sick and her twin sister to see me. The grandmother wanted me to see how much the child had improved since I had provided medication and food for her.

She lived for several years and completed her secondary education. However, after secondary school, she left the area, and we lost touch. She went to live with relatives a distance from her home. The relatives told her she didn't need that medicine, and they threw it away. She soon passed away.

PARENTS DIED

Jesus said to them, "I am the bread of life; whoever comes to me shall not hunger, and whoever believes in my shall never thirst."

John 6:35 (ESV)

Soon after our return to Zimbabwe in 2004, a grandmother brought a little boy to see us. The little boy was one year old. On our previous trip, this baby had been brought to me early one morning when he was only a few days old. He was brought to us by the grandmother, one of the Orphan caregivers. Orphan caregivers are women in each village who volunteered to check in on orphans in their respective villages and report any needs to Mr. Bondeponde.

This woman was at the end of her patience. The mother of the infant, her daughter, had passed away just a day or so after giving birth to this little boy. The father had passed away just ten days prior to the baby's birth. The deaths were due to AIDS, which was so prevalent in Africa in the early years of the mission. Antiretroviral therapy (ARV) was not yet available in this part of the world. The grandmother had tried every way possible to feed the infant, but all he did was cry. There were no wet nurses that the grandmother could find in the area. She pleaded with me to help her provide for the infant.

This was a new problem that we had not encountered before. Ralph and I discussed what to do. We quickly decided it was necessary to go to Harare, and hopefully, we could find baby bottles and formula. It was not going to be an easy find. Women in Zimbabwe did not use bottles. Mothers all breastfed their babies. Where to begin? We visited two or three large grocery stores with no luck. Next, we checked with pharmacies. I finally found a few bottles, but they were plastic. I was not sure about using plastic and boiling them to sterilize them. In case that was all that was available, I bought all that the pharmacy had in stock. Ralph and I kept looking. Finally, at one pharmacy, we found a couple of glass bottles, which we purchased. After the bottles were purchased, it was necessary to find formula. Fortunately, the pharmacy that had the glass baby bottles also carried the formula.

Because of the experience described above, we began to collect baby bottles and formula to add to the shipments of clothing, school furniture, books, etc., going to Zimbabwe. There always seemed to be a need.

On the trip back to the rural area, Ralph and I discussed the need to explain to the grandmother how to sanitize the bottles. We feared that with no experience with bottle feeding, she might not think of the need to keep all things related very clean.

The grandmother was so grateful when we returned and produced the bottles as well as the formula. I had to explain to her how to mix the formula with sterilized water. Emphasizing cleanliness was the biggest challenge. How anyone survives in their culture is a mystery to Westerners. Keeping things clean is nearly impossible.

The grandmother brought him to see me when Ralph and I returned the following year. When I held out my hands, the child came right to me. I was really surprised that he wasn't afraid. I think perhaps we had a bond from all the efforts in helping him survive. I would ask the grandmother about the boy over the years when we would return to Zimbabwe, but I never happened to see him to know who he was.

On what turned out to be my last trip to Zimbabwe in 2018, the woman who had come to Ralph and me for help when the grandchild was just a few days old brought her grandson to meet me. I had not seen him to know who he was since he was one year old. How exciting to see him after so many years. He had grown into a fine young man and was preparing to graduate from secondary school. This was such a special treat. A happy story for one orphan.

A BRIDGE IS NEEDED

But let all who take refuge in you rejoice; let them ever sing for joy, and spread your protection over them, that those who love your name may exult in you.

Psalm 5:11 (ESV)

It was a rainy morning, so I decided to visit some of the classrooms, interact with the children, and teach them some English words. I stopped at a first-grade classroom that happened to be Mrs. Bondeponde's class. When I entered the classroom, I was surprised to see only a few children. Typically, the room would have been overflowing with children. The classes were normally forty children and often larger. Teachers who had classes of sixty children or more divided the class and sent half to the playground. Later in the day the groups would be switched, and the playground group would come to the classroom for their lessons.

Mrs. Bondeponde reminded me that it had rained very hard during the night. This meant the river behind the school would be running rapidly and very deep. That was the first time I had heard about a river. The children would not be able to cross the river to come to school. Teaching on such days was wasted because more than half of the enrollment came from the far side of the river. Any lessons taught would need to be retaught in the future.

Mrs. Bondeponde told me that the river had been an issue for as long as the school had existed. She explained that the river was infested with crocodiles and snakes. In the past, several children had been injured or killed in attempting to come to school by crossing the river. During the flood stage, children could easily be swept away. Even a nurse from the government clinic had been nearly swept away as she attempted to cross when it was flooded. The nurse needed to check on sick children who lived on the far side of the river.

During the rainy season the children missed several months of school. As many as half the enrollment came from the far side of the river. This concerned me because either teachers had to hold back the children who did attend school or play catch-up with those who missed so many days. There had to be a better solution.

Later that day, I told Ralph what I had learned from Mrs. Bondeponde when visiting her classroom. Ralph and I walked to the river to see the situation for ourselves. We saw firsthand the muddy water and how fast it was running. We did not see any crocodiles but knew these creatures inhabited the river as well as snakes. We also saw a father carry his son across the river when the water was running high. Later, Ralph discussed the problem with Mr. Bondeponde, the headmaster. A bridge was needed so the children could come to school safely. People on the far side of the river had no way to get their produce to market in Murewa, the business center that was closer than Harare.

When we were in Harare, Ralph tried to meet with Dr. Parirenyatwa, MP for the local district. He was never available and we suspected we were being avoided because Ralph felt they should contribute many of the supplies needed for constructing the bridge.

The bridge should have been built by the local authorities long ago. Ralph began talking to the authorities in Murewa whenever he was in town. They were not especially cooperative. Ralph asked the district office to provide the culverts, rebar, and wire mesh for the cement. He promised that he would supply the cement and labor that would be needed. The local people were willing to haul the sand and gravel for mixing with the cement. They were also willing to provide much of the labor.

It took a couple of years for the authorities to get on-board with our request that a bridge be built. When we returned in 2001, work was well underway but the rains had halted the project. It had rained some every day. It wasn't wise to pour cement when the weather was not clear. They didn't want rain to fall on freshly poured cement.

The high water had washed away much of the sand that the local people had hauled in for mixing with the cement. The workmen indicate that it will not take long to finish the bridge when the weather finally cooperates.

In early August, it was announced that the bridge was now complete. It has been nearly two years since the work began. Many things had caused delays. Since we arrived in 2001, Ralph had pushed to get the job done. It was difficult to get pebbles delivered because of the shortage of diesel. This was the year of long lines at the gas stations. Much of the delay on the bridge was due to the lack of push by the engineer the district had hired. A new engineer was hired. He told Ralph it would be done in fourteen days. It was actually completed in twelve and a half days. Ralph checking two and three times a day on progress may have helped. It had been difficult for Mr. B to get to the bridge every day since he had no transportation and had to walk. As headmaster, he had lots of responsibilities on his plate.

As we were preparing to return to the U.S. that year, the headmen from the villages on the far side of the river gathered to express their appreciation to Ralph for the bridge that had been built. They were thankful that the children would no longer miss school or be in danger of crocodiles. The bridge would also allow the people to get their crops to market. A big job was completed, and the community was grateful.

A year after the bridge was completed, the bridge was underwater. This did not happen because of local rain. There had been history-making rainfall upstream some distance. This flooded the new bridge. Children had missed school one day. I am not sure that ever happened again. Missing one day of school is not like missing months during the entire rainy season. The bridge has been a lifeline for those families living on the far side of the river. While Ralph had planned to build a footbridge, this bridge benefited the entire community, not just the school children. It allowed community members to get their produce to market.

A Bridge Is Needed

RALPH—THE LOVED ONE

His master said to him, 'Well done, good and faithful servant. You have been faithful over a little; I will set you over much. Enter into the joy of your master.'

Matthew 25:23 (ESV)

Ralph and I were married for fifty-seven years when he died in 2011 of brain cancer. Part of our journey as a Christian couple was dedicating many years of service to orphans in Zimbabwe. For Ralph, that was fifteen years, and for me (who kept going after his death), it was more than twenty years. "Everyone in Zimbabwe loved Ralph!" Why would the natives over a hundred miles outside of the largest city (Harare) come to love this white-skinned male from America? He was sixty-eight years old the first year the Pippitts arrived in Zimbabwe (1997). At first, many of the children were "suspicious" of any white-skinned people. Most of these children had never been far from their rural home. No white people lived in their area of Zimbabwe. The children, especially the very young ones, were frightened when they saw the strange white people.

Within a short period of time, the people came to love both of us despite our white skin. They came to think of Ralph as "the guy who could do anything!" The children learned that if they came by the classroom door of where we were staying, they would get a cookie (biscuit) from me. If they saw Ralph walk toward his truck, they would run after him and get a ride in the back of the truck to the edge of the school property. In the beginning, there were no vehicles anywhere in the area. People in the rural area didn't know how to drive and did not own vehicles. The people can't afford to buy a vehicle, and they didn't know how to care for one. Over the years, Ralph would observe that a teacher would save enough money to buy a used car and drive it until it wouldn't run. Ralph discovered they didn't know that they should check the oil level or make certain there was water in the radiator. Ralph had a new job: teaching auto maintenance.

Ralph and I raised two sons, and eventually, we shipped some of our boys' old toys to Zimbabwe in containers packed with clothing and blankets for the people in the rural area where we were working. The toys included Lincoln Logs, wooden puzzles, Tinkertoys, and Legos. Ralph loved showing the boys how to assemble Legos; it was great fun for everyone! These children had never had anything to play with that would stimulate their creativity. The toys helped them develop coordination skills. What a gift! The people have no materials or toys, such as balls or even knives or forks, so they don't learn fine motor coordination. The people eat with their hands.

One of the early years, the morning after our arrival from the U.S., Mr. and Mrs. Bondeponde came by to say good morning and to see if we were ready for the day. Mr. B wanted us to be present when the toys were unpacked. Nothing like jumping in with both feet. We were off and running already. We hadn't even had time to completely unpack from our trip.

Mr. Bondeponde said that he had instructed that the toys from the recent shipment be brought to the new library. The kindergarten teachers were bringing the little children to see the toys and learn how to play with them. I believe that the kindergarten teachers were more excited to see the toys than the children. Most of the children had never seen toys before. There was no such thing in the area where we were working. Ralph had to show the children how to build with the Legos. However, the little girls knew exactly what to do with the dolls. I soon noted that they had found toy blankets and had the dolls tied to their backs as they see their mothers do with new babies.

Many soccer balls were carried in luggage or packed on shipments going to the Zimbabwe mission. The balls would replace the plastic grocery bags they gathered and stuffed inside one bag until it formed a ball. They then wrapped old string or strips of tree bark around it to help form it into a ball shape. The balls that were shipped from the U.S. were given to the schools to be used at recess time. No balls were given to individual children, or an unending line would have formed with everyone wanting a ball.

Playground equipment was shipped on large pallets. Ralph, with the help of local men in the community, installed the swing sets at the primary schools. The children loved it. Preschoolers loved climbing the steps and going down the slide. This was the first time the children had ever seen such equipment.

The local men received lessons on how to sharpen their cross-cut saws. When Ralph was back in America, he shopped at places like antique stores to find more saws and sharpening tools to take back to Zimbabwe. These men loved working with Ralph. I laugh in recalling the used saws that had hardly any teeth left on them that were brought to Ralph for sharpening. How great to get ones that really worked!

Early one morning, Ralph was summoned to the secondary school. The headmaster had fallen off his bike and thought he had broken his ankle. Ralph took an ace bandage and drove to the accident site. At 110 degrees and with no refrigeration, we have no ice for such injuries. Ralph wrapped the ankle with the ace bandage and then took him to the local clinic. Of course, they didn't do anything. They didn't even have an ace bandage. Again, there was no point in going to the hospital because no doctors or services were available on Sundays. So, the next day, it was obvious that someone (probably Ralph) would be taking the headmaster to the hospital for X-rays and a cast.

When in Zimbabwe, Ralph and I traveled to Harare about once a week to take our laundry to a laundromat and to get groceries and ice for the ice chests. In addition, there was always something that needed attention, such as getting visas stamped once a month, meeting with the member of parliament for the area, etc. The headmaster always warned us to be back before dark. It was good advice because it was not uncommon to find a bus running without lights on the highways. One-eyed cars were also another hazard. There were always people walking along the highway or on the edge of the highway, and they were very difficult to see until the vehicle was almost on them. In addition, cattle roamed freely and had the right of way. Hitting an animal was dangerous and very valuable to the owner. The local people did not understand an animal being struck and probably killed.

Sometimes, it would be just getting dark when we turned off the highway, and we still had twenty miles to drive over a very rough dirt trail. One evening on just such an occasion, we still had ten miles or so to go when Ralph realized we had a flat tire. There was no place to get off to the side of the road, and we just hoped another vehicle would not come along. We knew we only had minutes of daylight remaining. As Ralph was struggling to figure out the foreign jack, four men came out of the tall grass along the dirt path. They had had plenty of booze to drink and were singing at the top of their lungs. When they realized why we were stopped, three of the four picked up the hind quarter of the truck, and the fourth fellow took off the flat tire and put on the spare. They threw the jack aside. Thinking back, they probably didn't even know what a jack was. What a blessing! Ralph gave each of them some money, and they went away nearly dancing. This could have turned out so differently. God's protection.

After a few years, when teacher houses and the feeding center were constructed, Ralph often traveled to Harare several times a week to order supplies or meet with the officials, no phones in the rural area at this point. It was years before there was reliable cell phone service in the area where we worked. So, that made it necessary to drive about a hundred miles to accomplish anything. A hundred miles may not seem far to people living in the U.S. However, in Zimbabwe, the roads are very primitive at best. The edges of the pavement were always broken, and in some cases, holes were deep. One had to be careful not to hit a spot like that. It had the potential to break a tie rod or do other serious damage to the vehicle.

Sometimes, it was necessary to get permission from government departments to do certain things. Mr. Bondeponde would always go with Ralph. In the beginning, Mr. Bondeponde would never let Ralph travel alone, especially to Harare. He would help Ralph source supplies or act as an interpreter. He was very protective of both of us. In the beginning, I was not allowed to leave the school premises without a teacher or someone with me.

BEGINNING OF ORPHAN CARE

For I know the plans I have for you, declares the Lord, plans for welfare and not for evil, to give you a future and a hope.

Jeremiah 29:11 (ESV)

On our early trips to Zimbabwe, Ralph and I were focused on repairing school buildings and drilling wells to provide clean water. We had no plans to continue this work once we had Nyamashato Primary School back in good condition. God had other plans! After we had made several trips to Zimbabwe, Ralph saw children out playing along the road during school hours. He asked Mr. B who these children were and why they were not in school. Ralph was told they were orphans and did not have anyone to pay their fees to go to school or buy uniforms. Upon inquiring where the parents were, Ralph discovered that there was a significant orphan population caused by the AIDS epidemic. Parents had died, leaving children with little to no way to survive.

At that time, many families were reluctant to take in children of extended families that had passed away. This was another mouth to feed, and they had very limited resources. In some cases, they were fearful of the bad spirits that might enter their home. This attitude would take a long time to change. Local churches were doing their best. Was God planting a new seed in our minds? This was not only new to us, but we didn't know how to deal with the situation. Many children who were left alone had to scavenge for food to survive. They had no money, so they had no food, and there was no way for them to pay school fees or buy school uniforms; they were not getting an education. We knew that it was necessary to find a solution.

We found families of children living alone. The oldest might be as young as twelve years old. These children had no financial resources, and they were starving to death. They would say they don't come to school because they are so hungry that they are sick. At a funeral for a grandmother who had been caring for six grandchildren, one of the grandchildren, a twelve-year-old, pleaded for help. As the casket was lowered into the ground, she sobbed that soon, the crowd would return to lower the bodies of the rest of the children into the ground as well.

In some cases, during the parent funerals, the children were left to fend for themselves. Traditionally, the children were split up among relatives and did not see their siblings very often. With limited resources in each family, these orphans were on the losing end of getting food and were often used as slave labor. In that culture, the father and sons ate first at mealtime, then the mother and girls would eat. The orphans in the home would eat only if there was any food left. Sometimes, this forced those children to scavenge to have anything to eat. They would climb trees to find fruit to eat (i.e., orange trees) and sometimes would fall out of the tree and need medical care. So much need!

About this time, we learned that Zimbabwe had reached the point of zero population growth. This was due to the AIDS pandemic that was sweeping the country. People were dying in large numbers. AIDS was something new, and the rural people had no knowledge of how to treat the disease. How to prevent the disease was not common knowledge either. Children were left to fend for themselves; they had no one who cared for them. Neighbors and extended family were barely surviving. Traditionally, extended family would have taken them in, but relatives were afraid of the children of a deceased family member who had died. They feared they might contract the disease. They were also concerned about an additional mouth to feed.

When Ralph inquired about how many children lived in such circumstances, he was told there were more than he might think. When Ralph began to ask questions in the community, he quickly learned there were a lot of orphans (perhaps hundreds). Ralph and I flew home after that trip and talked about what we could do for these children. Building and running an orphanage would be way too expensive to consider, especially with the potential of hundreds of orphans. The need was immediate, and building a facility would take time. Putting children in an institution would Westernize them, we were told. When they aged out of the institution, they would be ostracized by the community since they had been Westernized. So, how could we help?

Thinking back to our first trip in 1997, Ralph and I were introduced to a British farmer named Fred and his wife, Denise. Our meeting came from a friendly Sunday afternoon dinner at their house with an introduction through a mutual American friend named Pat. That's so God! Denise was trained as a nurse in the UK, and she helped improve the quality of medical care at a local hospital in Concessions, north of Harare. This hospital served the large population of farm workers in the area. This couple became lifelong friends with Ralph and me. We would go to their home on some weekends for a respite. During these visits, we would discuss the situation in our area. We asked for their ideas on the best way to help.

Fred and Denise were part of a group of farmers in their area that sponsored an orphanage not far from where they lived. Fred supplied all the milk to the orphanage from his dairy. We attended church with our friends at the orphanage on Sundays when we visited them on their farm. They made suggestions based on some of their experiences.

One weekend, Denise received a call from the police. A newborn had just been found in a culvert in Harare. They needed a place to care for the infant. So, Denise went to the orphanage the local farmers supported to receive the infant when the police delivered it. This facility had a house on the orphanage property that cared for only infants.

Fred and Denise had lived in Zimbabwe for many years and had run a school for the children of families who lived and worked on their farm. Fred employed about sixty-five men and their families. He provided housing for the workers' families in a village on the farm. There was also a school for the children of the workers and a clinic on their property to care for their farm workers.

Ralph and I gained many good ideas from their experiences. The suggestion was made to leave children in their homes and provide education, medical care, clothing, and food for them. Ralph and I talked at home in Colorado about what we could afford to do and decided to follow this path when we returned. Fundraising began to enable us to build a facility on school grounds where orphans could come for assistance. Nyamashato school grounds occupied approximately twenty-five

Beginning of Orphan Care   99

acres, so there was space to build a feeding center where the old teacher housing had been torn down. These homes were being replaced with new houses in a different location on the school property.

Ralph and I returned the following year, 2001, and built the first "Orphan Care Center" on the cleared land. It opened its operation in January 2002, when the new school year began. The center would provide a meal each day for all the registered orphans and pay school fees for them. School uniforms, made by the sewing women, and school supplies would be provided in addition to medical care. The exchange rate for the U.S. dollar was strong, so school fees were less than one U.S. dollar per child. Every year, the exchange rate got better, so Ralph and I were able to make our money go a long way. I remember having stacks of Zimbabwe dollars behind the back seat of our truck as we made our way to the rural area where we served. Ralph paid the workmen in cash. We could have been easily robbed, but I believe God had His protective hand on us and our work from the beginning.

Ralph went to an auction house in Harare and was able to purchase metal shelving for the various storerooms in the feeding center that was nearing completion. He returned with a truckload. Even the back seat was stacked with shelves. The shelving allowed the cooks places to store their pots and utensils.

At the back of the building, there was an office for the orphan care program and a large storage room for storing uniforms made by the sewing women and bulk food supplies that were shipped from the U.S. or purchased in Harare. This area also received some of the shelving Ralph had brought from Harare.

Initially there were less than a hundred children that were being fed. It wasn't long until it was suggested that these children needed more than one meal a day. It was at that point that the orphans were given a cup of nutritional drink when they had recess in the morning. Lunch was not served until the afternoon.

Ralph and I did not travel to Africa in 2002 because of the political unrest in the country. White people, especially white farmers, were being attacked and, in some cases, were being brutally killed. The area where we were working was especially volatile.

This situation was created because white farmers, over many years, had gradually acquired the fertile land that originally belonged to the native people. The land was taken over because the native people did not have the financial means or the knowledge necessary to use the rich land to its optimum. Over the years, the native people were relocated to communal lands. This is where we were working. It was not safe during this time to travel and work where there were no white people. This area reminds me of the Indian reservations in the United States and how they came about. The government in Zimbabwe, during the colonial period, had moved the native people from the rich land in the Mazowe Valley to the communal lands. This is the area where we had been called to go and help.

In January 2002, when the new school year began, the feeding center opened for business. The center began providing meals for the children who were orphans, not only for the primary school but for the secondary school nearby. Mealtimes for these two groups were staggered because of the large number of children. Initially, we provided one meal each day during weekends and holidays, but we found that most children were not coming to eat. Finally, we put together food packets for the orphans who lived alone with no adult supervision to provide for the weekends. The orphans would pick up their weekend or holiday packets on Fridays before they left school.

It wasn't long before the number of children began to increase. Orphans from neighboring schools in Ward 1 enrolled at Nyamashato Primary so that they could benefit from the food being provided. This required the children living in other school areas to walk many miles to come to school. Our program quickly had to expand to all the schools in Ward 1. The feeding program was just for orphaned children in Ward 1. These limits were established when children began coming from outside Ward 1. We had to set some limits. At one point, we had more than 1,200 children coming for assistance. Now, the numbers have stabilized at just under 700 children.

For some of the very poorest children, the mission purchased shoes and decent clothing since the children had none. This is when Ralph and I began collecting clothing to ship to Zimbabwe. That made an enormous impact on the children and the community. At that time, we were able to do this at no cost to the mission through USAID. With a lot of volunteer helpers, we shipped twenty forty-foot sea containers loaded with clothing, classroom furniture, books, etc. One year, when there was a shortage of food, we also shipped forty-foot sea containers loaded with rice, beans, and corn from grain elevators in Colorado and Kansas. About the time Ralph passed away, this program through the government ceased. It became very costly to ship containers overseas. As a result, we are unable to do much about clothing the poorest children at the present time.

Nyamashato Secondary School was located a short distance from Nyamashato Primary School. It served all the secondary children from the three primary schools in Ward 1. The orphans registered at the secondary school walked to Nyamashato Primary School to eat the meals provided. Gradually, kitchens were built at the other two primary schools (Inyagui and Guzha) in Ward 1. The orphans would pick up their plate of food in the kitchen and carry it into the new library recently constructed and sit at tables to eat. Those two schools were several miles apart. It was too far for the children to walk to Nyamashato Primary for their meals.

Teachers often told either Ralph or me what a difference the feeding program had made in the lives of the children. Attendance improved, and even behavior improved. Children who had not attended school began to attend on a regular basis. Children who had been too weak to walk to school began to attend regularly as well. The teachers began to point out to me that they were able to see a difference in the children being fed and those not eligible.

Our reward was when Mr. Bondeponde informed the staff that the overall pass rate had gone from 53 percent to 85 percent in the period the children were fed. This was proof that the program must continue.

Teachers are paid by the government, but the mission pays salaries for anyone who is employed to care for the orphans, such as cooks, maintenance people, gardeners, poultry workers, and a nurse aide. Eventually, the budget expanded to include a registered nurse, an administrator, an accountant, a social worker, and a chaplain. This was a very gradual development over many years. Local people from the community are hired to run the poultry project, and gardeners raise the vegetables used to feed the children. There is also a group of workers that manage the moringa fields and others that work in the processing facility. The workers are all paid by the mission. These people are all "helping the orphans."

A young man from the community who had recently completed his A-level education was hired to run the office and keep books for the organization. It was his first introduction to a computer. Just before we left to return to the U.S., I had to spend time teaching him how to run the computer. Thank goodness he was a quick learner. He has remained with the organization all these years.

In 2006, the focus of the mission grew, and twenty-five acres of land for the work of the mission were granted by the government to the Orphan Care Project. Mr. Bondeponde is largely responsible for getting this grant from the provincial government. It allowed the work of the mission to expand and to have its own location away from the school. The new property was fenced with an electric fence, and a guard building was constructed at the entrance. This was staffed full-time. A new house was built at the site for the manager and his family. Over the years, an office complex has been constructed in addition to several houses for staff that do not live locally. Wells were drilled for water at the site, and Ralph was able to get ZESA to bring power to the location.

A poultry project was started at the far end of the land that had been granted to the organization. This was an effort to help the organization begin producing some of its own income. The project started small and eventually expanded. With the support of USADF, it now has the capacity to raise 20,000 chickens at one time. Each building can house 5,000 birds. The flocks are rotated so that there is a flock ready for market on a regular schedule.

Unfortunately, the economy in Zimbabwe is such that many people cannot even afford to buy meat for their families. As a result, the market for poultry has been hit hard, and now the poultry project has been mothballed for the foreseeable future. The mission is still raising a few chickens for the feeding program for the orphans. Now, it is not possible to make any profit by marketing the poultry.

The Bible talks about helping widows and orphans.

"Religion that is pure and undefiled before God the Father is this: to visit orphans and widows in their affliction, and to keep oneself unstained from the world" (James 1:27, ESV).

Beginning of Orphan Care

Now, here I was, standing in front of an orphan and a widow, seeing their grief spread raw before my very eyes.

This was the experience of Ralph and I, and we followed God's call.

PIPPITT HOUSE

My people will abide in a peaceful habitation, in secure dwellings, and in quiet resting places.

Isaiah 32:18 (ESV)

Finally, after three and a half years, we had a house to move into. This was originally a teacher's house that had been unsafe for occupancy. Ralph had it torn down to below the windows. It was rebuilt from that point. With all the construction going on, it took a while to get everything complete. Finally, we were able to move into the house in May of 2001. It was just in time. The school was growing so fast, and all the classrooms were now occupied. The school needed the classroom that we had been occupying.

The house had a room that we turned into a kitchen. Ralph built a work counter and installed a sink. Water was piped into the house from the tank on the stand just outside. This upgraded our living standard considerably. Some cabinets from one of the shipments came in handy. One of the cabinets served as a pantry for food storage.

We cooked with a three-burner bottle-gas stove. Our refrigerator was two large ice chests that did an excellent job except in extremely hot weather. We were unable to keep ice for more than five days when the temperatures were very high. It was necessary to plan meals accordingly. I didn't complain, it was such an improvement over what we had been doing.

A small room in our house was turned into a bathroom with a shower. Ralph purchased a camp shower from a camping store. When the water in the tank outside was cold, we heated water in a tea kettle on the stove in the kitchen and carried it into the bathroom.

We could cool the water down by adding water from the tank outside the house. It wasn't like home, but it was an improvement over our previous arrangements.

I felt guilty in such nice surroundings when a couple of teachers were living in old-type housing. Mr. Bondeponde insisted that we had lived in a classroom for several years, and it was only fair. New houses were still being built.

I made some simple curtains for the windows. It was difficult to accomplish much because the sewing women were so curious to see what I was doing.

In the Shona culture, it is tradition to hold a shower for anyone who moves into a new house. The sewing women insisted that they have a party. I didn't want the women to spend money on me when they worked so hard for what little they made. However, there was no way to say "no." So, they had a "housewarming party" for me. What fun was had by all the women!

RALPH'S HELPERS

Likewise, you who are younger, be subject to the elders. Clothe yourselves, all of you, with humility toward one another, for "God opposes the proud but gives grace to the humble."

1 Peter 5:5 (ESV)

Young boys had a way of finding Ralph wherever he might be. They watched every move he made and followed him around like little puppies. Often, when I was looking for Ralph, I would look for a group of boys, and usually, he was in the middle. Some of the boys would be sons of some of the teachers, and others would be children who lived in the surrounding community. They often ranged in age from four years to fourteen years or older. Usually, Ralph found something for them to do. Often, he used them to pick up bricks that littered the ground from a house being torn down or following the builder who was building a house or other structure. Ralph would have them load the broken brick in the back of our truck. Ralph would drive the truck to an area in the road that was a problem when it rained. Of course, the boys enjoyed the ride in the back of the truck. The boys would unload the brick into the mud holes, and Ralph would drive back and forth, pushing them down.

When the holes in the road were filled there were always deep gullies down near the river. Ralph would drive toward the river, and the boys would throw the broken bricks into the deep ditches. This got rid of the broken brick and reduced the washing away of the soil during rainstorms. I never knew if the boys liked to work or just liked the possible ride in the truck.

Ralph paid them according to how much work they had done. They immediately headed for the bottle shop to buy sweets. I am sure the owner of the shop is grateful to Ralph.

The amount of work accomplished always pleased Ralph. He plans to use the bigger boys to tear down the two old houses to make way for new structures. He says the boys are very good workers and accomplish more than the men with ox carts he has hired in the past. Ralph suggested to the older boys that they use their earnings to pay next term's school fees. He had already talked to them about saving most of their money and only spending a small amount on sweets. He says he is going to monitor their savings.

DEDICATION CELEBRATION

Rejoice always, pray without ceasing, give thanks in all
circumstances; for this is the will of God in Christ Jesus for you.

1 Thessalonians 5:16–18 (ESV)

Near the end of our stay in 2001, Mr. Bondeponde told us that there
was a special day planned before our departure back to the U.S. The day
was for the purpose of showing all the local people as well as many dignitaries what had been accomplished in the last five years. This was to be a
huge affair. Many dignitaries from Murewa and Harare had been invited.
Preparations were being made to feed hundreds of people. Ralph and I
would have preferred not to have them go to all the effort and expense,
but we chose to remain supportive; they have so little to celebrate.

Mr. Bondeponde came to me and told me that we needed boutonnieres for distinguished guests. Obviously, he was expecting me to come
up with something. I had only a few days and no supplies of any kind.
Ralph and I made a trip to Harare, and I looked for a fabric store that
sold fabric for fancy dresses. I found some white netting. I had no idea
how much I would need. I had to purchase needles and thread as well. I
spent several days making boutonnieres for all the honored guests who
would be attending. Mr. Bondeponde was so pleased when he saw what I
planned to make. I don't recall how many I made, but I worked late into
the night for several nights to accomplish the project on time.

There was a feast held after all the festivities. The food was all cooked
over an open fire. Cooking was done in fifty-five-gallon drums. Three
fifty-five-gallon drums were used just for cooking the sadza. What an
effort to do all of this. I think some of the women were up all night
cooking. I am sure it took a long time to clean up afterward, but everyone

enjoyed the day. It seemed the entire community, as well as surrounding communities, turned out for the celebration.

The orphan center is named in honor of Heather, who grew up in this community and brought Pat to visit the area and the school. Pat had relayed her experience to us and so was God's messenger. The story touched our hearts, and the rest of the story is history.

At the time of this celebration, the first orphan feeding center was under construction at Nyamashato Primary School. Soon after this building was complete and operational, centers were constructed at both Inyagui and Guzha primary schools in Ward 1.

The dedication day was a big day in the life of this community. They have so little to celebrate. Everyone told us there would be a big crowd and that it would take a lot of food because it was necessary to feed everyone. That was fine; we just didn't know that we were expected to pay for everything. We thought the day was to say "thank you" to us for the projects completed since 1997. We thought it was something the community was doing. It finally dawned on us that what seemed like a lack of planning was a situation where they were waiting for us to do it. It was a day of saying *thank you* for sure, but it was also an excuse to come together and celebrate and have a big feast. Our problem is that in the U.S. if you want something done, you delegate someone to do it. Here, we are learning, slowly, that when someone says we are planning to do something, they are really asking you to provide the funds. It is a much softer-spoken culture than in the U.S. We encountered this type of situation more this particular year than we had in the past.

Mr. Bondeponde had planned the celebration for just the Nyamashato Primary School and the work done at their school. However, other areas refused to be left out. Inyagui and Guzha schools dismissed for the day and brought all their students to the celebration. Both schools had prepared song and dance numbers. Chingwaru, who we had given only a small amount of support, also came with their children and an adult entertainment group. Their group was so good it brought the crowd to their feet.

During the program, a woman, Tracey, who had graduated from seventh grade at Nyamashato Primary School in 1973, made one of the speeches. She is the dean of the Faculty of Commerce at the University of Zimbabwe. She gave an inspirational speech directed at the students. She presented Mr. Bondeponde with twenty copies of the recommended text for grade seven. She told the crowd that she was embarrassed to have to admit she had not been at the school since she picked up her graduation certificate. She also said that it had taken some Presbyterians traveling 19,000 miles to this place to cause her to come here. In addition, she said that it was now time that she began giving back to this community. Mr. Bondeponde has requested that she serve on the Board of Trustees for the Orphan Care Center, and she accepted.

People came from all around. Some came from many, many miles. There were upwards of 5,000 people there. Mr. Bondeponde was disappointed that only one radio station showed up. He had contacted the TV station and newspapers, but no one came. We felt certain they were not given enough advance notice. It is necessary that ministers of government be given months of advance notice if one expects them to be in attendance. Late notice was the reason the minister of education did not come. The deputy regional director of education came instead and was the one who cut the ribbon for the official opening of the library/administration building. Most of the officials from the regional office and the local district offices came. Pastor Chigwida and his wife from City Presbyterian Church came as well. We attended their church when we were in Harare. They had become good friends and we sometimes stayed at their home when we were in town for more than one day.

Since the pastor is a Zimbabwean, we talked with him after the celebration about some of the things that were unsettling to us. He understood our feelings and concerns about the cost and our need to be responsible to our donors. However, he did say that this day was especially important for the community. He went on to explain that there was no way they could have afforded such an occasion. It was a time of bonding with us. I will say that there is no way I can explain how much the people appreciated the work that has been accomplished here over the last five years. The projects were made possible through donor gifts. The pastor went on to tell us that we now had an opportunity to do some teaching about some of the things that really concerned us. He feels we must do this. We followed his advice. It was a most difficult task.

BIBLE STUDY

All Scripture is breathed out by God and profitable for teaching, for reproof, for correction, and for training in righteousness, that the man of God may be complete, equipped for every good work.

2 Timothy 3:16–17 (ESV)

Ralph and I spent time with our Bible in the evening after a long day of work. Since Mr. and Mrs. Bondeponde visited us nearly every evening after dinner, they asked to join us in the study. After the Bible study, Mr. and Mrs. B. would stay on and visit. In the beginning, they asked questions about America and our home. They were curious about the types of food we ate. Mrs. Bondeponde was curious about sadza. She wanted to know if we had such a food in America. We explained that in the Southern part of the U.S., they made cornmeal mush that was very similar to sadza. Mrs. B felt she couldn't visit us unless she could have sadza. That became a joke between us. Most of the discussion would center around the work taking place at the school and making plans for future development.

Many of the teachers joined our Bible study. As the group of teachers grew, it was necessary to bring in more chairs. Eventually, there were so many people coming that the teachers had to each bring their own chairs as well as their own Bibles. Some teachers had no Bible, so Bibles that had arrived in a recent shipment were sourced from the library. Those times turned into more than Bible study. It was truly a time of bonding. The teachers became real friends.

One evening, as people were gathering for our time of Bible study, Mr. Bondeponde appeared with two mailbags of Bibles. He had picked them up at the post office while we were out and about. They had been sent by our church in the U.S. The group was anxious to open the mailbag. Teachers who did not have a Bible were able to select one. Mrs. Bondeponde already had a Bible, but she found one with a large print and latched onto it. She said it was easy for her to read this Bible. The bag included some guidepost study books that proved to be very helpful.

Soon after we began using some of the guidepost study materials, the teachers began to comment about how helpful the material was in understanding what they were reading in the Bible. I began to type the study questions on the computer and then printed off copies with my portable printer for the teachers. They were so excited to each have their own copy. They made comments on how much more meaningful the lessons were. We began to really make some headway in our study.

One evening, as we were concluding our study for the evening, a messenger came to our door to report that Mr. Bondeponde's father had passed away at three the previous morning. Mr. Bondeponde had made plans to go and visit his father the next morning. The family seemed to rely on him for everything and so he felt it necessary for him to leave immediately. At about ten at night, Ralph offered to drive Mr. B where he needed to go, not knowing where that would be. Ralph left with the truck full of family members. Two male faculty members went with Ralph so that he would not be returning in the night alone. Ralph reported that he had driven back into the bush where there were no roads or even a trail.

Eventually, the last distance was on foot; there was no way for a vehicle to get through. Ralph did not return until eight thirty the following morning. All he wanted to do was go to bed.

Several days later, Ralph retraced his trip to collect Mr. Bondeponde and the family. At dinner that evening, Ralph shared that it was a 109 km round trip over incredibly rough roads. Mr. B returned earlier than normal because we had a trip planned to go to the other side of Harare to observe how one community was dealing with the orphan population. Mr. B felt it was critical that he be involved in that visit.

After Ralph's fall, time in the hospital, and weeks of recuperation in Harare, we finally were able to return to Nyamashato. The Bible study group was so relieved when Ralph was out of the hospital and returned to the school. They all arrived at our door the following evening. They requested that we have a prayer service instead of our regular Bible study session. I assumed they had planned this earlier in the day. Nothing had been said to me about it. They had prepared a very nice service, and I was surprised. Everyone is terribly concerned about Ralph's well-being. Their prayers were truly from the heart. They were praising God for Ralph's recovery.

The Bible study group continued for several years. However, as time went on and we became busier, it was difficult to come up with time to have teachers come in the evening. Often, as has already been mentioned, Ralph would return very late from one errand or another. Sometimes, he had not eaten during the day. He would be anxious for his supper. He was also very tired. We were retired and we were working harder than we had ever worked in our lives. Driving on the roads was exhausting because it was necessary to keep shifting gears.

Working with the sewing women took up nearly all my time. I just didn't have enough hours to do any kind of preparation for the study. Since there was no one who felt called to lead the group in study, the group finally fell apart. This is one of my greatest regrets. The teachers seemed hungry for the study, and I just did not have time to do the necessary preparations. I felt the teachers deserved informed instruction and I didn't have time to properly prepare. If I wasn't answering questions that the sewing women had, someone was at the door with a need of some kind or a medical emergency.

During this time, I had a young man who came to visit me on a regular basis. He attended the secondary school nearby. His reason for coming was to ask me questions about the Bible and about Jesus. It wasn't long until he started bringing a friend and then two friends. When the mailbags arrived, which contained some religious reading materials, I suggested that he pick out a book to read, and when he finished, he could return it and get another book. If he had questions, I did my best to answer them. That continued for a long time, and then other boys came with him. It wasn't long until I had several groups of boys coming and asking questions and checking out some of the books that had come in the mailbags.

Note: we were unable to ship religious materials on sea containers. Those items had to ship separately and came in mail bags by snail mail. It was these books that received the most use.

Bible Study

One day, some of the boys asked for novels to read. I took them to the library and showed them where they could find those books. I quickly discovered it wasn't novels they wanted but the religious books that I had recently received.

When it was time for us to return to the U.S., I had to take the books that had come in mailbags to the library. I asked Mr. Bondeponde to appoint a teacher to hold the key to the library so that those interested could come and check out books that had come in the mailbags. Those books receive a great deal of use.

RALPH'S ACCIDENT

Behold, I will bring to it health and healing, and I will heal them
and reveal to them abundance of prosperity and security.

Jeremiah 33:6 (ESV)

In 2001, it was in the tearing down process that the accident happened. Ralph had climbed an African ladder to inspect the work taking
place on the roof of an old teacher's house being torn down. One of the
cross pieces on the hand-built ladder broke, causing him to fall backward
to the ground. He landed on his back on a broken brick. The pain was
severe. I was not on site when the accident happened because I had driven
the truck into the community to check on a girl who had not been in
school and was said to be seriously ill.

Focus quickly changed, and preparations were made to transport
Ralph to the hospital in Harare. I gathered food together that I had
promised the little girl, as well as a couple of bananas and a bottle of
milk. I sent the food to the child by a teacher. My focus had to be on
caring for Ralph.

The back of the front seat in our truck was reclined as far as it would
go. Ralph was rolled onto a board and carried to the truck. There was no
way to get him into the truck on the backboard and it wasn't wise to put
him in the bed of the truck. Four men moved Ralph into the passenger
seat, padded with pillows. I drove the truck, and Mr. Bondeponde directed the way. It was a different route than was normally taken to Harare.
Supposedly, it was a smoother road, but Ralph seriously questioned that
after the fact.

Ralph was X-rayed and immediately put into traction. He was wheeled
to a private room already set up for traction. Ralph spent a week in the
hospital and then was moved to the home of friends, Pastor Chigwida

and his wife. There, he was confined to a bed for a couple of weeks, with a board under the mattress. Finally, Ralph couldn't stand it any longer and he insisted on getting back to the mission. The doctor prescribed a brace for him to wear. He promised to lie around most of the time. That never happened! He wore a back brace for eight weeks and was eventually released from the doctor's care.

Ralph was unable to do any work, but he could walk around and observe. A cane gave him some stability. He wore the back brace until just days before our scheduled departure. We had changed our return to the U.S. until the doctor felt it was safe for him to travel. This gave me more time to work with the sewing ladies. The trip home was long, but Ralph managed well. He was ready to return to the mission the following year. He pushed forward with the work that was so needed.

Memorial Stone

Ralph passed in May of 2011. While I was in Zimbabwe in 2011, just a few months after Ralph passed, the staff planned a memorial service for the community. Many hundreds of people from all around attended the service. Several officials from Harare and Murewa were present. Schools in Ward 1 had been dismissed for the day. People gathered to celebrate Ralph's life. It was estimated that there were 1,500 people who attended, excluding children from Ward 1 schools. People attended from the district offices as well as many local people. Some of our friends from Harare also attended. Many spoke of the things that had been accomplished over the fifteen years we had been coming to Zimbabwe.

The sub-chief of the district was present. For the community, this was a very important occasion. Everyone knew Ralph Pippitt and all he had done for the community, especially the children of Ward 1.

A garden near the entrance to the HCOC property was set aside in memory of Ralph. The headstone was installed while I was at the mission in 2011. The builder had made a cement bench near the headstone where an individual could sit and meditate.

Shrubs and young trees were planted near the headstone to allow for some shade. Over the years, a stone pathway was built, and flowers and a hedge have been planted. It is a place where people can have a quiet moment.

TREATING FOR RINGWORM

Whoever is generous to the poor lends to the Lord, and he will repay him for his deeds.

Proverbs 19:17 (ESV)

One day, I was out among the children as they were playing at recess and noticed many children with scabs on their faces, especially in their hair. I questioned Mrs. Bondeponde (referred to as Mrs. B) about this and learned that it was probably ringworm. I had heard of ringworm but had never seen it to know what it was. I quizzed Mrs. B about what could be done about it. Mrs. B did not give a definite answer. She did say the clinic at the township probably had nothing to treat it with.

I decided to attempt to treat it with the ointment that I had brought with me. Mrs. B helped with the effort. However, I quickly decided that medicine would do no good if the heads were not clean. So, water was warmed in the sun, and Mrs. B and I shampooed heads. Even then, some of the children had so much hair that there was no way to get the medicine on the scalp where it could do some good.

The children were instructed to go home that night and have their parents shave their heads. This is normally done during very hot weather because it is cooler that way. The next morning, Ralph was up early. When he opened the curtains, he called for me to get up. He said there were children lined up outside our door. About thirty-five children were lined up in front of the house. They had come to have their heads treated. They had all bathed and everyone was shiny clean with their heads shaved.

After the abrupt call to get up, I dressed quickly, put on rubber gloves and my day began before breakfast. I applied ointment everywhere I saw a scab. It took several hours to get through all the children. As some children were treated, more joined the line.

Mrs. Bondeponde later informed me that there were a lot of children with scabies. That was something that I was not familiar with. Mrs. B explained that it usually appeared in the crotch area. So, I suggested that Mrs. B bring some children to me who were suffering from scabies. They were told to bring clean clothes with them to school the following day. Mrs. B explained to the children what we planned to do.

Mrs. B and I filled all the five-gallon buckets that we could find with water and set the buckets in the sun, hoping to warm the water a bit. The following afternoon, each child was given a container of water and soap and sent to the bathing area to remove their clothes and wash their bodies. When they had done that, I put some medicine on their finger and instructed them to apply the medicine to the infected areas.

It wasn't long before stories got back to us about the miracle workers at Nyamashato. My heart ached for these children because of the suffering that existed. People didn't know how to care for themselves, nor did they have the means to do so. The clinic never had adequate medicine to treat these ailments or claimed they didn't know what it was.

Children can't learn when they are hurting. Ralph and I ached for the children who really had no one to turn to. This experience was the beginning of plans for a clinic for children located at the school.

BOYS WITHOUT PARENTS

Learn to do good; seek justice, correct oppression; bring justice to the fatherless, plead the widow's cause.

Isaiah 1:17 (ESV)

Everywhere we turned, children were in need. Mr. Bondeponde came to us early one morning in September to give a list of orphans that had been brought to his attention. It was necessary that the center be finished as soon as possible. How we could have worked in the community for more than three years and these situations had never come to our attention was puzzling. God's timing? It was difficult for Ralph and me to understand how people could live very nearby and not be aware of the needs of children, especially children living alone. Mr. Bondeponde attempted to explain to us that in their culture, people did not get involved in issues of people outside their immediate family. I believe the struggle to survive is such an ordeal that people cannot be concerned about others.

Ralph was still in a back brace and had been very careful about riding in the truck over rough terrain. However, this day he seemed to need to see these situations with his own eyes. He would not listen to me about not riding in the truck on the rough terrain. One family of boys lived not terribly far from the government clinic to which we had given so much help.

We loaded supplies into the truck. The plan was to check out some of the situations that we had been told about. Mr. Bondeponde usually went with us but was unable to join us on this day.

Most of these children do not live near a road, so we had to drive cross-country. It was not an easy trip. I worried about Ralph's back, but he was determined to see the needs for himself. Our first stop was at the home of a family of five boys living on their own. The oldest boy was sixteen. The youngest child, only a toddler, was living with grandparents some distance away and not in our area of operation. The oldest boy had gone to gather firewood, and the other three were herding cattle. They were grateful for the food supplies and asked God to bless us. Ralph went inside the rondavel since I was filming. He said the building was neat and clean, but there were no signs of food supplies. We had brought food supplies with us that we left for the boys.

The second stop we made was at the home of three boys. It was a pathetic situation. The oldest boy was absent. He had gone to a commercial farm on the other side of the big river. It was miles away. The farmer lets people go into the fields after harvest and pick up anything edible left on the ground. The two younger boys were out picking and eating mulberries, the only food they could find. The three boys live in a small rondavel with only a dirt floor. They had no toilet or bathing area that we could see. Their clothes were ragged and dirty, as were the blankets on the single bed in the room. I am certain the younger boys sleep on the rough dirt floor. Junk was piled everywhere along the walls of the rondavel. There was no sign of a cooking utensil. A large stirring spoon was on the dirt floor. There were no dishes that we could see. A piece of tin had been pounded into a bowl shape and contained a few grains of roasted maize. It may have been the remains of their breakfast. There was a small amount of mealy meal in an open bucket. The water buckets were open and filthy. How they survive is a question. There is no place to store the food supplies that we had brought for them.

Ralph feels the rondavel is about to collapse. The door jamb is only a post driven into place. The hinges on the door are made of barbed wire. The beam above the door is collapsing, and the thatched roof will not last much longer. It can't be good for the boys to sleep on the floor breathing dust. I didn't see any mice, but they were undoubtedly there. The door would not keep out snakes, thieves, or much else. These children have been reduced to the very lowest level of society; they are living like animals. How neighbors can ignore these children is beyond me. Even though there was a family living nearby, no one came near when we stopped to check on the boys and leave food.

When we arrived back at school, we sat with Mr. Bondeponde and discussed the situation and determined where to go from here and how the Orphan Care Center could help. God is not going to allow us to build just a feeding center; it must truly be an Orphan Care Center. Again, the subject came up about involving the community and ways they could help. Ralph suggested building a small one-room house about ten by twelve feet. If we furnished the cement, a door, and a window, the community would have to make the brick and supply the labor, sand, and pebbles. Mr. Bondeponde explained again that it is foreign to their culture to help anyone outside the immediate family. I read to him the scripture from Matthew 25:31–46 and Luke 10:29–35. I explained that by the people not helping their neighbor in time of need, they were acting as the priest and the Levite. He pricked up his ears and said that he would use that during the meeting with the home-based caregivers and the management team scheduled for the next day.

Horrors

I had just been told by one of the caregivers that the boys where we had left food on Saturday had it all stolen this morning. Ralph had worried about the door that, even though it locked, was not secure. The boys told us about leaving to get water from the borehole in preparation for coming to school, and when they returned, the rondavel had been broken into, and all the items we left were gone. How can people steal from children who have nothing?

Yesterday, I had prepared some beef stew. There had been some leftovers. We took some to the children whose food had been stolen. They were so grateful; one of the boys had tears in his eyes. The older boy still had not returned, and the two young ones had been alone since Saturday morning. Mr. B gave all the boys the lesson books they needed from the supply we had purchased last week in Harare. He also told the older child that in the future, when he had a problem, to come to him because he should not leave the younger boys alone.

God does provide! Today, there is talk in the community about building the children a one-room building that is secure. One of the builders working here at the school has offered to furnish the labor free when the sand, pebbles, and bricks are donated. Some of the community members have come forward and donated these materials. The school has a few old sheets of roofing that are still usable, and Ralph has promised the cement. Ralph worked with the lumberyard in Murewa he had been buying materials from to donate the windows, door, and doorframe for the boys' proposed home.

A gentleman from the community promised Ralph that he would build the house for the three boys. Others from the community had just finished hauling a pile of sand for mixing cement. The boys would soon have a sound structure to live in.

MADANHA FAMILY STORY

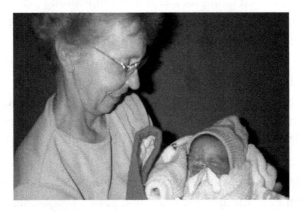

God said, "No, but Sarah your wife shall bear you a son, and you shall call his name Isaac. I will establish my covenant with him as an everlasting covenant for his offspring after him."

Genesis 17:19 (ESV)

Note: Names mean something to God, and they are also precious to human parents; Roberta helped a family, and they named their daughter after her—that is a big honor.

One afternoon, Mrs. Bondeponde came to get me. She wanted to go visit a friend who lived not far from the school. In fact, we passed the homestead every time we went in or out of the mission. The father works in Harare and comes home often on weekends.

Mrs. Madanha became a good friend over the years.

I met two of her children on that afternoon visit with Mrs. Bondeponde. Both children are unable to walk. The mother wanted wheelchairs for the children so that she would be able to move the children around. They are growing and are becoming difficult to move. The mother feels that if she had wheelchairs, the children would be able to attend Nyamashato

School. I learned that afternoon that she had another child that was also crippled, but he had passed away before our coming to Zimbabwe.

The mother locks the children in an empty room by themselves when she goes to the field to work. The fields are near a river several kilometers from her house. She attends to the children's needs when she returns from the fields. In my observation, the children are desperately in need of stimulation. The children have no books or toys. I find it difficult to think about children being locked in a room for long periods of time. I promised Mrs. Madanha that I would find wheelchairs for the children, but it would take time for a shipment to arrive here.

I sent a message home requesting two wheelchairs to come on the next shipment that was being prepared. A member of our board spent time outfitting the donated wheelchairs with solid tires and wider tires to be able to handle the rough terrain. Supporters of our mission were very helpful. Unfortunately, one of the children died while the shipment was en route to Zimbabwe.

Mrs. Madanha was so happy to receive the wheelchairs for the crippled children even though one child had passed away. One evening, she brought the little boy to tell us thank you for the wheelchair. He was so happy. It was the first time I had seen him smile. It meant that he could get outside and interact with other children.

Mrs. Madanha reminded us that she had the extra wheelchair at her homestead. She wanted to give it to anyone who needed it. Sometime later, a child was brought to us by ox cart that needed a wheelchair. The boy that was crippled lived in the Guzha Primary School area. The extra wheelchair was soon put to good use.

Another child dies! Madanha's little boy died while we were still in Zimbabwe. This was the third child to have died from apparently the same ailment. The doctors, to my knowledge, never gave them a diagnosis. All three crippled children of the Madanha family had died before they reached the age of ten years.

Ralph and I, along with several members of the faculty, walked to the Madanha home when we learned of the little boy's death. The men were all gathered outside under the shade of a tree. That is the custom in this culture. Ralph joined the group of men. Mrs. Bondeponde and I entered the home. The mother was sitting on the floor in a corner with the child totally wrapped in a blanket at her feet. A group of twenty-five or thirty women were sitting around her on the floor. We shook hands with everyone. When I finally reached the mother, she began crying, and instead of shaking my hand, she threw her arms around me and sobbed. It was difficult to hold my composure. I was expected to sit on the floor with the other women. They began to sing in Shona. After a time, I was asked to offer a prayer. I am sure most did not understand any English. Later, Mrs. Bondeponde motioned for me to come with her. We went outside and she explained that I could return to school but that she would remain there for a time. The men had disappeared. I was told that they had gone to the grave site and would be digging the grave. At that point, I returned to the school, and Mrs. B remained with the women.

Outside and a distance from the rondavel, another group of women were cooking, preparing sadza. A huge pile of plates was stacked nearby. Apparently, everyone must have brought their own eating plates. Ralph told me later that when they finished digging the grave, the men all returned to the Madanha homestead. Food was served: sadza, fried cabbage, and small fish (*kapenta*). The fish are found in Lake Kariba. They are caught, dried, and are often served with sadza.

Much later, when Mrs. B returned to the school, she came by to tell me how much everyone appreciated my attending the funeral. She indicated that the family wants us to come and get the wheelchair and take it to someone who has need of such.

A year later: As is the custom in their culture, a memorial service is held one year after the death of an individual. We were expected to attend and were usually called upon to make a speech. The community saw the wheelchairs that we had provided as the ultimate expression of the love of one human for another.

Later that same year, one of the teachers appeared at the door of the classroom that Ralph and I were still occupying. She had a very elderly lady from the community who had come to see me. I recognized the woman; she walked with a cane. She was the grandmother of the Madanha children, who had passed away. The woman had brought me a bouquet of flowers that she had picked from her yard. It was her effort to say thank you for all that we had done for her grandchildren. I would love to have communicated with her, but she knew no English and I knew very little Shona.

I saw Mrs. Madanha from time to time and she always waved to us when we drove past her house on our way to Harare or just running an errand in the community. She would walk to Nyamashato from time to time and visit me. Sometimes, she stopped at Bondeponde's house and visited with Mrs. Bondeponde.

Mrs. Madanha had another little boy. He was a cute little guy and would always wave to us when we drove past their house. One day, we went back and forth numerous times past their house, checking on the progress of the workmen. This little boy would run out to the road and wave at us. We thought he was just being friendly and had no idea his mother needed our help.

Later that evening as we were sitting down to supper, a knock came on our door. It was a man wanting Ralph to come quickly; Mrs. Madanha was in labor and needed to go to the hospital. So, Ralph left his supper and went to Mr. Bondeponde's house and asked him to go along. I think Ralph was afraid he would have to deliver a baby on his way to the hospital.

Later that night, Ralph returned, but the baby had not yet been born. He was tired and still had not had anything to eat. It was a couple of days later that we learned that Mrs. Madanha had a little girl, and they named her Roberta after me.

A year or so after Roberta was born, the Madanha family moved to Harare. The husband's work was in Harare, and he had been able to find housing for his family. Ralph and I did not have contact with the family for several years.

Roberta Madanha and Mrs. Madanha came to see me one day years later. They were in the rural area checking on things at their property. Roberta was the baby that was born on one of the early trips to Zimbabwe that Ralph and I made. Roberta had just completed fourth grade. She had placed number seven in a class of 400 children. She was very excited to share her achievements with me.

BILHARZIA, A PARASITE

Heal me, O Lord, and I shall be healed; save me, and I shall be saved, for you are my praise.

Jeremiah 17:14 (ESV)

Bilharzia is a disease caused by a parasitic worm found in freshwater. It is not a disease found in the United States but is common in Africa. A certain type of snail that lives in freshwater is the carrier. The parasite from the snail can live in the water for about forty-eight hours. The parasite penetrates the skin of a human being who wades, swims, bathes, or does laundry in contaminated water.

After several weeks, the parasite matures into adult worms and lives in the blood vessels of the human body. Eggs from the female can travel to the bladder or intestine as well as the heart and lungs. It can be deadly if it goes untreated.

One day, I was called to a sixth-grade classroom. A child had what I thought was an epileptic seizure. The teacher panicked. It happened twice in one day. I found out later that it had happened before but never at school. I learned immediately that the children from that family had nothing to eat. I wondered if this might have triggered the attack. At the time, I wanted to take him to the hospital in Murewa. Our truck was in Harare for repairs, and Mr. Bondeponde had gone with the Orphan Care truck. Those were the only vehicles in that area at the time. What was I to do?

Our only resource was our recently opened first-aid station. It was not prepared to handle this type of emergency. The local government clinic had no source of transportation and no ambulance. The child was moved to the first aid room, where we were able to have him lie down.

When he recovered, he wanted to go home. Several children walked with him so that he would not be alone.

When we were able to transport him to the hospital, we learned that he had a severe case of bilharzia. He was treated and released from the hospital the following day. The treatment required one dose of the proper medication. Ralph and I had never heard of the disease.

We learned that it is something the children get from playing in the water of streams and ponds. You will recall that one of our earliest projects was the building of a bridge across a small river that many children waded through daily to get to school. It was important that the children be taught to use the bridge and not to play in the river.

About a week later, another emergency—the nurse aide called for me to come to the first aid station. She had a child in severe pain, and she didn't know what to do. When I arrived, the child was on the examining room table, writhing with pain and crying for help. I suspected appendicitis. Ralph drove him to the clinic at the township. He was given an aspirin and sent home. The wrong treatment if it is appendicitis. I drove him to the hospital in Murewa. The boy was admitted with a suspected strangulated hernia. When the doctor saw him the next day, he identified the problem as bilharzia and treated the child. The boy was dismissed from the hospital the following day.

We soon learned that most people did not know the seriousness of the disease or how to prevent it. The nurse aide from the dispensary came to me a few days later to inform me that she had identified nearly 200 children with bilharzia from the four schools in Ward 1 that she visits. There was no way we could transport that many children to the hospital in Murewa for treatment. What were we to do? We were informed by Albert Mukondwa, the environmental health technician and Advisory Board member, that possibly there are three times that many children who were infected.

The following day, while we were trying to decide what to do about screening all the children, we received a call from Albert, the health technician from the local clinic. Yes, after years of no phones or contact with the outside world, cell phones became available in the rural area. Albert informed us that three people from the hospital in Murewa will come here and spend the day screening the children attending Nyamashato

Primary and Secondary Schools and will treat them for bilharzia. Ralph had to go and pick up the hospital personnel, bring them to Nyamashato Primary, and take them back at the end of the day. The hospital has no transport, we were told.

The staff from the hospital spent a day and a half treating children from Nyamashato Primary and Secondary Schools. Because of the large enrollment, they tested only the children who came voluntarily. Four hundred twenty-five children in a population of approximately 1,200 children were tested, and 88 percent tested positive. That was a higher percentage than had been previously estimated. The total enrollment of Nyamashato Primary School at that time was about 600 children. I do not recall what the enrollment at the secondary school was at that time, but I would estimate it to be about the same number as the primary school. The secondary school serves the entire Ward 1 children. Ward 1 is made up of three primary schools. Nyamashato Primary is the largest of the three schools. Not all children attend secondary school. Some of the children cannot pass the required exam for entering a secondary school.

Ralph and I requested that the team from the hospital come back and screen all the children in Ward 1, where we are working. Ralph was told no; the medicine was too expensive. Yet we were told that this is a life-threatening ailment. How could a government turn their backs on their own people?

We then requested an extensive educational program for not only the school children but the community at large. This was something that could be conducted by the local government clinic.

Life in the communal lands of Zimbabwe is tough at best. The local community receives few, if any, services. Yes, there is a government clinic locally, but they provide few services and seem to never have medicine for various ailments. They freely hand out aspirin for anything and everything.

Early in our stay the following year, Ralph was contacted by the hospital in Murewa. They informed him that they were prepared to treat all the infected children in Ward 1. Praise be to God. That was certainly an answer to prayer. Yes, Ralph was their chauffeur each day. He had to drive that awful road to and from Murewa twice each day. The hospital sent a much larger crew of nurses, and every child was tested at all the schools in Ward 1.

Bilharzia, a Parasite

When the nurses were finished at each school, a meeting was called of all the staff and children. The nurses explained how the people could check for themselves to see if they were infected. They were shown samples of what their urine would look like if they were infected. Those individuals were told how serious this was and that they should come to the hospital for treatment. The head nurse stressed the importance of not playing in water, whether in the river or standing ponds. The children were instructed to teach their parents that evening when they returned home. Many of them did exactly that because we heard from the parents.

Beauty, the nurse for HCOC, has been concerned about cases of bilharzia. UNICEF does not supply the testing kits or drugs in their routine deliveries to HCOC clinics. The clinic has not had enough money to buy what is needed. The medicine is very expensive and sometimes is even difficult to find. Some of your donations made it possible for us to fund this very important project. With the proper medicine, Beauty has been testing children and treating the ones that test positive. The number of children testing positive is alarmingly high, as high as 75 percent. Our truck became a traveling clinic. Testing was done on the spot, and medicine was dispensed from the back of the truck.

OSWALD: A TEEN STORY ABOUT AIDS

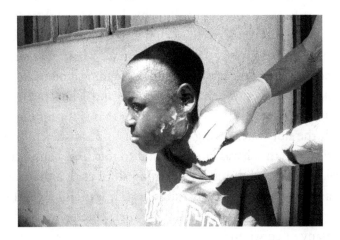

Then they also will answer, saying, 'Lord, when did we see you hungry or thirsty or a stranger or naked or sick or in prison, and did not minister to you?' Then he will answer them, saying, 'Truly, I say to you, as you did not do it to one of the least of these, you did not do it to me.'

Matthew 25:44–45 (ESV)

I recall an amazing experience that happened in 2006. It involves a young teenager. Mr. Bondeponde, the headmaster of the Nyamashato School, periodically took a load of orphans in the back of a one-ton truck to the hospital in Murewa (more than an hour's drive from the Orphan Center) for check-ups or because of illnesses. Oswald had just returned from one of those trips.

The doctor in Murewa had instructed Mr. Bondeponde to have me care for this child daily. I did not know where the child lived or what kind of care he needed. I also did not know how the doctor knew about me, but God did. When Ralph returned in his own truck, Florence, a nurse aide for our First Aid Station, and I proceeded to the home of Oswald. Florence, the nurse aide, went with me because she knew where Oswald lived. When we arrived, we found Oswald sitting outside a small two-room building. The people standing around were skeptical of a white woman, but Florence explained that the doctor wanted Roberta to dress their brother's wounds every day.

Initially, little was known about AIDS. It was a death sentence in most people's minds. Families usually abandoned members who became ill. They were fearful of becoming ill themselves because they didn't know how the disease was transmitted. Ralph and I would ask the Lord daily to see the needs and give us the courage to face what came our way.

I sometimes asked the family members standing around to boil water. That took time over an open fire. Florence and I had carried medical supplies with us. I carefully cleaned the pus that was running down his neck with the hot water, being careful not to burn the child. His skin looked so fragile that I was almost afraid to touch it. I suspected it was AIDS-related, but I did not say anything since such a diagnosis is like leprosy, and everyone would abandon him. It was also a good thing we carried rubber gloves in our vehicle for such emergencies so we could deal with any open wounds.

There were no band-aids large enough to cover the entire wound. I made a pad out of a roll of gauze and applied Neosporin. When my supply of gauze ran out, it was necessary to use strips of sheeting to tie around his head to hold the gauze in place. His skin looked so fragile that tape might have pulled the skin off when removing the bandage. The following day, when I returned to redress the wound, the bandage was saturated with pus, and the dressing was coming off. (Note: Ralph and I had shipped discarded sheets from local hotels in forty-foot sea containers "for such a time as this.") Such items were also sent to other rural hospitals in Zimbabwe. I used torn sheeting for bandages. I tore the sheets into various widths and lengths. The only way to sterilize them was to iron them with a very hot iron and place them in a new zip-lock bag. This method would not pass here in the U.S., but it was all that I could do.

I went daily to check on the boy and dress his wounds. Often, there would be no other person around—they were clearly fearful. The child was alone and usually had not been given anything to eat. Families were

136 Hope for Zimbabwe Orphans

afraid of AIDS at that time and really ostracized the patient. It was obvious that Oswald's infection was as bad inside his mouth as outside. The pain had to be severe. Oswald never complained or gave any indication that it hurt.

I always brought something for Oswald to eat when I visited him. If the rondavel (the cooking area) was locked, I would be unable to cook any food. Eating was a problem for Oswald. His mouth had sores in it, and his throat was so swollen that it was difficult to get anything other than liquid down it. He required food that would go down easily, such as bananas or soft, cooked eggs. Cleansing the wound and bandaging was the purpose of my daily trips. Even though he knew little to no English and I knew no Shona, he always tried to say thank you. This routine went on for months. It took a lot of time to drive to Oswald's home and back again besides the time I spent with him. When the wound got worse, I often went twice a day to clean him up and redress the wound. Oswald and I built a special bond between us.

We became aware that families often do not want to be bothered caring for sick relatives. In this case, I think they are ignoring Oswald and not giving him his medicine, hoping he will die soon. Ralph and I knew that Oswald would not survive, but we could not abandon him. It is heartbreaking, but all we can do is check on him daily and administer as much care as possible. I always took a bit of food for him or sent it to him by Florence, the nurse aide.

Florence and I went early one morning to dress Oswald's wounds. Florence could not go later because she was going to the doctor in Murewa with eight other orphans that day. She and I had decided Oswald was not able to make the trip. However, when we arrived at his home, Oswald was dressed, ready to go, and wanted to go, and so he did. However, the doctor did nothing for him. He said the dressing was well done and did not want to change it. He prescribed some medicine, but we knew that Oswald was not going to get well.

It was difficult to lose Oswald, but I knew from the beginning that he would not survive. AIDS was a death sentence at that time. The people in Zimbabwe were just beginning to learn of the disease and were fearful. As time went on, I discovered that in families with several children, it was always the youngest that contracted AIDS. I assumed that the older children had been born before the father began going to Harare seeking employment. The father would stay there for long periods of time where prostitutes were present and often shared disease. The youngest child was conceived on a visit home. We saw this situation repeated many, many times.

The reader may be wondering why this young man, a secondary school student, was so severely infected with AIDS. This is a disease passed through direct contact with bodily fluids. We can only speculate. I do know that sexual abuse is common in this area, often by an older family member.

Oswald continued to decline. Florence indicated that Oswald was now critical. I decided the end might be near and so I decided to go see him. This might be the last time. Florence and a visitor from Denver went with me. Since Florence had dressed his wounds earlier that day, no additional dressing was done. We found Oswald seated in the house. His breathing was rapid and shallow, his feet were swollen, and he had a fever. He had just wasted away; he was only a skeleton with skin stretched over it. He coughed, and it sounded like his chest was full of congestion. I felt certain his lungs were filling. I felt helpless, and taking him to the hospital would be futile. They do nothing. Florence washed his face and chest with cool water to help bring down the fever. He is refusing medicine, saying that it makes him vomit. The left eye that appeared to have a boil forming on the eyeball the last time I dressed him was bulged, and I knew he no longer saw out of that eye. I suggested that Florence close the eyelid and put a patch over it.

Days later, Florence came to find me and told me that I needed to go and see Oswald. I told her I would go when Ralph returned with the truck, and he could go with me. Florence told me no, that I must go immediately. So, I walked there with Florence, and several others accompanied us—it took over an hour, and it was very hot outside. I found Oswald in bed in the building where he always sat outside. He was so frail. He motioned for me to come close. He whispered thank you for caring for him. He said he was happy. Oswald passed a few hours later. The uncle came to our house at five the next morning to tell us that Oswald had passed.

With the severity of Oswald's case and others, we began to wonder if there was a need for a hospice center. We also saw a need for a place where abused children can seek refuge. One day, a child came to school complaining of chest pains and a headache. She would talk to no one. Even Florence, our nurse aide, couldn't get her to talk. She lay in the dispensary all day, facing the wall and talking to no one. I was certain she was an abuse case. She was one in a family of six children that lived alone. Vincent, who died, was a member of this family of children. I doctored his leg wound early in our mission.

When we left the U.S. in June, we thought that possibly this would be our last trip to Zimbabwe. After this experience and others, we began to feel that God may be opening a new door for this mission. As I write this, it is 2024. The mission continues under new leadership. The number of orphans is less than in the early years, but we still provide the needs of nearly 700 children. It is speculated that this number will decline only slightly in the coming years. In the rural areas, food is so dependent on the weather and the rainy season. Irrigation is not an option for most families in the communal lands where the mission is located.

KNITTING CO-OP

I will greatly rejoice in the Lord; my soul shall exult in my God, for he has clothed me with the garments of salvation.

Isaiah 61:10 (ESV)

From the beginning, the sewing women had been given access to a classroom for them to operate from. This room was in seriously poor condition. They did the best they could for a few years. In 2008, Ralph was finally able to see a clear way to build a building dedicated to the sewing co-op and the recently formed knitting co-op. It was constructed on school property just inside the entrance gate. The building housed the sewing women, and a smaller room was used for the knitting co-op that had recently formed. The knitting women made sweaters for the children that go with the school uniform.

The knitting co-op began with only five women and one knitting machine. Since the women had no knowledge of how to use a knitting machine, it was necessary for them to receive some training. I arranged at a shop in Harare that sold yarn and supplies to train the women at their shop. Two women from the group were taken to Harare and lived with relatives for one month. The two women spent their days learning to operate and maintain a knitting machine. When they returned to the rural area, they would be responsible for training the rest of the women in the co-op.

A couple of weeks after we had taken the two women for training, we were in Harare and decided to stop in and check on their progress. They were so excited to see us and fell over themselves, attempting to show us the sweaters they had made.

The women were doing an exceptional job. They still needed to learn to knit sweaters using more than one color of yarn. It was good that we checked on them because they needed more yarn for the lessons in the last two weeks of their training. The cost had gone up by 1,000 ZD per package. I just hope that after the training they will be able to sell the sweaters and make a bit of profit. In the beginning, we only had one knitting machine for the five women in the group. They made out a schedule of when each woman would come to work. One woman would knit in the morning and then assemble the pieces in the afternoon, while a different woman would knit a sweater in the afternoon. Mr. Bondeponde sent out a notice to the community that they could purchase sweaters from the knitting women.

They did well, and later, two new manually operated knitting machines were shipped from the U.S. in one of the shipping containers. In addition to making sweaters for the school uniforms, they made baby layettes. These were sold in the community, along with sweaters for the school uniforms.

The knitting women came to me one morning so excited. They came to tell me they had received a lot of orders for sweaters from the secondary school students. The sweaters they have been making are for primary children. Now, they need to make some larger sweaters for the secondary students.

When Ralph could find some time, he spent time building cabinets for the sewing co-op and the knitting co-op. Both groups needed a place to store supplies. They were finally completed and delivered to the women. Ralph said the women were so happy that they were dancing and singing. When the cooks in the feeding center saw what he had done, they decided they needed a cabinet, too. So, Ralph built cabinets for them as well. Thank goodness for the generator we bought in South Africa. It has made it possible for Ralph to use a Skilsaw for cutting such large pieces of lumber.

As this book is being written, things in the country have declined to the point that if fabric and yarn can be obtained, the cost is so expensive that there is no way for the women to break even with their expenses. So many people have no jobs, and money needs to be reserved for the purchase of food. In addition, the quality of the supplies is extremely poor; it really is not worth the time and effort required to make the garment.

It is heartbreaking to see this effort fail because of the cost of supplies if they are even available.

In 2018, the last year I was able to travel to Zimbabwe, I was unable to find yarn in Zimbabwe in the colors needed. I flew to South Africa and purchased all the yarn I could find in the correct colors that would work on the knitting machines. The yarn was on large cones that were very heavy. I was able to check several large boxes as luggage on the return trip to Harare. That supply has been made into sweaters long before the writing of this book. They are now unable to operate because of the lack of supplies or the cost of the yarn.

Children were always so proud of new clothing. Most had never had anything new in their lives. They would often walk past our house to show us their new clothing. A boy wanted us to see his new sweater that the knitting co-op had made. He was so very proud of the sweater.

PRESCHOOL & CLINIC BUILDING

Train up a child in the way he should go; even when he is old he will not depart from it.

Proverbs 22:6 (ESV)

As soon as the feeding center was ready for occupancy, Ralph and I decided to build another building about the same size as the feeding center inside the fenced area. We planned for the building to have two classrooms for preschoolers with a storage room between the two classrooms. This was a place where teachers could prepare for the following day, and it also provided storage space for supplies. The building also housed a small clinic where children could come when they had a medical issue.

A woman who lived just outside the school grounds was hired to staff the clinic. She had been previously employed at a clinic as a nurse aide. She had to go for a refresher course in Harare before we could hire her. The building was completed and ready for occupancy in 2003. It quickly became a very busy place. The children loved Florence, our nurse aide.

It wasn't long before community members began coming for help with medical issues. We explained that this was just for the care of orphans. We told them that they needed to go to the government clinic at Madamombe town center. They explained that the government clinic had no medicine. We couldn't turn them away, but any child was given priority.

One of the classrooms in this new building was for infants. These children were just toddlers. The other room housed the children who would be preparing for first grade the following year. The classes were large and began to grow when word spread that they had regular classrooms. Fortunately, one of the shipments had tables and chairs for young children. A room full of forty to sixty wiggling bodies is something to be dealt with.

The preschool teachers were elated to have real classrooms for the children. Previously, they met their classes under the mango trees on the school grounds. The trees give dense shade but what to do when it rains? It was time that they had a real classroom.

Teaching English to that many children was nearly impossible, but it was so much fun! The teacher would take half the children outside to play on the equipment that had come in a recent shipment. I would switch groups with the teacher at the halfway point. It was fun, and the children learned quickly. I tried to make it a time of activity. I would call on them by name to show me certain items in the room. They loved it because they could get up and walk around. When they showed me the item, they had to say the English name for the object.

The teachers reported to me that the children were giving their parents an English lesson at home in the evening. Some of the children were even going to the infant room and teaching those children some of the English they had just learned. These children were so young that I am not sure how much they really understood.

The children came to me when they saw me out and would try to talk to me in English. They got so excited when I responded in English to what they had said. Our time was not all work. I loved working with the little ones. They were always so happy.

EXPANDING SUPPORT FOR ORPHANS IN WARD 1

The Lord is a stronghold for the oppressed, a stronghold in times of trouble. And those who know your name put their trust in you, for you, O Lord, have not forsaken those who seek you.

Psalm 9:9–10 (ESV)

In March 2003, we began to expand the orphan care program throughout Ward 1 of Mashonaland East Province. We were way beyond the two-year commitment we had originally made. There was no way to walk away. It just wasn't possible.

A meeting was held at Inyagui Primary School for the purpose of informing the community on how to begin caring for their orphans. Mr. Bondeponde informed the gathering about how to select orphan caregivers from each village. He also gave them some guidelines to follow when determining who is really a child in need of the services the Orphan Care Center provides. He also warned them of pitfalls that they may encounter. The plan was to begin feeding a nutrition drink to the identified orphans when the second term begins in May.

At the end of our meeting, parents lined up to express their appreciation for the last shipment of clothing that had been received. The thanks really go to all the many people who helped make these shipments possible. My gratitude goes to all those who collected and donated clothing and time involved in packing boxes for shipment. Once items were collected, the real work of sorting, folding, and packing boxes began. It takes many willing hands and a lot of time. In addition, many man-hours are required when it is time to load a container. The support many people gave Ralph and me, enabling us to make these shipments happen, is so rewarding.

The day following our meeting at Inyagui, we made a trip to Guzha Primary School for the purpose of meeting with the headmaster and the

School Development Committee (SDC). Mr. Bondeponde spent a great deal of time teaching them how to select the neediest children. He cautioned them to be on alert for those who would try to force registration but do not fit the criteria. He related some of his own experiences in the last year as an example.

The village headmen were encouraged to organize for the purpose of each village growing a specific vegetable crop for the feeding program. It was pointed out that this would help reduce our operating costs.

After the meeting, the headmen showed us an outdoor cooking facility that had not been used for some time. It is a rondavel with a cooking pit in the center. With some minor repairs, it can be made usable until a proper structure can be built. The village headmen offered to do the necessary repairs so that we could begin operation when school resumes on May 6. We were grateful for their support.

Ralph was in frequent contact with the MP (member of parliament) over the area we were working in. He had promised Ralph to track the shipment of maize that would soon be arriving from the port in Durbin, South Africa.

Cheunje, a boarding school, nearby but not in Ward 1, invited us to come for the opening of their new library. This was the result of the school receiving boxes of books from a recent shipment to Ward 1, our area of operation. This school had been an O-level secondary school. They are in the process of becoming an A-level secondary school with boarding facilities. They are requesting our assistance. We had to explain that the books were a gift. Our area of work encompasses only Ward 1. It is important that we do not overextend our ability to be effective. There are many requirements set by the government before they can become a boarding school. We just don't have the funding to help them achieve their goal. This is another example of why we had to restrict our area of operation.

The books arrived at an ideal time. Their new library did not have one book. The school had a long list of needs for their library. We had to explain that we had supplied the books because Ward 1 had more books than they needed. We shared with them the extra books that were shipped. We also explained that we could not expand our work beyond Ward 1. Our resources just couldn't cover all the needs in the area.

148   Hope for Zimbabwe Orphans

FEEDING CHILDREN

For I was hungry and you gave me food, I was thirsty and you gave me drink, I was a stranger and you welcomed me.

Matthew 25:35 (ESV)

The new feeding center at Nyamashato Primary School was built in 2001 and opened for service at the beginning of the new school year in January 2002. We were unable to be present at the opening because of the unrest in the country at the time. We were advised not to travel there until things were more peaceful.

One day in 2002, we received a call from Mr. Bondeponde. He was requesting permission to provide the nutrition drink the orphans received at morning recess to all the children enrolled at Nyamashato Primary School. The local people were finding it impossible to provide food for their families because of the poor crop year in 2002. He reported that during recess the children who were not orphans were hanging on the fence crying because they were so hungry. Ralph told him to proceed with his plan, and he would find a way to send money for the necessary supplies. I don't recall the actual number of orphans we had registered at that time, but we began supplying nutrition drinks to approximately 700 children, including orphans.

This service continued for the balance of 2002 and until May 2003. Two thousand two had been a very bad crop year, and there was little or no food available. At the beginning of the second term of 2003, families in the community were beginning their harvest and had food to provide for their families. That was the worst crop year that we had ever encountered in all the time we spent in Zimbabwe. It was during this time that we shipped container loads of rice and beans from Colorado to the area we were working in rural Zimbabwe. Our contact at DOD for humanitarian shipments enabled us to get a container when needed.

It took time to get Inyagui and Guzha organized and a cooking facility built for the cooks. It was late in 2003 that they began to cook for the orphans at Inyagui and Guzha. In the interim, the orphans were fed a nutrition drink during morning break. The drink helped the orphans significantly.

Building a building where meals could be prepared at the two schools was put on hold because it was impossible to get cement at that time. We looked forward to a time when cement would become more readily available. This was one of many hurdles we encountered. Finally, in late May 2003, the cooking facilities at Inyagui and Guzha Schools opened. The cooks at each of the schools had a proper kitchen in which to prepare food for the children.

LOADING SEA CONTAINERS

I was naked and you clothed me.

Matthew 25:36 (ESV)

When Ralph and I made our first trip to Zimbabwe, it didn't take long for us to realize the need for clothing was critical. Everywhere a person looked, there was a need for something. All we could think about were the things that were going to the dump in the U.S. that would be so useful in Zimbabwe.

That was the beginning of exploring ways to get things to Zimbabwe. Finally, Ralph, through a friend, made a connection with DOD in Washington, DC, and learned that they made humanitarian shipments all over the world. This opened a whole new endeavor for the work in Zimbabwe. There were specific things that could and could not go on these shipments. However, it was not an issue for the mission. The things being shipped were all for humanitarian relief.

Ralph contacted various school districts in the area. He requested permission to look through their warehouses where items were stored that were no longer of use to the district. His initial request was for school textbooks and library books. That was only the beginning. While collecting books he saw so many things that could be used in the schools in Zimbabwe.

On our first trip, Ralph and I discovered that the classrooms had nothing in them in most cases. There were no student desks or tables, no teacher desks or chairs, no books, and no sign of a pencil or paper. There was no dictionary or anything else, only a bare room. Collections eventually went beyond just books to include teacher desks, file cabinets, student desks, and even cafeteria tables. These items were stored in the basement and garage of our home until enough had been collected to fill a forty-foot sea container.

Church friends were the support needed in preparing shipments for Zimbabwe. This work took place in Ralph's shop and in our garage. Churches that heard about the work taking place in Zimbabwe got involved. Many of them collected clothing for children in Zimbabwe.

Shoes were so important. I learned from some of the children that they had never had a pair of shoes. After a recent shipment had arrived, I noticed a little boy walking to school one morning carrying the shoes that he had received from a recent shipment. When I inquired why he didn't wear his shoes, he told me they were too heavy. The child had never had shoes and so it is easy to understand that they probably did feel heavy to him.

When Ralph and I would return home from Zimbabwe, Ralph spent many days collecting discarded but usable items from various school districts in the Denver Metro area. Over the years and with the shipment of twenty forty-foot sea containers, four schools have been completely furnished, including desks for teachers. The saying is, "One man's trash is another man's treasure." This has proven true repeatedly in rural Zimbabwe. Even wooden desks that had a leg broken during shipment have been repaired and are in use.

One year, someone suggested that Ralph contact hotels to see if they had things that they would be willing to donate to the mission. Contacts were made with various hotels requesting bedding and especially blankets that were no longer usable. Hotels even donated drapes and bedspreads, as well as the terry robes that were no longer up to the hotel standards. Often, there was not very much wrong with the items. In Zimbabwe, nothing is thrown away. Everything can be used for something. The sewing women were very ingenious. They used some of the drapes that were shipped to make dresses or matching skirts and jackets for themselves and for sale in the community. Nothing was wasted; a use was found for everything.

Ralph spent many hours hauling twenty-foot trailer loads of items that were being discarded by different school districts and hotels. The items included folding chairs, cafeteria tables, teacher desks, file cabinets, out-of-date textbooks, and even culled library books. Bath towels, sheets, blankets, and even drapes from hotels were collected and shipped to Zimbabwe. The blankets were probably the most coveted item. All these things were stored in our basement and garage. They remained there until a packing party was organized, and friends would gather to help pack boxes.

One year, Sunday school children in Castle Rock, Colorado, packed shoe boxes with all kinds of things that they thought the children in Zimbabwe would like to have. They sent pencils, pens, toothbrushes, toothpaste, small notebooks, small storybooks, toys, and many other things.

These boxes were given to the orphans. A shoebox would bring smiles to children's faces that had no reason to smile. What joy for a child who had been left without parents to receive a decorated shoebox full of all kinds of small items. Most of these children had never had a gift in their lives.

One little girl found a baby doll in her shoebox, as well as a pair of flannel pajamas. The smile said it all. Yes, there is a cooler season in Zimbabwe when the nights can be chilly. The flannel PJs were welcomed because the child possibly did not own a blanket.

Waste Management was a source of items to ship. They donated several bales of blue jeans for the shipments. We wondered if the jeans would even be wearable. It was soon learned there was no reason for concern. The community was so excited when jeans began to be handed out. It amazed us how excited the people were to have a pair of blue jeans. We were also surprised to see what good condition many of the jeans appeared to be in. A hole in the knee of the jeans was of no concern to the local people. Just having a piece of clothing was a blessing.

Project C. U. R. E. in Denver was also a source of supplies for the many shipments made to Zimbabwe. They donated baby cribs, bandages, wound ointments, hospital beds, and mattresses, and the list goes on. An autoclave was one valuable piece of equipment that was needed for the local government clinic at Madamombe township in the area where Ralph and I were working. The head nurse said their only means of sterilizing equipment had failed recently. They had no way to sterilize any of their instruments.

It was not necessary for Ralph to haul all the donations from C. U. R. E. to our house. He was able to arrange for a container to be delivered to C. U. R. E.'s warehouse. The supporters of the mission gathered at the warehouse on a Saturday and assisted in the loading of the container. The shipper picked up the container on the following Monday.

When enough things had been collected and stored at our house, a packing party would be organized. Church friends would gather on a Saturday at our home. The basement would be a buzz with people packing boxes with books, clothing, bedding, etc. When all the donated items were packed, Ralph would set a day with the shipper when a forty-foot sea container would be delivered to the Pippitts driveway. Friends would gather again on a Saturday and help load the container. The container would be picked up on the following Monday and driven to an assigned port for shipment. It usually took two to three months for the container to arrive in Zimbabwe.

Mr. Bondeponde would be notified of the container's expected arrival date. He then would get the container released from customs. This was not always easy to accomplish. Once released from customs, the container would be delivered to the school where community members would assemble for the unloading.

The shipment would be unloaded into the new feeding center until things could be unboxed, sorted, distributed, and/or stored in the proper places. Books were left in their boxes and carried to the library. A group of teachers would be there to unbox, sort, and shelve all the books. In the beginning, there was no shelving for books. In fact, the school did not have a library. Once the library was constructed, Ralph spent time building many bookcases to hold all the books that were shipped.

The container that contained clothing was a challenge to handle once it arrived in Zimbabwe. There were so many boxes that the feeding center could not hold all of them. It was necessary to set tables outside to have space to unbox some of the clothing. Thank goodness it took place at the time of year when rain was not likely.

Mr. Bondeponde, along with village headmen, selected specific days when orphans from a designated village could come to Nyamashato Primary School. The headman for each village would be present on the day of distribution for the orphans in his village. He made a record of everything each orphan in his village received. The orphan caregiver for the respective village would assist their orphans in selecting items of clothing and shoes that would fit them. Adult clothing was kept for a separate distribution date.

At the end of each day, the group that had received clothing would wait in a shady area until all children for a given day had received their allotment. They would expect Ralph and me to come out so that they could express their appreciation. There would be singing and dancing. What jubilation! It is difficult for people in the U.S. to comprehend the joy they felt.

Ralph and I tried to explain that there were many people in the U.S. who worked to make this all happen. It is uncertain whether the local people ever really understood the hundreds of man-hours required to make the shipments.

SHIPMENTS

For I was hungry and you gave me food.

Matthew 25:35 (ESV)

We learned a lot through the process of making shipments to Zimbabwe. It doesn't sound difficult but it turned out to be a challenge. The first shipment was not even a container load. We packed a few boxes of books and some briefcases we no longer had use for. It was obvious to us that Mr. Bondeponde needed a briefcase to carry things when he was going for a meeting either in Murewa or even Harare.

There were a few other items included that we thought would be helpful for the staff. The entire shipment fit on one pallet and was wrapped with shrink wrap.

The shipment did arrive, but no one could tell Mr. Bondeponde where it was. After three months, we gave up. We decided that it was too much for Mr. Bondeponde to have to run down shipments. His plate was full without having to go by bus to Harare to oversee shipments. It was apparent that we needed someone in Harare designated to receive shipments.

During the first year we were in Zimbabwe, we met one of the MPs (member of parliament). Before we left the country, Ralph asked him to receive our shipment and make sure it was delivered to Nyamashato Primary School. He had agreed to do that, and we returned home feeling more encouraged.

Our second shipment (a forty-foot sea container) included many books, classroom furniture, and some clothing. Ralph received news that the shipment arrived in Harare on November 11. When we arrived in Zimbabwe in February, the shipment had still not reached the school. Ralph was so upset. He went directly to the MP's office, and of course, he wasn't in his office. Ralph did not give up. He waited and waited.

Finally, he got to the bottom of the issue and discovered the shipment had been delivered to the district offices in Bindura, a long distance in a different direction from Nyamashato. That happened to be the MP's district. This was a new step in our learning curve. Apparently, jealousy is a cultural thing!

On March 11, we left Nyamashato Primary School early in the morning with Mr. Bondeponde as our guide. The destination was Bindura. On our way there, we passed a truck that we later learned was headed to Bindura to pick up our shipment. Was this a coincidence? I like to think the MP was getting the hint that Ralph didn't give up. When we arrived at the district offices, we found the shipment. It had been dumped on the ground in front of the office building and had been there for a month. Remember, the shipment had arrived in November, and we never knew where it was in the months prior to our arrival in Zimbabwe.

Yes, it had rained during that month, and some of the boxes were dissolving. We loaded on the big truck all the things Ralph thought were salvageable. Mr. Bondeponde was so upset he insisted we take every single item. Mr. Bondeponde took the responsibility of drying out the wet books, and he was surprisingly successful. Many boxes had survived, and for some reason, most of the clothing had not gotten wet. Those boxes apparently were protected by the boxes of books on top of them.

We were told by a worker that the MP had told the governor to call Murewa and have the shipment for Nyamashato picked up. He obviously refused to make the call. We learned along the way that this is an example of jealousy in the culture. It wasn't our last time to experience this kind of jealousy. We were on a steep learning curve.

Businesses also have individuals who are out to get all they can, especially from greenhorns like us. CMC Freight had brought a letter to Mr. Bondeponde threatening court action if they did not receive payment for the shipment that had arrived. The bill now had reached 200,000 ZD. Remember, this was a humanitarian shipment through the U.S. Government. Our government had paid the shipping costs. Mr. B. was beside himself. He was so afraid that they would come and take everything and sell it. He had heard nothing from them for three months and thought the issue had been resolved.

Several days later, Ralph and Mr. B. went to SMS Freight Distributors in Harare. They were to have received the shipment. Ralph was determined to get to the bottom of the issue.

They spoke first with an individual that Mr. B. had dealt with in January when the shipment first arrived in Zimbabwe. As Ralph began asking questions and requesting paperwork, the manager appeared. Things were resolved in our favor. The manager plans to deal with CMC Freight; he was puzzled about how they got the shipment in the first place. He indicated that they were a very small concern. At the end of the meeting, the manager gave Ralph a list of clearing agents to specify for future paperwork.

After this meeting, Ralph took Mr. B. to the U.S. Embassy to report the issue. Ralph presented the case along with Mr. B. Now, he will know where to go in the future if there is a problem receiving a future shipment.

In 1999, Mr. and Mrs. Bondeponde were given a lot of credit for getting a shipment delivered to the school. If it had not been for Mr. Bondeponde's persistent effort, it was feared the shipment would have been misplaced. Because of his aggressiveness, the shipment was not opened in Harare. Mr. Bondeponde personally rode on the first truck coming out of Harare. He broke the seal when it arrived at the school. Because of the excessive amount of rain, they were unable to deliver the shipment to the school. The trucker had to stop at the school sign on the main road and a neighbor that had a pick-up truck brought a small load at a time down to the school. The school is located about a mile off the main road. One container was unloaded at night. The other two were unloaded in daylight. Obviously, three containers in one shipment were too much for them to handle at one time, especially with the heavy rains they had.

On occasions, there would be some damage to items during shipment. It was important for the containers to be packed tight so that there was minimal shifting in transit. Despite the care that was used, there was often some damage. Ralph became very skilled in repairing furniture that was damaged. That was usually his first task once we arrived on a following trip. The items were put in what was the old school office waiting for Ralph to return. Nearly everything was salvageable once he had a chance

Shipments   159

to work on the items. The items, on occasion, served a new purpose, but nothing was thrown away.

An interesting observation was the increase in enrollment once the classrooms had adequate furnishings. As the years progressed, there were many additional shipments. Every time we thought we knew the correct procedure for getting the shipment released from customs in a timely manner, the rules changed. It became a game of guessing what the next challenge would be. I probably don't need to add that the entire process was extremely frustrating, and it would have been so easy to just discontinue the shipments. Then, we would witness the need, and all the frustration would be forgotten. Once we experienced the joy of the people when a shipment arrived, there were no more doubts about continuing the shipments. Through these experiences, we learned a lot that was always useful.

I want to give credit to Mr. Bondeponde, headmaster at Nyamashato Primary School, for his persistence in getting shipments released from customs and delivered to the school. Without him, I fear all would have been lost. He was able to somehow make certain the containers were not opened in Harare. Once he knew the procedure, the seal was never broken until the container arrived at Nyamashato.

Mr. Bondeponde was a true warrior and did not give up easily. The U.S. Embassy was a big help when the shipper in Zimbabwe tried to charge us an enormous fee. These shipments were all funded through a program in DOD. Without Mr. Bondeponde, I believe more would have been lost. Over the years, twenty forty-foot sea containers were shipped, loaded with many humanitarian items. It was always like Christmas when a shipment arrived. After the first lost shipment, Mr. Bondeponde became very skilled in working through all the red tape.

Mr. Bondeponde was never contacted to say that a container would be delivered at a specific time. He might have been expecting a shipment, but its arrival was always a surprise. Community members were quick to respond. In the early years, there was no form of communication, but news traveled rapidly. Often, as many as sixty people would show up to help unload the container or containers. We had just arrived on our trip in 2003 when two forty-foot containers appeared. People appeared from everywhere to help with the unloading. A line would form at the truck leading into the feeding center. People would pass the boxes from one person to the next. The boxes were stacked in the dining hall until the container was emptied.

These containers had left Colorado on the 19th of October and had taken over three months to arrive in Durban, South Africa. The containers must have sat in Durban for some time, or perhaps they were in the line of trucks we had encountered at the border crossing when we traveled up from South Africa. Possibly, the containers had been sitting at the border for weeks, waiting to be cleared. It was such an eye-opening experience to be present to witness an unloading. Witnessing the joy of the community made all the work worthwhile.

When shipments arrive, it makes feeding the children a challenge. Tables are set up outside on the veranda. Children would line up and get their plates of food and then sit at tables outside. The children didn't care that they weren't in the dining room.

The orphan caregivers spend many hours opening boxes and sorting and stacking the contents. When they ran out of space, we set aside some days for the distribution of clothing that had been shipped. Orphaned children came by villages. The village headman kept track of the orphans in his village and noted the clothing they received. The orphan caregiver assisted the children in her village in finding clothing that would fit them. Once the children of a specific village were all served, another village would be contacted to send their orphans.

During the commotion of distributing clothing from a shipment that had just arrived, three student nurses from Parirenyatwa Hospital in Harare arrived. They were sent to view our setup and learn all that they could about our operation. Apparently, our feeding program had caught someone's attention. While I was talking to the students in the feeding center, a very little girl about six years old came and gave me a hug around my legs and said thank you for the jean dress she had just been given. A little boy following her shook my hand and told me thank you. These are only a few examples of why we come and work as hard as we do.

The distribution of clothing generated so much excitement. I tried to catch it on camera and there is just no way. The atmosphere was electric. Some little girls paraded past our house on their way home. They were hoping we would see them in their new clothes. Secondary school girls refused denim skirts and dresses; they wanted jeans, and they took jeans. It is almost unheard of for women to wear trousers in that culture. Although, over the years we have noted things are slowly beginning to change.

The orphan caregivers were responsible for unpacking boxes and sorting clothing by size and for boys and girls. It was an enormous task, and I know they left at the end of the day totally exhausted. One day during this time, Ralph happened to enter the area where all the sorting was taking place. One of the orphan caregivers who had come on countless days brought some money to Ralph and gave it to him. She explained that she had found it in the pocket of a pair of jeans she was sorting and folding. It was eleven dollars. Ralph gave it back to her and told her that "finders were keepers." She nearly jumped for joy.

Days later, when she saw Ralph again, she told him that in the evening, when she went home with the money, she received a notice that her daughter was in critical condition. Her presence was needed in Harare. She explained that the money she had found paid for her bus fare. It was the only money the woman had. Her daughter had died in childbirth. She thanked Ralph again for allowing her to keep the money. God provides!

Sunday evening, one of the village headmen from Guzha came to our house to welcome us back. He especially wanted to thank us for the bale of jeans that they had received at Guzha. He told us that men who had nothing to wear now had two pairs of jeans each. They wanted us to know how much they appreciated the shipment.

A young boy had been hanging around the school for several days. He wanted a job with our builder. He had dropped out of school to care for a younger brother and sister and an invalid mother. The father had passed away previously. Mr. Bondeponde had felt so sorry for him that he had given him small jobs and paid him a bit of money so that he would be able to buy some food for his younger siblings and himself.

While he was not from the area we were working in, Ralph could not turn him away when he asked for some shoes and some clothes. He came back the next day to thank us. He fell on his knees in front of Ralph and told him how much he appreciated the assistance. Then he presented Ralph with two five-dollar bills that had been in the pocket of the trousers he had been given. Ralph changed it for Zimbabwe dollars.

162   Hope for Zimbabwe Orphans

At that time, local people could not purchase anything with U.S. dollars. The boy nearly cried. It was more money than I felt he had ever seen. He told Ralph that now he could buy food for his brother and sister and sick mother. God provides for our needs in unexpected ways. Do we always remember to thank God?

This same boy began acting as a runner for the builder who was working near our house. He came very early each morning to work with the builder. He often sat on our veranda in the mornings, waiting for the builder to come to work. I would feed him whatever I had left over. He never turned anything away.

Clothing distribution continued for several weeks. After all orphans had received their outfits, other children who were not orphans but certainly needed clothing had a chance to pick out an outfit or two. Mothers with infants and toddlers also had an opportunity to come on specific days when clothing for small children was laid out. Some remaining clothing was shared with neighboring schools outside Ward 1. The remaining clothing was shelved in the storeroom according to size. This was stored for future needs.

Blankets were a coveted item that came on some of the shipments. Many of these blankets were donated by various hotels in the Denver Metro area. Some blankets were purchased in bulk by some of our donors. They were stored in our storage area until the weather began to get cold, and then they would be distributed to child-headed households first. Some of the blankets were given to families that had taken in an orphan. We tried to make certain that all orphans had a blanket.

Thanks to all of those who donated many hours to the packing of hundreds and hundreds of boxes. We were blessed by your support. The work of our many friends blessed many children.

BLANKET DISTRIBUTION

I was a stranger and you welcomed me.

Matthew 25:35 (RSV)

Very soon after our arrival back in Zimbabwe, one of the early years, a distribution of blankets was made to the orphans in the Nyamashato area. A sea container had arrived just prior to our arrival and contained many blankets. Mr. Bondeponde decided to wait to distribute the blankets until we arrived. The day of the distribution of blankets brought out many people, even though the distribution was for orphans. We had one of the orphan caregivers check them off her list as they entered the building. Others were made to remain outside.

Ralph discovered that one girl had walked ten or twelve miles to come for blankets. She was only twelve years old and was caring for five younger children. One of those children was a sister. The rest were related, but all the parents had died. This twelve-year-old had assumed the responsibility of caring for all these children.

When Ralph learned how far she had walked, he said there was no way she could carry all the blankets that far. He put the bundle of blankets in our truck and told the girl he would take her home. Since the bridge across the river had not yet been completed, it was necessary to go the long way around to take the girl home. Dodging tree stumps hidden in the tall grass was a new experience. The entire trip was an experience. It was truly cross-country. The young girl had to direct Ralph because there was no road.

Once Ralph arrived at the rondavel, he helped the young girl unload the stack of blankets. He asked the girl where she stored the food. He learned that she had nothing to eat except what they could find growing. This brought to our attention a much bigger problem. We were going to have to make sure these children, who lived without parents, received help, and they needed it now.

Ralph returned to where we were staying. After hearing what he had learned, we put together some emergency supplies, and he drove back to the girl's home. By that time, the other children had returned. They had been unable to find anything to eat. How could the local people not know what was going on in sight of their own homes? No wonder many children were just skin and bones.

STORIES OF APPRECIATION

Not that we dare to classify or compare ourselves with some of those who are commending themselves.

2 Corinthians 10:12 (ESV)

In 1998, the second year we made a trip to Nyamashato, we still lived in a classroom that had been made available to us. One evening, a group of community members came to visit us. They were so grateful that we had returned and had come to have a prayer meeting. Mr. Bondeponde opened a classroom next door to where we were living, and we all gathered in that room. It was dark, and there was no electricity. Some of those who gathered had stubs of candles they had brought. It didn't give much light, but at least we didn't trip over each other.

One of the men in the group acted as the leader. He read some scripture and then talked about how it applied to us and the work we were doing. They knew that God had heard their prayers. At the end of the service, they took up a collection. When the meeting broke up, the money was given to Ralph to help with the work. I don't recall how much it was, but it was all that they had, I am certain. This was an example of giving *all*. Ralph used it to pay for materials for projects that were in progress.

Khumbulani Mangena was on assignment from school, acting as our social worker for one year when I was in Zimbabwe. It was after 2011, after Ralph had passed away. This was a year soon after the mission had moved from the school to the site given to us by the provincial government. Khumbulani still had schooling to complete but was on attachment at HCOC for his term of hands-on experience. He loved the work. One morning, Khumbulani brought a mother to see me. She came specifically to thank me for caring for her six children. Three of the six have completed their A-levels and are working to help support the younger children. One of her children is employed in Harare as a dressmaker. This mother brought a blazer that her daughter had made at her workplace and donated it to HCOC for a student to use when they go to boarding school. I was very surprised and pleased. Thank yous are always appreciated.

Khumbulani was himself an orphan. His mother passed away when he was in grade three. His father passed away when he was in grade seven. A teacher was instrumental in helping him get a scholarship to the University of Zimbabwe through Econet, a cell phone company in Zimbabwe. Khumbulani will graduate in one year. His hope is to come back to HCOC and be employed. Albert has nothing but good things to say about this young man. Khumbulani visited with me at some length on Saturday about his life and his hopes and dreams.

Donations such as this woman brought to us are very special. We often do not hear success stories. It is so heartwarming when things like this do happen.

It wasn't long after the mother had donated the blazer that Albert came to find me. He had just learned that one of our orphans at Cheunje Secondary School did not have a blazer. This is required by all boarding schools. Albert said that he wanted to take the donated blazer to the girl at Cheunje and present it to her. Albert wanted me to go along. She was so surprised and delighted to receive the blazer. Another example of God providing.

After a very long day of clothing distribution, a mother walked back several miles the following day to return to see Ralph and me. She wanted to personally thank us for the clothing her children had received the day before. Mr. Bondeponde, the interpreter, had come with the woman to tell us thank you. She wanted us to know how much she appreciated the help we were providing for her children and all of the orphans. She explained how badly her family needed clothing.

I invited her into our house when she knocked. However, the woman refused to enter the house. We were told later that she didn't feel worthy to enter our house. This mother had heard that we had been given gifts the previous day at a farewell event. She had not known of the event and so this mother presented us with a reed sleeping mat, the only thing she had. I need to add that the bamboo reed sleeping mat had obviously been

168 Hope for Zimbabwe Orphans

well used. She wanted us to know how much she appreciated what we were doing for her community and especially her family.

She explained that her husband had passed away and that she had no way of providing for her children. I found it very difficult to accept the sleeping mat, but I knew that there was no way to refuse. It would have been rude. I also knew it would mean the mother would have nothing to sleep on that night. She would have to sleep on the cold floor with nothing to protect her, perhaps. It was difficult to cope with situations like this. The experience was truly humbling.

WHEELCHAIR FOR A CRIPPLED CHILD

If we are being examined today concerning a good deed done to a crippled man, by what means this man has been healed.

Acts 4:9 (ESV)

The Madanha family lived near Nyamashato Primary School. They had several children. The two youngest children became crippled between the ages of four and five years. Mrs. Madanha had requested a wheelchair for each of the children on our first visit. We had promised to do what we could. The wheelchairs that were donated were outfitted for rough terrain by a member of the ZMP (Zimbabwe Mission Partnership). The chairs had wider tires and solid tires, so no inner tubes were needed. The wheelchairs would be used on rough ground and needed to be sturdy. Unfortunately, one of the Madanha children who needed a wheelchair passed away while the shipment with the wheelchairs was in transit. We told them to just keep the wheelchair until someone needed it.

One of the children we worked with was non-verbal, and he was crippled. He lived with his parents in the Guzha Primary School area. He had become too big for his parents to manage. The child was brought to us at Nyamashato from that area in an ox cart, the only mode of transportation they had. The child was too big to be carried such a long distance. They had to travel about ten miles. The mother rode in the ox cart, but the father walked beside the oxen. The parents were requesting a wheelchair to assist them in caring for the child.

We knew that one of the Madanha children had passed away a short time before our arrival back in the country. We promised to see what we could do about getting one of their wheelchairs for this child.

The Madanhas were most happy to share the chair with the other family. They had experienced how difficult it can be to move children around when they get bigger. Madanha had lost two other children to this same ailment. The doctor gave the family no explanation as to why the children died.

The day that Ralph and I delivered the wheelchair to the crippled child was one of pure joy. It was difficult to determine who was the happiest, the parents or the crippled child. The parents said that the child rarely showed any signs of emotion, but they knew he was happy because he was smiling when he was put into the chair.

GOD'S CHILDREN

Behold, children are a heritage from the Lord, the fruit of the womb a reward.

Psalm 127:3 (ESV)

Activia was the only living member of a family of six children we fed during one of the early years of our work in Zimbabwe. Mr. Bondeponde had brought her to me early one morning. She is alone because the other members of her family have all died due to various illnesses.

The girl has been out of school for more than a week because of illness. She says she is better, but she is still a long way from feeling very well. She told me she had to walk to the clinic each day for an injection. I had no idea what they were giving her; hopefully, it was an antibiotic. She is not playing with the other children, so I could only assume she didn't feel like it. I felt walking miles to come to school had taken all her energy. I fear she is going to end up like Vincent, one of our orphans who passed away.

This is just another sad experience. After a while, it begins to get to us, and it is so depressing. There is nothing I can give her to make her better. Why are these children all so sick? AIDS is not a childhood disease. Most children who die of AIDS do so before the age of five years. These are the children who have contracted the disease during birth. In such cases, the child usually does not live beyond five years. Young children should not have AIDS unless they are being sexually abused. That does happen more than I care to elaborate on. This little girl was in second grade at Nyamashato. I have no proof that she has AIDS, but my guess is that is why she is so sick, and the injections the clinic is giving her are doing no good.

One young boy was so ill with AIDS. Both parents were dead. He lived with an older brother. The child was very weak. However, he insisted on coming to school. He was unable to walk very far, so his older brother would carry him to school each day on his back. At the end of the school day, the brother would come to get him. The child did not play at recess but would find a sunny spot and sit in the sun to get warm. He was so very thin. He had wanted to come and see me so that he could thank me for his new school uniform. His brother had carried him to our house. I don't know how he held his head up in class because he obviously was very ill. Even in this condition, he still came to school every day until the very end. There were many children who died in 2001. The last time I saw him, his brother had taken him to school, but he was too sick to remain. Three boys from his class carried him back home. He passed away a few days later.

NEEDING TO BE IN SCHOOL

It was brought to Mr. Bondeponde's attention that there was a boy in the community who had not been attending school. He had no one to pay his school fees. Apparently, this had been the case for a year and a half. The young man had no parents and had been living alone all this time. People in this area are so intent on surviving each day that they frequently are not aware of the needs of others. This is difficult for most of us to understand.

Mr. Bondeponde had put him in a sixth-grade classroom just two weeks prior to our becoming aware of the situation. He had told the child that he did not have to write the exam that the rest of the children were writing since he had not been in the class. He also told the boy his school fees had been paid. The boy insisted that he wanted to try to write the exam. The following day, Mr. B. brought the boy to meet Ralph and me. He had placed twenty-ninth on the test in a class of forty-two students without the opportunity to come to school for more than one year. When he was brought to meet us, his clothes were filthy and nearly falling off him. Ralph and I looked at him, and immediately, Ralph took him to the sewing ladies and purchased a new uniform for him. I didn't have a camera with me, so I missed getting a picture of the biggest smile I have ever seen on a child's face. He tucked his old clothes under his arm and started running home.

FIRST AID

One afternoon, a woman came by with her little girl, who had a serious cut on her finger. It probably should have been stitched. I wasn't equipped to do that, and Ralph was gone with the truck. I had no transportation. All I could do was clean it and treat it with an ointment.

The mother told me she had been to the clinic, and they said they had nothing to treat it with. Word is out that we have first aid supplies. The little girl was terrified of me. She had never seen a white person before. I treated the finger the best that I could. I left supplies with Mrs. Bondeponde and told her what to do over the weekend while we were gone. We usually went into Harare on weekends to take laundry, purchase groceries, and always planned on attending church.

I had just returned to the sewing women after doctoring the little girl when a man came for help who had stepped on a big thorn. (These thorns are the hardest things I have ever encountered. You cannot break one in half with your hands.) Ralph gave him a bucket of water and soap for him to wash his foot and then proceeded to doctor it with what we had. Ralph thought the thorn was out of the man's foot, but it was terribly infected. He hasn't returned, so we had no idea if the foot was healing.

Try to imagine the only medical facilities are miles away and there is no way to get there except to walk or to ride the big green bus. If you have an injured foot, walking for help is not an option. Most people don't have the money necessary to ride the bus. I can't understand why clinics are built and then are not kept stocked with at least first aid supplies.

***

An orphan was brought to Nyamashato in a wheelbarrow. She was in a great deal of pain from some serious burns. She had lost her hold on a bucket of boiling water when she was preparing to bathe some younger siblings that she was caring for. Both parents had died of AIDS, and she was the oldest child, probably eleven or twelve.

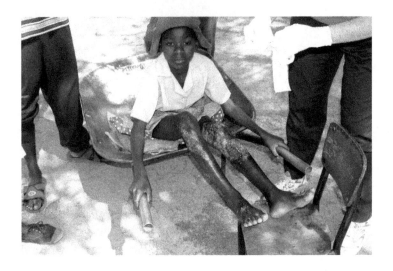

The siblings brought her to us for help after having walked long distances to two different local clinics, wheeling her in the wheelbarrow. The distance between the two clinics, I estimate, was more than eight miles. After all of that, they brought her to us. In both instances, the children were told that the clinic had nothing to treat her with. No one knows how many hours they had walked trying to find help. The young girl was obviously in serious pain. I was afraid to treat her with the supplies that Ralph and I carried with us. I did not have burn ointment.

Ralph picked her up as carefully as possible and placed her in the back seat of our truck. Ralph told me to take her to the hospital in Murewa for treatment. Ralph could tell when he picked her up from the wheelbarrow that she was in some serious pain. The road to Murewa is rough despite how carefully one might drive. It took a very long time to make the trip because of the pain the child was in when I hit any bumps.

The child was in the hospital for a week or so, and then she was released. She came to me one day to show me that she had no scarring. I was very surprised that she was completely healed. Praises to the great healer!

ASHLEY—A GRANDDAUGHTER'S IMPRESSIONS

And we know that for those who love God all things work together
for good, for those who are called according to his purpose.

Romans 8:28 (ESV)

As I sit at my computer debating how to start this chapter, I think
about the years of stories I heard from my grandparents, Ralph and
Roberta Pippitt. These stories started when I was just six years old. Of
course, back then, I didn't understand the extent of poverty and the needs
that these people had. I remember my grandparents telling me about kids
who walked to school and some who unfortunately didn't make it because
they were eaten by crocodiles as they crossed a local river. I remember
hearing about how the classrooms had no furniture and a very limited
number of books and supplies. I recall the stories of them building the
orphanage for those children who had lost their parents, most of them
from diseases such as AIDS. I am thankful for the life I have been granted,
but I still wonder about those children and families who suffer traumatic
loss far worse than mine.

In the months leading up to this trip, I had to receive several vaccines,
such as typhoid, tetanus, meningitis, and hepatitis A. I was at risk of
contracting malaria, so we were prescribed fifteen weeks of Mefloquine
to take weekly prior to leaving and to continue for several weeks upon
our return. While preparing for this trip, I collected items to take to these
children, including crayons, medical supplies, emergency food supplies
(protein bars, tuna packs, and crackers), and items from home to make
this trip a little easier. I packed and unpacked my suitcase too many times
to count to make sure I had everything I could possibly need for the next
seven weeks as I would be far from home and have a limited number
of resources. Most teenagers plan to pack a cell phone or tablet, but I

packed a book and activities to do with the children at the orphanage. I was fifteen and about to start my freshman year of high school. My plans for the summer were much different than my friends who planned to spend time at the pool or local amusement parks.

On June 23, 2006, I boarded a plane with my grandparents in Denver, Colorado, flying to London, England. We had a long enough layover where we could get a few hours of rest in a hotel room, along with a hot shower and change of clothes, before we boarded our next flight. The second half of the trip was traveling from London to Johannesburg, South Africa. When we arrived in South Africa, my grandparent's friends Magda and Faan picked us up and took us to their house. We stayed with them for a couple of days before we traveled on our way to Zimbabwe. From Johannesburg, we drove to Zimbabwe. It took several days to get there as we drove through Kruger National Park. This was a once-in-a-lifetime trip to see the wild animals in their natural habitat. We also made a stop at The Great Zimbabwe, a medieval African city known for its large circular wall and tower. This was part of the wealthy African trading empire that controlled much of the East African coast from the eleventh to fifteenth centuries. I remember studying about The Great Zimbabwe in middle school, but I never thought I would experience it in person.

Later in my stay in Zimbabwe, my grandparents took me to visit Victoria Falls for a few days. Victoria Falls is one of the Seven Natural Wonders of the World. Victoria Falls is located on the border of Zimbabwe and Zambia. Watching the water rush over the falls was stunning. We saw wild animals along the way. Seeing the poor living conditions of the people along the way was something I will always remember.

Traveling to Nyamashato proved to be difficult with road conditions that were less than impressive, making a one-way trip about one to two hours. There were also brief stops along the way where the Zimbabwe police would ask for your visa and passports. At times, this was scary. I didn't know what they were really looking for. When we arrived at Nyamashato, a hundred miles from Harare, the capital of Zimbabwe, we were greeted by so many smiling faces. These people were over the moon to see my grandparents return. After years of traveling to Zimbabwe and providing great improvements, the community members had taken my grandparents in as family.

After we settled into our "home away from home," I toured the Nyamashato community. The area was set up like a small neighborhood. In the center were the classrooms and library and surrounding that was huts for teachers and their families. There were very few houses like ours.

Our house had a small cooking area. We had a sink to wash our dishes, but there was no hot water. The water was boiled on the propane stove. We had no electricity, meaning we didn't have a refrigerator to keep our food cold. When we went to town and bought food, we packed it in a cooler with ice to keep it cold for several days. We had a small living area that we used for our dining room and living room. We did have a water tank that supplied clean water into our house. We had a small bathroom with a shower and sink. We had a bucket and stool that we used at night for our bathroom needs. I learned quickly that the best time of day to shower was in the afternoon. The water was warmest from the heat of the midday sun. The shower was not pressurized, so it was a gentle trickle. Our bathroom facility was located behind our house. This had no running water. It was a large hole in the ground with a mounted toilet seat. There were also two small bedrooms. Our beds were inflatable mattresses on top of a plywood frame. Around our beds were mosquito nets to eliminate the number of mosquito bites while we slept. As for laundry, most of it was done by hand washing using a bucket of soapy water and hanging the clothes along the chain link fence.

Right next to our home was the Heather Chimhoga Orphan Care Center, where meals were prepared and served to the orphans, and extra supplies were stored. I ate with the orphans one day. Cooked beans were served with sadza. Sadza is a cornmeal porridge. This was not a favorite thing to eat, but you can't be picky. This was one of the many projects that my grandparents had completed over the years. On the other side of our house was where the headmaster lived. Then, there was a row of houses for teachers and their families.

On an average day at Nyamashato, I spent my time in various classrooms, at the orphanage serving food, or playing games with the children. The teachers and children would dance and sing in their native language. I also spent some time helping the nurse care for several children. I saw children with malnutrition; they had large, rounded bellies and small arms and legs. I saw several children with ringworms, which were treated using an antifungal medication. There was one boy who had a serious bone infection, and my grandpa had made several trips to Harare to obtain the appropriate medications. I helped the nurse make rolled bandages, like gauze here, by taking strips of sheets or clothing and rolling them neatly.

While I was there, a young boy came up to me with open wounds to his lower legs. He had a mint green/blue paste around the outside of his wounds. I had asked him what was on his wounds. He told me, "Colgate." I was confused, so I asked again, and he told me, "Colgate, toothpaste." He thought that since Colgate cleans your teeth, it would also clean his wounds. I will forever remember this young boy.

I visited many classrooms while in Zimbabwe. The classrooms had no electricity. They may have had a few desks and long lunchroom-type tables that were sent over from the U.S. Many of the walls were eaten by termites. One day, I went into a classroom and found several students sitting and reading. When I asked where their teacher was, they told me she hadn't come to school that day. I sat down with the students and started reading out of a biology textbook. The students loved listening to me read. I also sat in on a younger class as the students were learning their alphabet, and I was able to learn as well. I also helped in a preschool classroom teaching the children their shapes and colors. I brought with me a crayon box with over 500 crayons.

I spent time playing with the younger children, teaching them how to play leapfrog and duck, duck, goose. There was a little boy about three years old who had a small handmade car out of wire, sticks, and Copenhagen cans. These children are so creative and have such a beautiful imagination to create something with very limited supplies.

Upon returning to my home in Denver, Colorado, my perspective of life and its necessities changed. Several months after returning home, I spoke at New Hope Presbyterian Church in Castle Rock, Colorado, about my time and the experience that I had in Zimbabwe. I made so many friends and memories while over in Zimbabwe that I will cherish forever. For a couple of years after going to Zimbabwe, I continued to communicate with my friends by sending letters. As an adult, I reflect on all the experiences I had as a teenager traveling to Zimbabwe. The things we take for granted in the United States are astonishing. The lights in our home, air conditioning for hot summer days, running water for bathing, having food on the shelves at the grocery store, or having medical supplies. My list could go on forever. I thank my grandparents for giving me this opportunity to travel across the world and help develop an appreciation for what I have, as there are so many other people who are less fortunate.

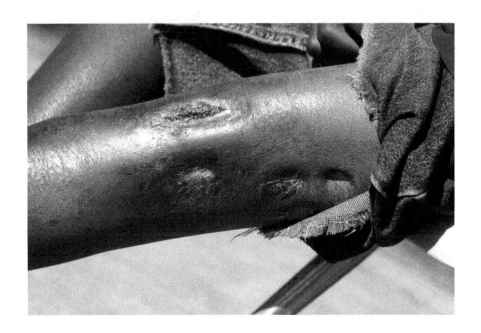

LEG WOUND HEALS: "MIRACLE WORKERS"

For I will restore health to you, and your wounds I will heal, declares the Lord, because they have called you an outcast.

Jeremiah 30:17 (ESV)

Things have not changed. When word gets out that we have returned, serious medical cases begin to appear. Ralph called me to the Orphan Care Center. A boy had been brought in with terrible wounds on his upper leg. See the picture above. The boy is registered with the OCC (Orphan Care Center) and has only a mother. The father has passed away. The mother was requesting help with the leg condition he was experiencing. The boy could only walk a very few steps because of severe pain.

Apparently, the leg has been like this for more than a year, and they cannot afford the recommended surgery. The child and the mother were taken to the local clinic to begin the process necessary to get him admitted to a hospital in Harare.

Ralph took one look at the young man's leg and immediately knew that osteomyelitis was the infection in the leg. (Note: Ralph and Roberta were not doctors, not even nurses; they both had only had first-aid training in high school.) Ralph knew what the infection was because he had the same infection in his leg as a child in the 1930s. Ralph had been treated by the doctor putting maggots in the wound to eat the infection. However, Ralph knew that in the U.S., they treated this ailment now with mediation.

The clinic sent the boy (Prosper) to the doctor in Murewa on Tuesday. The doctor said that he would do the necessary paperwork to try and get at least a portion of the surgery paid for by Social Welfare. The doctor indicated that the surgery would be very expensive.

The surgery meant amputation. Ralph insisted that this ailment could be treated with medication. He did not give up.

Ralph received word one day that a pharmacy in Harare had some Gentamycin. We hoped that they still had it when Ralph arrived. If Ralph could obtain it, it would be an answer to our prayers. We were concerned about saving the boy's leg. Another trip to Harare was necessary, something neither one of us ever looked forward to. Ralph finally located the medicine, Gentamycin, after some searching in Harare. We were so grateful to finally be able to treat Prosper. God does answer prayers.

Florence, the nurse aide, had to go to the boy's home each day to administer the injection. However, we learned on Friday that she was scheduled to take a refresher nursing course in Harare. That left me to give Prosper his injection. This was not my favorite thing to do. I told Prosper that it would hurt me worse than it did him. On the day of his last injection, he told me that he was already feeling a bit better. This was truly an answer to prayer. Without Ralph's perseverance in finding the medicine, the outcome would have been very different.

The leg was slow to improve but it did finally heal. Before we returned to the U.S., the young man was back walking and beginning to work in the fields. God was watching over that young man for certain. We soon learned that the community expected miracles from us. Little did we know what we had gotten into. Someone was always at our door with an illness or a need, and we helped in any way we could. Thank You, Lord.

VISIT TO ORPHANS

Religion that is pure and undefiled before God the Father is this: to visit orphans and widows in their affliction, and to keep oneself unstained from the world.

James 1:27 (ESV)

When Ralph and I could find some free time on a weekend, we would load the truck with supplies for orphans. Sometimes, Mr. Bondeponde would load the Orphan Care truck also and lead the way. The trip would take us to remote areas where the orphans lived.

One year, the Sunday school children in our church in Colorado had packed hundreds of shoe boxes filled with things for the children in Zimbabwe. This gave us an opportunity to distribute the boxes to the neediest children. In addition to the shoe boxes, we carried blankets, clothing, and food supplies. One little girl was all smiles because Ralph had given her a box to open. The look on her face said more than many words.

What an adventure and eye-opener as well! It gave Ralph and me an opportunity to see what life was like for many of these children. On one such trip, we visited nine child-headed households. Three of the families of children had managed to raise a crop of maize. Two of the three families had a good yield, possibly enough to supply them with mealie meals for several months. One family of one girl and four boys not only had a good maize crop but had also raised soya beans that they had shelled and laid out to dry.

I recall one stop we made. The family consisted of two boys and a mentally disabled mother. This family is in danger of starving to death. Inside the rondavel, the floor was only dirt. The only blankets they had were worn out, and the mother and two boys had to share them. They obviously slept on the floor. The dishes that were given to us to put the food in had holes in them and were not usable. We ended up having to leave the supplies in plastic bags. We left a new blanket and a hygiene packet for each of the boys.

One such trip took us to the Guzha area. This is the furthest point in the Ward we operate within. It became necessary to drive up mountains where there were no roads. The children we found were mute. I never learned whether they could speak or not or whether they were just shocked at encountering white people. The rondavels in this area were made of bamboo. Some were plastered with mud on the inside. The shelter might be good for air circulation, but I often wondered what they did when it rained or got cold. It never gets cold like it does in Colorado, but when the temperatures are consistently in the nineties and above, even eighty degrees can be a shock.

The region is extremely poor and there was little ground where crops would grow. We drove up mountains where no roads existed and through dense forests in some places. These children had a very long walk to get to school. One might expect to encounter some wildlife. It was explained that all the wildlife had been killed during the war. Occasionally, people say one might encounter a warthog.

So much need. It is just mind-boggling. People are scavenging for food just as wild animals do.

INYAGUI PRIMARY SCHOOL

The headmaster at Inyagui School had sent a written request twice to us during the past year, asking us to visit his primary school. In our letter to him, we had promised that on our next visit to Zimbabwe, we would try to come and visit his school. Unfortunately, things kept happening and we had run out of time. We had not intentionally ignored his requests. On this day, very near the end of our stay, we made a special effort to visit the school. It is located about four to five miles from Nyamashato and in Ward 1. The children were on term break, so we knew we would not see classes in session. We would have an opportunity to visit a few of the staff and have a look around the school.

The deputy head greeted us and showed us around the school, but the school head was not available. The school appeared to be in much better condition than we had expected. Their greatest need was for water, and the school gardens were suffering because of a lack of water. They also needed fencing to protect the school grounds and the things they were trying to grow from the cattle that roamed free.

Ralph made a special effort to find funding for a well the following year. To make a long story short, we drilled four wells at the school over the period of many years. None provided a sufficient supply of water. The last well drilled did provide water for a time and then, after several years, went dry. The driller came when we were not on site. When he hit the water, he stopped drilling instead of drilling into the granite layer. He stopped drilling because drillers did not like drilling into the granite layer since it consumed a lot of time and a lot of wear and tear on equipment. As a result, the water dried up in a very dry year.

Finally, a mission board member, Julia, in the Denver area made it her personal mission to raise money for another well. The funds were made available through several Rotary Clubs and private donations. This well was drilled off school property and a distance from the school. The well is pumped by solar power and piped underground to the existing storage tank on school property. This project required much fundraising but is such a blessing to the school after numerous disappointments.

When we first began work at the school, the most critical need was for teacher housing. I went inside a house which had only two rooms. Six members of one family lived in it. There was a danger to those living in the house. The building was crumbling away. We learned that the other eight members of the faculty and their families occupy three other very small three-room houses. I didn't go inside those houses.

A serious concern to me was the facility where the preschool and kindergarten classes met. There were forty-six children meeting in two tiny rooms smaller than a jail cell with only one window too high to see out of. There was no sign of a book or a toy. I have no idea how they worked with the children. I know that we collected story books and small toys for the next shipment going to Zimbabwe.

We explained we had no funds left this year. We promised to take their request home with us and see if we could find another church or churches to support their need. We promised to assist in any possible way.

The needs were overwhelming. Raising funds was difficult and not something either Ralph or I felt comfortable doing. We were more hands-on people. We explained we would do the best we could with whatever monies we were able to raise in the U.S. I am certain they saw us as their only ray of hope. We returned to where we were staying with a heavy heart. There was so much need everywhere we looked. We kept asking ourselves what Jesus would have done if He had been in our shoes. What was God trying to tell us, or was the devil trying to frustrate us so we would quit? Both of us were overwhelmed and didn't know what to do next. Need was everywhere we looked. Money was always an issue. We had to make every dollar go as far as possible.

The following year, we returned with funds that enabled us to build three new teachers' houses. What a welcomed accomplishment for the teachers at that school. While it didn't satisfy all their housing needs, it was a good start.

After the houses were complete, the school fenced a garden plot and the classroom buildings and playground. Keeping cattle off school property was a big step in the right direction. One of the shipments that was delivered to Nyamashato contained two outdoor playground sets. One of the sets was delivered to Inyagui since they had fenced the school grounds. Ralph supervised the setting up of the equipment. It was impossible to capture the joy of the children. They quickly figured out how to use the equipment. Remember, these children had never seen such equipment before. The last time I visited Inyagui, the set was still in good condition and being used.

The thing that gave us the greatest joy was that after we built three new houses for staff and later built an administration building and library combination, the school began to improve in small ways. The community installed more windows and larger windows in most of the classroom buildings. The floors and doors in these buildings were upgraded. One building that was severely damaged in a storm was rebuilt with funds that were provided from the U.S.

The well at Inyagui was drilled while we were in Harare on business. In the past, teachers had to get up at 2 a.m., walk a long distance, and stand in line with other community members at the only well around to get water. This attempt was after several previous attempts that only produced a dry hole. The outcome of this well was remarkable. We met the driller as we were returning from Harare. He had indicated that he hit water at forty meters. Ralph knew that was not deep enough for long-term use. The driller said that when he hit water, the teachers were dancing everywhere. Apparently, the entire community turned out to watch the event. This was a pleasant surprise since several attempts have been made in the past to get water and they have all failed. We rejoiced with them.

With this new source of water and being so close to the agricultural land for the school, they were able to raise a good crop of maize. They are planning on starting a poultry project to raise money for school fees and to provide funds for building maintenance. With a supply of water for irrigation, the school should be able to receive a good yield from their crop. They should be able to grow enough maize for the feeding program at their school, as well as have enough maize to feed the chickens.

A garden plot was fenced after the well was drilled. A local man volunteered his time to the school to plant and maintain the garden. The vegetables from the garden were used in the feeding program for the

Inyagui Primary School 191

orphans who were starving. A building was constructed near the new administration building. This building served as a kitchen where the meals were prepared for the orphans. The orphans picked up their plate of food at the serving window and carried it into the library room of the administration building. The children sat at tables to eat their lunch. When the children finished eating, they returned their plates to the kitchen. These children were so appreciative. They were always thankful for the food. If I happened to be around, the children would come to me and clap their hands in front of me as their way of saying thank you!

While Joan and Amanda were visiting us, I took Joan with me to Inyagui to distribute uniforms to the orphans at the school. The uniforms were all made by the sewing co-op. What a fun experience! The children were so happy to receive something that was new. Some ran to put on the new their new uniform. There were about a hundred boys and girls who were issued a new uniform that special day. The orphans each receive one new uniform each year.

GUZHA PRIMARY SCHOOL

Vickie, my traveling partner on one trip, and I made a visit to Guzha Primary School. We had the opportunity to visit a second-grade reading class. The class met in the shade of a mango tree due to a shortage of classroom space. Mango trees give very dense shade. The children read the lesson first in Shona and then in English.

Children were sitting in the sand because there were not enough classrooms or furniture for the size of the school. There is never enough money to do all the projects that are needed. The new secondary school that had been started by the parents had no classrooms at this stage. So, some of the classes were occupying classroom space at the local primary school. This caused the primary classes to meet outside.

Obviously, they need additional classroom space. This seems to be the case at most of the schools I have visited. Ralph made certain many of the classrooms in poor condition were renovated but no new classroom buildings were constructed. I did not feel qualified to take on the planning and overseeing construction of new facilities. I am not certain that contractors would have worked with me. Women in that culture were treated as worker bees. Men do not take directions from women in their culture. Over the years, I have seen some change in women doing all the work, but not in the very rural area where we were located.

Building was always Ralph's responsibility. He is terribly missed by everyone at the mission. Ralph had the ability to figure out how to repair most things. There was no end to the things that needed repair in the rural area. One thing we learned early on is that repair is not something the local people knew how to do. When something broke, it would be left where it broke, and the person would move on.

Guzha is so overcrowded with students that we found the preschool meeting in the library because there were no available classrooms. The books and bookcases that had been shipped to Zimbabwe from the Denver area had to be put in the back of the library to make room for this class of kindergarteners.

Unfortunately, we did not have the time or resources to do renovations of buildings at Guzha before Ralph passed away. An administration-library building was constructed at Guzha when the same was constructed at Inyagui. That was a big help for their overcrowding issue. However, more buildings were needed. So many needs and inadequate funds to cover all the needs.

The parents at the end of Ward 1 (Guzha area) are attempting to start another secondary school because it is necessary for their children to walk as much as fifteen kilometers each morning and evening to attend Nyamashato Secondary School. As mentioned elsewhere, there is only one secondary school for the entire Ward 1. This seems like poor planning on someone's part. However, there is no real development beyond the Madamombe town center, where the government clinic is located.

While a new secondary school is slowly being constructed, the classes are meeting in some of the Guzha primary classrooms. As a result, there is a shortage of classroom space for primary school classes. The preschoolers are using the library as a classroom. I have no idea what happens to the classes meeting under a tree if it begins to rain. I would guess that they will crowd into the library with all the preschoolers.

I have been traveling to Zimbabwe for more than twenty years. During those trips, I have, on rare occasions, seen an albino person. Two thousand thirteen is the first time I have seen one locally. There is a child enrolled in pre-school at Guzha. He has suffered from the intense sun, even though he wears a hat, long sleeves, and trousers in spite of the temperature. We had brought a supply of sunscreen with us. This had been given to the nurse to dispense a tube at a time to the child when needed. This child has a younger sibling who is also suffering from the same condition. The child is to share the sunscreen with his sibling. A supply of sunscreen was left with our nurse to dispense as needed. The child faces many challenges as he grows. This culture is not very supportive of anyone with a disability.

ELECTRICITY (2006)

As you, the reader, may recall, electricity was finally connected to the government clinic in one of the first years of our work in Zimbabwe. It took some insistence on Ralph's part to get the job done. Ralph requested the district council many times for electricity to be brought to Nyamashato Primary and Secondary Schools at the same time. However, it was many years and numerous requests later before the task was accomplished.

One day, six or eight years later, as I recall, power poles were delivered to an area between Nyamashato Primary School and Nyamashato Secondary School. Perhaps electricity was going to become a reality after all this time.

The plan was to put electricity in the house that we occupied as well as all the teachers' housing. We planned to electrify the administration/library building at both the primary and secondary schools. This would enable holding evening classes for community people who wanted to learn to read and write. The teachers could not believe that they would no longer have to deal with candles for lighting.

We were unable to electrify Inyagui or Guzha primary schools. The power stopped at Madamome Clinic. There was no power service to the distant part of Ward 1.

Electricity was installed in the faculty housing at both Nyamashato Primary and Secondary Schools, as well as the library/administration buildings. Poles were set and wire strung. Everyone was celebrating. Unfortunately, the ZESA people left without connecting the power to the buildings. It was necessary for Ralph to take an entire day to drive to Bindura and speak with officials. He learned they had left because more money was needed for the meters, but no one informed Ralph. So close and yet so far. I don't think we had planned on this expense. There was no turning back at that point. Another trip would be required to get the workmen back to connect everything once Ralph paid for the meters.

Surprise, ZESA appeared the following day to connect our power without Ralph having to drive to Bindura to get the workmen. All was completed by 5 p.m. It was so good to be able to flip a switch and have lights. The teachers were celebrating because they had hope of not having to use candles, which had become very expensive. They can go to the library in the evenings to do their work because there is power in the administration building. The cooks at the feeding center are looking forward to the day when electric stoves can be provided in the kitchen, and they will no longer have to cook outside on a wood fire. Early in our stay, we had hoped to have enough funds to provide stoves this year but the cost of getting electricity installed has consumed most of our money. Cooking for so many children (approximately 800) required a lot of firewood, and that has become very expensive, as has everything else.

As years went by, electricity became very unreliable, especially during the rainy season. The infrastructure is poorly maintained. The service trucks have broken down, and there is never any money for repairs. Or other issues interfere. One of the causes was the unstable power poles falling over. Once a pole fell, vandals often stole the cable for the copper wire and would sell it. Now, in 2024, the electricity, if available, is too expensive to use. In some cases, especially at the HCOC property, solar power is being used almost entirely.

There were plans to build a structure to house the sewing co-op and the newly established knitting co-op. This building would need electricity as well. The women needed to be able to have an iron to press the garments they were making, etc. Charcoal irons were dangerous. More than one uniform was ruined by ash or sparks from a charcoal iron. The treadle machines were beginning to show the use they had received. Electric machines would speed up the process and enable the women to put in machine-made buttonholes. At this point, the uniforms would look like store-purchased uniforms, and the fabric would be better quality.

The secondary school and staff houses received power when Nyamashato Primary received power. The expanded administration/library building was electrified, as was done at the primary school. This allowed them to have evening study time for students who planned to go on with their education after secondary school.

Ralph thought it was necessary to electrify the feeding center as well. This was accomplished at the same time. The dining room served many purposes over the years. It became a community gathering place for meetings. Having electricity was a change even for us. I found myself fumbling around in the dark, mumbling, and Ralph would flip a switch. That was good for a laugh at me.

In recent years, much has changed. Electricity has become very erratic at certain times of the year, and there are months during the rainy season when there is no power at all. Some of the times, there is no power due to the lack of proper maintenance of the generation system or the power lines need maintenance. Remember, the holes for the poles were dug by hand, not drilled as here in the U.S., and so were frequently not set deep enough to support the poles during the rainy season. One year, when there was little or no power, the cause was the Kariba Dam Power Station. The Zambezi River level was so low due to little rain that there was insufficient water going over the dam to generate electricity. This was beyond anyone's control.

When there is no power, the offices at HCOC (Heather Chimhoga Orphan Care) cannot function properly. They had generators to connect at such times, but fuel for the generators is very expensive and, at times, not available. The nearest source of fuel was Murewa, an hour's drive one way to a filling station. The station may or may not have a supply once someone arrives. This is yet another hurdle to deal with in a third-world country. Solar power has more recently been installed in the office building and the housing for staff so electric power use is limited. Electricity is still very unreliable. It has also become very expensive. I don't think many of the teachers can even afford the expense. It is so very discouraging.

Solar power is the only solution. However, batteries must be replaced periodically. The cost to replace them is very expensive; more than $600 for batteries for a small home.

Electricity (2006)

TRUCK FOR HCOC

Transportation for the mission became an issue as the work began to grow, especially during the periods we were in the U.S. Ralph and I were not able to be on-site twenty-four seven. We did not feel comfortable leaving our truck on-site while we were out of the country. It was obvious that the mission needed its own vehicle.

One of the board members in Harare began to search for a used vehicle. He learned of a way to get used vehicles from Japan at a significantly reduced price. This was a new program, and the board member thought it was worth a try. He signed up for a one-ton truck.

The truck that arrived for us from Japan cost $3,000. It required a great deal of work before delivery to the mission. It needed tires all around, plus some engine work. Mr. Bondeponde had a driver's license and so he was designated as keeper of the keys. A couple of the men teachers knew how to drive, and Ralph asked them to go and take a driver's test, which they did. Ralph felt that Mr. B could not do everything and would need individuals he could call on for help.

The truck was put to good use. It was used to transport food supplies from the main storeroom at HCOC to the kitchens at Inyagui and Guzha primary schools. The mission was able to buy food supplies as well as school supplies in bulk from Harare. With the truck, it was possible to transport these supplies to Nyamashato. Firewood would need to be collected and then transported to the kitchens at the different schools. Mr. Bondeponde used the truck to transport orphans to Murewa to the hospital for check-ups. The truck ended up being in constant use. It was a good purchase. Ralph and I were concerned about transporting bulk food supplies from Harare during the rainy season. Supplies were also at risk of being stolen when Mr. B was stopped at a stop light. Such theft happened frequently. It was decided that it was necessary to take the truck to Harare and have a metal frame built over the bed of the truck. A canvass cover was purchased that fit snugly over the frame on the bed of the truck. This would protect the supplies from getting wet if it rained and give some protection from theft.

It proved to be an excellent purchase. The cover also protected children being transported to the doctor for check-ups.

Later, as the work expanded, the truck was used to bring baby chicks to the poultry project. This didn't happen until about 2006 or 2007. Several vehicles have been purchased over the years. They have received much hard use and the roads that are driven are not kind to any vehicle.

FOUR MOTHERS WITH INFANTS

Blessed are those who mourn, for they shall be comforted.

Matthew 5:4 (RSV)

One morning, I was called to the Orphan Care Center to meet with four women, each with an infant. They had come asking for food assistance. All four women had lost their husbands, but only two had death certificates to prove the fact. Food assistance for the babies was issued for two weeks, and the women were told to bring the death certificates of their husbands to receive more food supplies. This may sound harsh, but we had been taken advantage of by grandparents bringing grandchildren from elsewhere in Zimbabwe to live with them and, therefore, take advantage of the services provided. We had to set some limits. It was necessary to see the death certificate to verify the accuracy of the claim.

One of the women had a child that was nineteen months old and was not even as big as a six-month-old child. It was not very responsive, and its mouth was full of sores. I doubted that the child could even suckle a bottle. The clinic had sent the mother here for formula because the staff indicated that the baby was undernourished. Obviously, they had heard that Ralph had purchased a bulk supply of formula on an earlier occasion. However, a nineteen-month-old should not require formula.

Because the baby was so listless, we decided to take it to the hospital. The child was admitted, and the doctor scolded the mother for not coming sooner. The baby died Saturday night. The truck had to go to the hospital Sunday morning to pick up the body. Ralph was the only person around to do that trip. He was terribly depressed after that experience, and it took him some time to recover.

When the body was delivered to the home for the funeral, five other children were seen at home. All the children were dirty and in tatters, and none looked very healthy. The children rarely attend school even though two meals a day are provided. Ralph reported that the adults looked reasonably healthy despite the condition of the children. I am puzzled by the fact that the mother did not look undernourished. One can only conclude that the children were not being fed.

Situations like the ones described above are extremely difficult to cope with. How parents can eat and not feed their children is beyond my ability to imagine. Children in this country become very vocal when they are hungry. Perhaps children denied food become numb to hunger! I only know that it was difficult to deal with situations like this.

ROOF DAMAGE

During one of our trips the time to leave had come. We were packing, preparing to leave before noon. There had been a bad storm during the night with wind and rain. It was a challenge to not get everything muddy in the process of loading the truck, including ourselves.

Suddenly, a gentleman appeared and was out of breath. He was hoping he was not too late to catch us before we left. He was a parent from Inyagui Primary School. During the storm the previous night, a classroom building had been severely damaged. He wanted Ralph to come and have a look. This was not a part of our plan for that day. But how does one turn their back when there is an unexpected need? This school was in Ward 1, just further down the road from where we were working. We could not turn our backs on their need. We had committed to helping schools in all of Ward 1.

Ralph stopped what he was doing and drove to Inyagui with the gentleman. Ralph assessed the damage and determined that it was obvious that the building was not worth the expense of a new roof. He talked with the headmistress and the members of the Parent Committee who were present. A plan was made to tear down what remained of the building. The men were instructed to salvage the bricks that were in usable condition. The plan was to rebuild the building as soon as possible. This emergency had delayed our departure but that had become a common thing for us.

Mr. Bondeponde checked the progress and kept us informed. He indicated that the men had been able to salvage a large amount of the bricks. Community members began making bricks to enable the workers to build a new building.

When Ralph and I returned the following year, the site was cleared, and all the salvaged bricks were cleaned and stacked, ready for use. The rubble had all been removed, and the site was ready for new construction.

That year, a new building was constructed while we were in the country. When the building was complete, Ralph had the workmen pour a new cement cap on the floor. New and larger windows were installed that provided better light. New doors were hung. The building really stood out. The children were excited about having new classrooms.

Soon after that building was occupied, we noted that the community was giving a facelift to the other classrooms. We were told the community wanted all the buildings to look like the new building. They even poured new cement floors in the other classrooms. The community just needed to know what their school could look like. It gave them an incentive to work together to improve their school. What a gift to be a part of this process! The pride of having a nice-looking school was wonderful to behold.

ORPHAN CAREGIVERS ARE TRAINED

Show yourself in all respects to be a model of good works, and in your teaching show integrity, dignity, and sound speech that cannot be condemned.

Titus 2:7–8 (ESV)

Ralph's back was continuing to improve but he was still walking with a cane and avoided riding in the truck because of the rough roads. Mr. Bondeponde and I left early in the morning to drive to Harare. Our first Board of Trustees meeting was to be held. It was to be an organizational meeting and an opportunity to review the constitution that the lawyer had been writing. When speaking to the lawyer recently, he agreed to register our organization as a non-profit organization, referred to as a Private Voluntary Organization. Once this was accomplished, it would pave the way for our shipment of food supplies. Mr. Bondeponde would then be able to expedite the matter. A lawyer and retired partner of the firm and a member of the City Presbyterian Church would co-share a spot on the Board of Trustees as an advisor in legal matters. During the meeting, the constitution was gone through with a fine-toothed comb and numerous changes were made.

The first board was made up of professional people in Harare. We applied for registration, and that dragged on for years. We finally decided we were getting nowhere fast. I became suspicious that they were stringing us along until we gave up. I suspected that they really wanted the local people to run the organization. Ralph and I could see that this would create new problems. Reluctantly, we did form a board of local people and we were able to be registered almost immediately. It ended up being a board mostly in name only. The people didn't understand what they needed to do. Nothing was accomplished, and elections were not held as required. Finally, the government stepped in and forced them to change the way they were operating. Very recently, a new board has been put in place. It is made up partly of professional people from Harare, and the rest are from the local community. This seems to be working well.

Before we were even registered with the government, we took five women who were chosen by the community to be orphan caregivers to Norton for training. There was a caregiver for each of the twenty-two villages, but only five were selected to visit Norton. They were to spend three days at the Tsungirirai Orphan Care and Training Center. The training prepared the women on how to deal with orphans in their respective villages. After the session in Norton, they were to return to Nyamashato and train all the orphan caregivers. We were anxious to hear about what the women had learned.

When I picked up the women after their training, they were so excited about all they had learned. They did complain that it was a lot of information to try to absorb in such a short period of time. They had also trained in how to give care to terminally ill patients. Since the children will know the caregiver in the community they live in, the caregiver will be able to help the children through the bereavement period.

Several weeks later, I took the Home-based Care Team back to Norton for additional training. When the training was completed, they were to be Red Cross certified and will work closely with the Murewa Hospital. Terminal patients at the hospital were turned over to the Home-based Care Team when there was nothing more that the hospital could do. These women returned and trained the rest of the orphan caregivers.

I sat in on a few of the training sessions. However, they were training in their native language since many of the women knew no English. I noted a man or two on the sidelines or standing outside the window, listening. Mr. Bondeponde laughed at me when I asked what they were doing listening to the meeting. He told me they were suspicious of us. They couldn't understand our sending their women for training. Their women were supposed to be at home working. They finally began to trust us and didn't continue to hang around checking on what was going on.

NYAMASHATO SECONDARY SCHOOL

For your Father knows what you need before you ask him.

Matthew 6:8 (ESV)

Before the end of our first trip, we had groups coming to us from many places requesting assistance. There was no end to the need; it existed everywhere one looked. The most difficult thing we did was to say we couldn't help someone. Where there is so much need, people would look at us and think we could do anything. We had to turn down a headmaster's request for help, who had walked more than a hundred kilometers to come and beg for help. Telling the gentleman no was the hardest thing we ever had to do. We knew that they were desperate for help, but we also knew that we were not superhuman and we could only do so much. Our funds were limited, and we knew the distance would be an issue when it was necessary to check on supplies or progress on projects. Close supervision was always necessary. All of this would have fallen on Ralph's shoulders. He was one person and could only do so much.

It was several years after our initial trip that we opened our eyes to the need at the secondary school almost next door. Nyamashato Secondary School is located just a short walk from the primary school. Remember we had only committed to one or two years to help a primary school remain open for the local children. We never intended to make this adventure long-term. Obviously, God had a different plan. The secondary school serves all the primary schools in Ward 1. Mr. Chivava, the headmaster, came to Ralph asking for help in completing a classroom building that had been started years previously. It had never been completed because it did not pass building standards, and the work had stopped. The school had run out of classroom space and needed the building. Ralph knew the school needed more classroom space because one of their classes used one room at the primary school. The new building was meant to house the science classes. Ralph began to make plans to bring the building up to the government building code.

Pillars were constructed at regular intervals to strengthen the walls of the building. A roof was put on, and a floor was poured. Walls were constructed on the inside to divide the building into two large classrooms, with a section in the middle devoted to teacher offices, a lab prep room, and chemical storage. Now, they have a science building, but the electricity that had been brought to the school is rarely available. I have been told recently that they only have electricity between midnight and 4 a.m. This does not enable classes to function. Teaching in the rural area certainly has its challenges.

***

In addition to the science building that needed help, there was another smaller building that also was only partially constructed. I learned that it was the sewing lab. The building had been constructed but still needed a roof and nothing had been done about finishing the inside. Doors were needed for the rooms. Window glass still had not been installed into the window frames. A proper floor was waiting to be poured. The inside and the outside of both buildings needed to be painted. Gradually, Ralph was able to budget funds so some of these tasks could be completed.

***

Sometimes, I felt that the sewing lab was pointless. The school's headmaster, who had recently been appointed, wasn't going to let go of any money for machines or fabric or sewing supplies. The girls could not afford to purchase fabric, even poor-quality fabric.

There is no way to teach sewing without sewing machines or fabric. The students had no money and certainly no money for fabric. The situation was so frustrating. The girls that came to the class had nothing to do. They could only sit and visit. So much need!

The school had one home economics teacher but very little for her to work with. The scissors she had for cutting fabric were so dull she couldn't cut anything with them. Over time, I was able to get fabric to the class. People in the U.S. gave me fabric they had purchased and then had not used. It was far better fabric than any available in the city shops. This donated fabric was boxed up and shipped in one of the many containers that went to Zimbabwe. With only two sewing machines, it was difficult for the girls to make much progress. The machines were hand crank machines like the sewing women would have liked for me to purchase for them. In my ignorance, I had purchased treadle machines. I had learned to sew on a treadle machine and just assumed that is what was used in Zimbabwe as well.

If the secondary girls could learn to sew, they could join the sewing women when they completed secondary school. The women I taught to sew many years ago are getting elderly, and many have stopped their work of making uniforms. New blood is needed to keep the sewing co-op alive.

Once we had the primary school moving forward, Ralph turned part of his attention to the secondary school nearby. In addition to the science lab that had to be reconstructed, Ralph added an addition to the administration building at the secondary school. The addition was added to have space for a library. Many of the books shipped over the years were textbooks needed at the secondary level. The headmaster was delighted with the quality of the books, especially the English books. He had majored in English.

In addition to the books the school received from the shipment, they also received many computers. One end of the large addition was devoted to the computers. The balance of the large addition was turned into a library. The school was also appreciative of the shelving that Ralph was able to acquire at an auction house in Harare.

A couple of new houses were built at the secondary school. One of the houses was for the headmaster and his family. They were overjoyed with a new house.

One of the projects was bringing water from the well some distance from the school to the school grounds. A 10,000-liter tank on a stand was erected near the school garden. Parents dug a trench from the well to the school grounds, where the storage tank was located. A water line was laid in the trench to the tank. The agricultural teacher was so pleased. They began dividing the garden into plots. Each class was assigned a certain area for growing vegetables. Teachers who requested a plot were given one for their own personal garden.

Nyamashato Secondary School

ORPHAN STORIES

For as the body apart from the spirit is dead, so also faith apart from works is dead.

James 2:26 (ESV)

A teacher brought a child to me who wore filthy clothes, and they were in shreds. I took him to the Orphan Care Center to find some new clothes. We first found a pair of shoes. I had to put them on him. He told the teacher that it was the first pair of shoes he had ever had. Next, I found a pair of shorts and a pair of long trousers, a short-sleeved shirt, and a long-sleeved shirt. Last, I gave him a sweater. He was so happy; there are no words to describe experiences like this. Those smiles are worth a million dollars. The boy walked away inches taller.

Initially, we began by outfitting the pre-school children first and then moved up by grade level. The process was slow, but it was so rewarding to watch the children's faces when they received new clothes. They tried hard to keep a sober face, but it was more than they could do. When one looked them in the eyes, they burst into laughter.

I asked one little third-grade boy if the clothes he had been given were okay. He looked at me and said they were too beautiful. He was grinning all over. My wish is that you, the reader, could have shared my experiences.

I noticed another little boy that I had given clothes to. It has made such a difference in his personality. He is now socializing with some of the other boys. Before receiving the clothes, he had been shunned by the other children. The teacher said that she had not been certain that he could even talk; however, since receiving the clothing, he has been participating in class. What a difference has been made in the lives of the children through the donations made by so many people in the U.S.

One day, a little third-grade girl was sent to me so that I could give her some presentable clothes. She left the storeroom so proud and with a smile as big as the sun. However, the next day, when she came to school, she was again wearing the dirty, tattered dress that she had worn to school every day. The teacher learned that her father would not let her wear the clothes I gave her. They were to be saved for special occasions.

This same little girl told her teacher that she had to do the cooking for the entire family. She also told of being given a bucket of tomatoes and being told not to come home until she had sold all the tomatoes. Apparently, she spent three nights in the forest alone with nothing to eat before she was finally able to sell all the tomatoes. Considering some other disturbing stories about the little girl, Mr. Bondeponde and another member of the Management Committee paid a visit to the home one evening. Their plan is to monitor the situation closely.

While it has been a joy beyond words to be able to dress these children in new clothes, there has been a downside as well. Seeing these children undressed and witnessing the distended bellies and deformed bodies is overwhelming. Some children have humped backs or crooked legs. Bony legs are standard. There is no fat anywhere. I did not see one normal child out of probably 400 that was helped to select clothes. Some children had sores on their bodies. I have no idea the cause, and I haven't enough band-aids to doctor all of them. My guess was that some of it at least is due to malnutrition. In a few instances, I felt the child was probably infected with HIV. This would complicate the healing.

One of the teachers at the primary school has taken in a girl of about ten or eleven who has no place to live. She is an orphan and ran away from her grandmother, who beat her so severely that her arm was broken. She has been thrown out of other homes. It is all due to being an orphan and she represents another mouth to feed. How awful it must be to be so young and not have anyone who cares anything about you. So many children in Zimbabwe have similar stories to tell. Clothes were given to this child a couple of days ago. The expression on her face was priceless when she was given the clothes.

Today, a boy came to me so that I could care for the burn in his hand. He was wearing the same dirty clothes he had worn all week. After I had cared for his hand, I took him to the storeroom to get some presentable clothes. When I told him goodbye, he thanked me and asked for a pair of shoes. I had forgotten to fit him with a pair of shoes. He had never had a pair of shoes before. When he left, he was looking down as he walked with a huge smile on his face.

One day, a father brought his little boy, six years old, to us. The child had the worst infection on his buttocks that anyone could imagine. I asked if the clinic had seen the child. He said they had given him a prescription for some medicine but that he couldn't find the money to pay for the medicine. I first thought the child was not cleaning himself after going to the toilet. Later, I decided that it was mosquito bites that he had scratched, and they were infected. Apparently, it is common for children to sleep naked. I first cleansed and treated the area with ointment. In the storeroom, I found a pair of pajamas for him to wear at night so that the mosquitoes could not bite that area. These situations nearly broke me. I feel for the child who is hurting and for the parents who cannot provide for the needs of their child. This has not always been the case in Zimbabwe.

The child continued to come to me for many days to be treated. One day, an orphan girl who is living with the family brought him rather than the father. I discovered she had something similar on her wrist. I now wonder if the infection is not from mosquito bites.

***

We took a fourth-grade girl to the hospital last week with what was thought to be a broken arm. The X-ray proved that it was only badly bruised. The girl said that she had slipped on a rock when getting water from the river to water the garden. However, this week an orphan caregiver came to tell Mr. Bondeponde that the girl had been raped. We are inclined to think the suspected broken arm was the result of a struggle when the girl tried to defend herself. It is reported that the aunt, who is the girl's guardian, took the child to the man and told him he was now responsible for her (a practice in this culture). The man is already married. What kind of a life does this child have? We needed to find a way to provide a place of refuge for children like this one.

***

One Sunday morning, a boy was brought to us in a wheelbarrow. He had been injured playing with other children the previous evening. We didn't think the leg was broken, but we couldn't be certain. He was obviously in a great deal of pain. So, he was given some aspirin, and Ralph said that he would take him to the hospital the next day. There was no point in making a trip to Murewa to take him to the hospital on Sunday. No services are available on a Sunday. On Monday morning, at seven, Ralph left here with a truck full of children, five total, including the boy with the injured leg, and the nurse aide. The boy's leg was broken, and he was in a cast and walking on crutches. Some of the children could not be cared for as there was no water at the hospital. So, another trip to the hospital is necessary on Friday. If we are lucky, the water will have been restored. How a hospital can operate, even for one hour, let alone days, with no water is beyond me (no toilets, no showers, no surgery, etc.). So goes life in rural Zimbabwe.

**

As I was eating breakfast one day during Joan's visit, I happened to look out of the kitchen window. I saw a young girl walking toward the school. She appeared to have a large goiter on her neck. I had never seen the child before. It was difficult to understand how we could have missed this child. Joan and I quickly ran out to her and began to question her about her neck. I walked to the dispensary with the child. Her name was Beauty. We learned the growth had been getting worse recently. This was going to require another trip to Murewa to the hospital to have the doctor evaluate her condition.

When the doctor examined her, he indicated that she would need surgery. She was admitted to the hospital, and surgery was scheduled for later in the week. In Zimbabwe, surgery is not taken lightly. The local people are very fearful of surgery. The surgery for Beauty was successful, and it was a cyst, not a goiter. When she was released from the hospital, she came to see us and was all smiles. She thanked us for taking her to the hospital. I am convinced that it was God bringing her condition to our attention. How mighty is our God!

**

A grandmother appeared with a three-month-old infant. She had a letter from the District Administration Office asking for HCOC's help. The baby is three months old and was born two months prematurely. The mother is critically ill and not expected to live. The grandmother has few resources. So, Beauty, the nurse, provided a blanket, several outfits of clothing, baby bottles, and formula from our supplies in the storeroom. This was made possible through all the money and items of clothing that friends at home have donated over the years for shipment to Zimbabwe.

***

A grandmother brought an eleven-month-old baby to me. She had the death certificates for the parents. The death certificate was a requirement to prevent some from saying they are orphans to benefit from services when they really are not orphans. The local clinic said the baby needed to go to the hospital. The baby was eleven months old and weighed less than eleven pounds. I suspect the baby was HIV positive and certainly had every sign of starvation. The mouth was full of sores and so the baby was refusing to eat. No one was around, so Florence and I drove to Murewa to the hospital. It was late afternoon when we arrived at the hospital, and there was no doctor on duty, but the staff did admit the child. She died mid-morning on Monday. The same day, another child died that I have written about previously.

Florence and I discussed the need for some classes for expectant mothers on infant care. When Florence completes her refresher course, we plan to outline a course that Florence will hold periodically for expectant mothers in the community.

***

On Saturday, Albert drove us to visit some orphan boys. It was explained to Erik and me that these boys had been living like animals until they were reported to HCOC. Both parents are dead. With a $1,000 donation from one ZMP church, $1,000 from Albert's Rotary Club, and $600 from ELMA, HCOC has been able to construct a toilet/bathing structure and a sleeping facility. The construction has been done by the environmental health technician from Madamombe Clinic at no cost to HCOC except for the materials.

***

A ten-year-old girl was brought to me. She has one older sister, about eleven or twelve, and three younger sisters. Her mother is mentally disturbed and left the family more than a year ago. The father has taken another wife who is little more than a girl herself, and she is pregnant. The child was raped by a forty-plus-year-old man about a week ago and spent several days in the hospital. Her six-year-old sister was also molested. The perpetrator was finally captured and put in jail. This is an example of a family of vulnerable children. They are in the care of two adults but are not being cared for or provided for. These children need to be housed here on-site where they would be in pleasant clean surroundings and have loving care. Dorothy, Albert's daughter, who has recently graduated with a degree in social work, is volunteering at HCOC and will begin tomorrow the process of getting HCOC registered to house children on-site. Please keep children like this in your prayers. They have so many strikes against them.

***

Bill, a Renewed Hope board member, and I joined Albert when he delivered food to an orphan living several kilometers from the school. The child was not at home, so I didn't have a chance to visit with the child, who is twelve years old. I did talk with the grandmother through Albert. The grandmother is blind and can barely walk. The grandmother said that a granddaughter was out collecting firewood. This is a case of a child living with a grandparent, but the grandparent is dependent on the child.

***

When my friend Susan paid a short visit one year, she was anxious to visit a child-headed household. One day, Albert drove Susan to visit Innocent. The child is only fifteen years old and lives alone. When asked about any problems he had, he said that the house leaked when it rained, and he wanted space so his young sister could join him. He says he gets very lonely living alone.

He had a hen and seven chicks confined in a box outside his home. There was a tomato plant growing by the door of his one-room structure. Innocent told us when he needs money, he sells a chicken. He uses some money from the sale of chickens to pay his school fees.

There is so much desperation in the area; people do whatever is necessary to provide for their basic needs. And if that means stealing, that is what they do. When Innocent was at school, someone stole his hen and six of the seven chicks. My heart goes out to these children, who, at too young an age, are forced to become adults.

***

Beauty took Susan and me to visit Maud on a Friday morning, Susan's last day, before traveling back to Denver. Maud is the girl who had been very ill in July when Deanna and Jackie visited the mission from Colorado. The grandmother resisted letting Beauty, the HCOC nurse, take Maud to the hospital. Eventually, Beauty and Albert were able to convince her that it was the only way Maud could survive. When we saw her, one would never know how ill she had been.

I gave Maud a quilt that Kathy, a friend, had given to me just before I came on this trip. It was made by some Syrian women living in a refugee camp in Jordan. In the four corners are the words "Faith, Hope, Love, and Peace," embroidered in both English and Arabic. The smile on Maud's face said more than words. She loved this quilt.

Maud came to see me yesterday. She wanted to thank me again for the quilt that I gave her recently. She is so happy. One would never know how seriously ill she was nine months ago.

We discussed the possibility of her returning to school. She indicated that she would like to do that. We discussed her not having a birth certificate, which is necessary for her to have so the ZMP could pay her school fees. I promised to see what might be done to obtain the document. Both her parents are deceased, and she is living with her grandparents, who are both elderly. That seems to concern her a lot.

***

Orphan Stories   217

Trosky came to see me. He had come here from Botswana, where his father had brutally beaten him and nearly killed him. He hid from his father for several weeks until he regained his strength from the beating. Only then was he able to travel. A donor provided his school fees and a uniform, and we registered him in the secondary school.

He wanted to proudly show me that his uniform now represents a top student at the school. Outstanding students wear white shirts or blouses to distinguish them from the rest of the student body. He was all smiles yesterday and very talkative. He wants to become an advocacy lawyer. A couple of years ago, he would hardly look at anyone and was extremely thin. Donor gifts are making a big difference in the lives of these children.

GOD'S PROTECTION

Blessed is the one who considers the poor! In the day of trouble the Lord delivers him.

Psalm 41:1 (ESV)

During the early years of our time in Zimbabwe, I mentioned that Mr. Bondeponde would always go with Ralph every time Ralph traveled to Harare. Ralph and I thought it was just an opportunity for him to escape for a few hours. However, it quickly became apparent that he did not want Ralph to go unless someone was with him. When it wasn't possible for Mr. B to go, he would send one of the male teachers.

We weren't in Zimbabwe long before we began to hear of women having their purses snatched off the front seat of their car when they would drive around a corner. I was warned to keep my purse (briefcase) on the floor behind my legs. We were also warned to keep our vehicle doors locked. Then we heard of bricks being thrown through a window and things taken, even when the vehicle was moving.

Over the years, we needed to travel in high-density areas when Ralph was searching for something specific. We were fortunate that we never had a problem. I must add that when Ralph went in anywhere, I stayed with the vehicle. I was the official car guard. It wasn't my favorite thing to do, but it was necessary. I am not sure I could have deterred a robbery, though.

One day, Ralph needed to go to the bank. It was necessary to park a block or so away, and, as usual, I stayed with the vehicle. There were mobs of people milling around on the streets. It was hot, but I kept the windows rolled up. Two young men tried everything to get me to check my taillight. They said it was broken. It could have been broken, but I knew I didn't dare get out to check. If I had been attacked, no one would have intervened.

***

Another time, Ralph had just come from the bank with a briefcase of money. He had workmen to pay and numerous bills to pay. It had gotten so few businesses in Zimbabwe, and no individuals would accept a check. Ralph paid all the local workers in cash.

When he got in the truck, I knew he was frustrated because of the time it had taken at the bank, and he was in a hurry. Ralph threw the briefcase on the back seat. I think this was the only time he had ever done that. We had made a practice of never leaving anything visible that would trigger an attack. The transaction had taken way longer than he had expected, and Ralph was frustrated at the inefficiency. As we approached a stop light, I saw, out of the corner of my eye, a young man run from the sidewalk toward the back door of the truck. I alerted Ralph to lock the doors on the truck, something we always did (but not this time). Just as the locks snapped into place, I heard the man try to open the back door. Saved in a split second. The brief case was saved and perhaps our lives. God was watching and teaching us a lesson. You must never let down your guard. This could have ended so differently, but God was watching over us.

SIGNS OF DESPERATION

Reproaches have broken my heart, so that I am in despair. I looked for pity, but there was none, and for comforters, but I found none.

Psalm 69:20 (ESV)

When people are hungry, they will go to great lengths to scavenge for food. Driving along the highway to Harare, I noticed grain along the side of the highway. It was probably maize that had leaked from a grain truck on its way to market. A bit further on, I noticed two women along the side of the road. They were down on their knees with grass brooms sweeping the grain out onto the edge of the tar road. They were picking up the kernels of maize and putting them into a container. I thought to myself, *One must be terribly hungry to do that*. I would not have believed it if I had not seen it with my own eyes.

Can any reader know what it is like to be severely hungry? Mr. Bondeponde came to our door one day to tell of a fourth-grade boy who had just passed out at school. When the child regained consciousness, the teacher questioned him. She discovered that he could not tell her when he had anything to eat. When Mr. Bondeponde went to visit the home, he discovered that the child lived with a stepmother. Both parents of the child were deceased. The stepfather, brother to the child's father, who was deceased, had gone to Mozambique to find work. The stepmother had no money. It was finally concluded that she scavenged for food for herself during the day while the boy was at school. The child had no food and no resources. The boy was slowly starving to death. How can one human treat a child in this way is beyond my comprehension. This was only one instance where children were not being fed. We often witnessed children that were just skin and bone and yet the parents would look reasonably healthy.

We gradually learned over time that living with extended family is not always a good thing. It certainly was obvious in this case, as well as in other situations we discovered. My heart ached for this boy and many other children like him. Ralph tried to speed up the work on the feeding center that was under construction. Building can progress only so fast. It just takes time to build a structure of any kind, especially when everything is done by hand.

At the time, I realized that we might encounter more desperate situations. Children were especially vulnerable. Living was becoming more difficult, especially without any resources. Many things that I was able to purchase when we arrived in March were no longer on the shelves in the markets. It isn't an issue of the items being too costly, they just weren't to be had at any price. On this trip we experienced stores with empty shelves.

When Ralph and I first arrived in Harare just five years ago, we were impressed with the city of Harare. As we drove into the city, we felt like we were in the UK. The streets were wide and maintained. The buildings were impressive. Boulevards were maintained with beautiful flower beds. In just five years, we saw significant deterioration. Water mains were broken in some places, and water was running in the streets. There was no effort made to repair the break. If one were to inquire why nothing was being done, they would have been told there was no money to purchase repair parts. Water continued to run in the streets, in one area, for several years. One day, in a different location, we witnessed the street give way under the cab of a semi-truck. That was an unbelievable experience.

Ralph and I went to a store in Harare like Sam's Club, except you can only buy in bulk at the store. We purchased 20,000 ZD ($4,000 USD) worth of food items to hand out to starving children until the feeding center is operating. The store had run out of salt the day before and didn't know if they would get more. Their supply of sugar was nearly gone. We purchased some of the last that they had. There was no margarine available. We did get items we could give to starving children to help bridge the gap until the feeding center was in operation.

When Ralph finished loading everything into the back of the truck, he asked me if I had his briefcase. I didn't! He had it with him when he left the store. He had laid the briefcase inside the backend of the truck when he opened the tailgate. When he had loaded all the grocery items into the backend of the truck, his briefcase was nowhere to be found. The briefcase contained not only important papers but also a lot of money, his passport, etc. The passport was the most critical item. We dare not get stopped and have no passport. Ralph had to go to the U.S. Embassy and report it stolen. Moral of the story: don't ever let your briefcase leave your hands. It does make loading groceries difficult while hanging onto it.

A couple of days later, Ralph was able to pick up a new passport, but he still was missing the papers he needed for a scheduled meeting, not to mention the money. A week later, when we were back in town, we stopped to see our friends that we often stayed with. They had received a call from the bank near the wholesale market where we had purchased all the groceries. We were never able to figure out how the bank knew to call our friends. That was truly a God thing. The bank said the briefcase had been left on their counter. When Ralph went to the bank to collect the briefcase, everything was inside the case except the money, even his passport. What a relief!

TIRIVANHU—STONE SCULPTOR

He has filled them with skill to do every sort of work.

Exodus 35:35 (ESV)

Tirivanhu was a young man from the Ward 1 community near Nyamashato Schools. Ralph and I met him the first year we were in Zimbabwe. He had come to visit us one evening near the end of that first trip. He had brought us a sculpture of a mother elephant and her baby. I have this sculpture displayed in my home. Tirivanhu told us that he had attended the school when he was a child and that now his children were attending the same school. He thanked Ralph and me for renovating the school facilities.

Tirivanhu presented us with a sculpture of an elephant and its baby to thank Ralph and me for helping his community and especially the school. He was so appreciative of what had been done and spoke of what a difference it had made in the entire community. The sculpture was exceptionally well done and is highly treasured by us.

Ralph became very interested in his work, and we went to visit him at his home. It was amazing to see what he could accomplish with homemade tools or discarded items that he had shaped for his purposes.

This was the beginning of a long relationship. Before we left to return to the U.S., we purchased several sculptures from Tirivanhu to bring back in our luggage. As it turned out, those sculptures were quickly purchased by people who visited our home. We began to wonder if this might be a way of raising funds for the ongoing work in Zimbabwe. Each year, we would bring back our empty pieces of luggage full of sculptures. Tirivanhu was very particular and insisted that he be allowed to pack them in the luggage. He did an excellent job. There were no casualties.

The following year, when we returned, Ralph presented Tirivanhu with a new set of real carving tools. Tirivanhu was speechless and had tears in his eyes when he saw the tools. He finally told Ralph he would be able to do some real carving now. And he did!

Ralph and I soon decided that it was necessary for us to ship crates of sculptures to the U.S. and display them at local art shows. It would be a good source of income for the work going on in Zimbabwe. Ralph purchased lumber and taught Tirivanhu how to build the crates. When Tirivanhu had the crates packed, he had to find someone with a pickup truck to transport them to Harare for shipment to the U.S. Once they arrived at Denver airport, Ralph would go in his truck to pick them up.

The demand for the sculptures at art shows was great, and the supply sold out quickly. Purchasing sculptures from Tirivanhu provided him with an income that he did not have access to in Zimbabwe.

Over a period of several years, we bought a ticket for Tirivanhu to fly to the U.S. for the art shows held locally. He stayed in our home for several weeks on each trip. The shows were a big success and generated significant income for the mission. In addition, Tirivanhu was able to support his family in a way that would not have been possible without the U.S. market.

One year, we were in Africa working at the time of the art shows. Tirivanhu was not here as a result. The sales were way down and did not even cover the expenses. We did not display at the shows in the following years. The work in Zimbabwe was consuming more of our time and we were unable to be here at the time of the shows. This left a hole in our funding for work at the mission.

INJURED HAND

I have seen his ways, but I will heal him; I will lead him and restore comfort to him and his mourners.

Isaiah 57:18 (ESV)

Ralph and I went to Harare, an almost weekly event. Ralph sometimes was in Harare several times a week, collecting supplies, meeting with contractors, etc. I would go along once a week to send emails, a frustrating task, take laundry to the laundromat, and purchase groceries and ice for the ice chests. The goal was to leave town by 4:30 so we would be off the highway before dark. That frequently did not happen. If we could just get to the dirt road and off the highway, we would feel safe. There was so little traffic on the dirt road that we didn't worry much about an accident. On this occasion, as we rounded the curve to go through Dandera, we were almost home (Nyamashato, where we were living) when both of us noticed headlights ahead and wondered what was happening. As we approached, Mr. Chivava, a teacher from the secondary school, flagged us down.

In the back seat of the car, they had a young man who lived very near Nyamashato Primary School. He had injured his hand in an oxcart accident. His hand had been caught between a fence post with barbed wire on it and the oxcart as the oxen made a turn into the homestead. Mr. Mafuta, one of the teachers at the primary school who had a car, had driven him to the government clinic at Dandera. The nurses refused to open the clinic because it was after hours. The young man was bleeding profusely. I knew the minute I looked at him that an artery had been damaged. I also knew there was no time to waste, or he would bleed out.

I quickly handed Ralph the flashlight and put on surgical gloves that were kept in the glove compartment of the truck. The gloves were kept clean in a zip-lock bag. I asked Ralph to get a clean towel from the fresh laundry to wrap the hand in. It was not sterilized, but we had no alternative. I asked the teacher, who was riding with the young man, to remove his necktie and give it to me. He really dug in his heels, so to speak. It may have been the only necktie he owned. Reluctantly, he finally gave it to me. I tied the necktie around the upper arm of the injured young man. Then, I directed a man standing near me to find a small straight branch that I could use to make a tourniquet. The stick was tied into the necktie and twisted until the flow of blood had stopped.

I instructed the young man to keep his arm elevated. The teacher was instructed to release the stick every few minutes, and when the blood began to seep from the wound, to re-tighten the tourniquet.

Our truck was loaded with groceries, laundry, and supplies for projects Ralph had going at the school. There was no room for one more thing. What to do?

Just then, another truck pulled up behind Ralph's truck. There was nothing in the back of his truck. The father helped load his son into the back of his truck. Ralph convinced the clinic to let us have a mattress to lay the young man on and a blanket to cover him. I instructed the teacher to be sure the young man kept his hand raised to reduce the bleeding. I used some of our clean towels to pack his hand. They were seen in the hospital in Murewa when they arrived. The hand was X-rayed, and the hospital transported the young man by ambulance to a hospital in Harare. God provided the second truck and driver just when it was needed. We later learned that the driver of the truck that appeared when we needed it was the young man's father. God's assistance when needed most!

Several years later, the young man came to see me at Nyamashato to thank me for saving his life. He said that I was responsible for him still having his hand. He didn't have full use of the hand, but the young man said it was so much better than having no hand.

ORPHAN CARE PROGRAM RELOCATES

He who has prepared us for this very thing is God, who has given us the Spirit as a guarantee.

2 Corinthians 5:5 (ESV)

Mr. Bondeponde was a real trooper in helping us to expand the Orphan Care Program. As I mentioned in another chapter, he led the effort to gain access to a piece of property designated just for the Orphan Program. He made many trips to Marondera, the headquarters of the government for Mashonaland East Province. He pleaded for the need for land for the Orphan Care Program separated from the school operations.

After we returned home from a recent trip, Ralph received a call from Mr. B one day inquiring about how much land he thought would be needed for his vision for the future. They settled on twenty-five acres of land not far from the school. This piece of land was granted in 2006. It enabled moving much of the operation away from the school. It also reduced the level of activity that could be disruptive to the classes. The feeding center remained at the school. Feeding centers were constructed at each of the other two primary schools in Ward 1. The secondary students walked to Nyamashato Primary for their meals. It is just a short distance away.

The first project was to construct a fence around the entire property granted to the mission by the provincial government. The fence is electrified to deter livestock from rubbing on the fence and to keep out intruders. A building was constructed at the entrance to the property to house the guard, especially the night guard.

A poultry project was started on a very small scale in the beginning and located on the back side of the property. It had two purposes. Meat would be provided for the children, and a bit of income for emergencies.

The project began with a small batch of chickens. It was a learning experience. They ignored a warning about putting medicine in the drinking water to prevent the chicks from getting sick. This was because they don't give their hens that run free any medication. They couldn't see the need for medication. However, after they lost an entire batch of chicks overnight, they learned an expensive lesson. Now they know.

Soon, a larger poultry run was built that would handle about 1,000 chickens. Over time, they were able to grow the project. USADF (United States Agricultural Development Foundation) heard about the mission and came to see what was happening. Soon, they were contributing significant funding for developing the project. Over four or five years, several buildings have been constructed that will hold about 5,000 birds each at one time. HCOC now has the capacity to raise more than 20,000 birds at one time. Each building can house chicks at different stages of development. This has the possibility of providing a steady income flow. As I write this book, the economy in Zimbabwe is such that most people cannot afford to buy meat for their families. The market for dressed chickens has been seriously impacted.

Expanding the project made it necessary to have piped water to the project rather than hauling it from the well. Rather than drilling another well, a trench was dug along the fence line from the main tanks to the poultry project. A 10,000-liter tank on a stand was placed within the poultry grounds. This supplies a constant source of water. Initially, automatic waters were purchased for the poultry run.

Over several years, USADF also donated a walk-in sharp freezer for the dressed chickens, in addition to slaughter equipment and an incinerator for the disposal of the waste. They have also donated some equipment for producing chicken feed. The goal was to make this an income-generating project in addition to providing meat for the orphan feeding program.

As the new site developed, it was necessary to build housing for the staff. Ralph dug the first shovel full of dirt for the manager's future home. Soon after this, the house was complete, and Albert was able to move his family in. This freed up the house at the primary school for Ralph and me to have a place to live when we returned each year.

Ralph's first effort was to convince ZESA (the power company) to bring power to the new HCOC site. This would provide electricity for future development. Wells were also drilled to provide water to the project. Water was essential for the development of a large garden and the expansion of the poultry project. However, we quickly learned that electricity was not sufficiently reliable. It was necessary to switch to solar power. Solar is expensive to install, so it all took time, but it is far more reliable than electricity. Four of the five wells are now solar-powered.

At present, there are five deep wells operating and one well is idle. Since electricity is so unreliable, it was necessary to install solar power for all the wells. One of the wells services the new, state of the art, child-friendly health clinic, the most recent structure to be built on site. This was accomplished by the perseverance of the ZMP (Zimbabwe Mission Partnership Board.) Many donors contributed, and fundraisers were held to sponsor this construction during COVID-19. It was a challenge, but the structure is now complete and in operation. Recently, a van was purchased to enable the transport of children as well as community members to the doctor or even the hospital in Murewa when necessary.

Over the many years since a manager's house was constructed, the mission has grown. An office building was needed and several houses to accommodate staff who live in Harare but stay locally during the week. There is also a house that was built in the beginning for visitors. It is the only accommodation within a thirty-mile area.

In addition to structures, a large garden is managed by a crew of workers. It provides all the vegetables for the three feeding centers. Excess produce is sold locally or sent to the market in Murewa. Much of the maize used in the feeding program is grown on-site. In a good growing year, it is necessary to purchase only a small amount of maize for the kitchens.

One bright spot that has very recently taken place is that one of the two girls we sponsored for their secondary education has recently graduated from the university. She graduated with a degree in agriculture. She is now volunteering at HCOC in the garden. Her focus is training the workers on how to manage the garden. This gives me hope for the future of the mission.

MORINGA

I have given every green plant for food.

Genesis 1:30 (ESV)

During one of the first years that we traveled to Zimbabwe, the headmaster requested that a garden plot be fenced so that the teachers could raise a few vegetables. It was also intended to generate income for the primary school. Fencing was necessary, or the cattle owned by the people in the community would destroy the crops. The cattle were let out of their pens at night to graze when the temperature was cooler. The garden plot was not fenced until the entire school property was fenced with barbed wire. This was done to keep the cattle off the playground. Cattle guards were put in place at the entrances of the grounds. This way, gates were not needed.

Once the garden was fenced, the next request was for water to be brought to the garden. A water line was buried from the tank stands to the garden and a standpipe inside the garden was installed. Teachers could fill their buckets at the faucet and carry them to their plot of vegetables. Eventually, a garden hose was purchased and could be connected to the faucet and pulled to the plot where water was needed. Each teacher who wanted a plot was given an assigned plot in the garden. Such a simple thing made a huge difference in the teachers' diet.

The fencing of the school property had a dual purpose. It also kept the donkeys off the school property at night. Prior to the fencing, the donkeys seemed inclined to graze near the teachers' bedroom windows. They would let out a loud bray that could wake the dead. No one appreciates being wakened in the middle of the night, and certainly not by the sound of a donkey.

Several years later, a group of university students from Scandinavia were going around the community, educating the local farmers about moringa and giving them seeds to plant. These young people came to Nyamashato because they had learned that the school had a fenced garden so cattle could not disturb the plants. They trained one of the teachers on how to raise moringa. The young people donated wheelbarrows and black soil to the school along with shovels, hoes, planting containers, and a bag of moringa seeds. Shade cloth was donated, and the students built a sunshade to protect the new plants from direct sunlight. The students also demonstrated to some of the teachers how to fill the containers with soil and how to plant the seeds. Their time ran out, and they needed to return to their country.

The local teacher who had worked with the students came to me and asked what he should do now. I had no idea and had not been involved with the group of young people. My time was totally involved with the sewing women. Instructions had been given to the teacher to transplant the plants to a spot in the garden when they were about eighteen inches tall. Ralph and I were leaving in just a few days to return to the U.S. When we returned home, I began doing research on moringa. I was not familiar with the plant and had no idea why it was being introduced into the local community.

Researching moringa was eye-opening. It is the most nutritious plant known to man and grows in most of the sub-Saharan regions of the world. It grows naturally in Zimbabwe but the people did not know of its nutritional value. It is of limited value when allowed to grow wild. The tree grows very tall and is very limber. The foliage is just at the top and too difficult to harvest. It provides minimal shade. As a result, no one paid any attention to it. All parts of the tree have nutritional value but it is the leaves that are most sought after. If the tree is meant to be used in the daily diet, which would be ideal, it needs to be kept trimmed so that it doesn't grow beyond five feet. This makes it possible to harvest the leaves for their nutritional value. When kept trimmed, it produces an abundant amount of leaves.

Ralph and I returned to Zimbabwe the following year and were prepared to develop the moringa for use in the feeding program for orphans. This plan was easier said than done. We quickly learned that the people tended to live as they have always lived for generations. In spite of the nutritional value, they were reluctant to try anything new. I did not give up but had an uphill climb that lasted many years.

In the meantime, a new person had been hired to manage the garden for the Orphan Feeding Program. He was very knowledgeable about gardening and was eager to learn new things. I showed him how to cut back the moringa plants to about twelve inches above the ground. The stalks that remained in the ground regrew into a bush, producing more leaves for harvesting. The new plants were not allowed to grow into a tree. The cuttings were then planted in the ground and kept watered. They soon sprouted and grew quickly into a bush that was easier to harvest.

When the mission moved to the new site, just a short distance from the school, a small area was staked to be planted with moringa. Getting workers to weed and water the moringa was a challenge. Before I had arrived, someone started a fire and it got out of control and burned up the trees and the new irrigation lines that were in place. I always felt that it was an effort to get rid of the project, and I couldn't be certain it hadn't been done on purpose. Little did they know who they were working against.

The trees were cut back near the ground. They are hardy, and they regrew from the root. The workers had to carry water to water the trees because the irrigation tubes were ruined. I refused to replace the irrigation tubes. Several years later, a well was drilled for the moringa field. The trees are now watered with hoses. Moringa is unique in that it has a tap root that goes deep into the ground and will seek its own water source. Once the plants are well established, they no longer need frequent watering. The moringa field has expanded over the years and now covers about a ten- to twelve-acre area. The trees are planted about two feet apart in the row, and the rows are four feet apart. The trees are doing very well.

I kept talking about the nutritional value of the moringa and how much healthier the children would be if moringa were added to their food. It has been a very difficult sell. However, this changed when a very ill child was brought to Beauty, the nurse. He was malnourished and had been abused. He couldn't even walk, and he didn't talk. The child was starving. Beauty kept him near for several weeks and included a bit of moringa in his diet daily. In just a few weeks, he was strong enough to walk around and has continued to thrive. It is truly a miracle plant.

Eventually, a building was built at the edge of the field, and a vermiculture project was started. The liquid from the worms drains to a trough in the floor of the building and is directed outside to a catch basin. This liquid is dipped into a five-gallon bucket, diluted with seven parts of water, and used to periodically fertilize the trees. The trees do very well when fed in this manner. No commercial fertilizer is used.

The leaves are harvested and dried. In the beginning, the leaves were dried on cloth mesh stretched between hooks on the walls. It was essential to dry the leaves indoors, away from as much light as possible. The leaves are high in vitamin A but sensitive to light, which destroys the vitamins. When the leaves were completely dry, they were put into a grinding mill to turn into powder. A small amount of the powder was added to the porridge for the orphans that came to the feeding center.

After the acreage of moringa was expanded, a processing building was constructed. A bathroom with showers and lockers is at one end. The women who do the processing can come to work and take a shower before they put on their clean uniforms. The building also has a breakroom, where the women can take a rest. Standing while stripping leaves from the branches can be very tiring.

In the processing room are long stainless steel tables and sinks where the moringa is washed before being stripped from the branches. The leaves are put on plastic screen mesh before being put into the electric dryer. Excess leaves are put on the same screen mesh and stacked on bakery racks to air dry. After drying the leaves, they are put through a grinder to make powder. The powder is bagged in plastic bags for use in the feeding center or to be sold at the market.

Dr. Chris Gadzirayi, the professor of science education at Bindura University, brought three of his students to visit our moringa field. He had heard about the work being done at the mission and wanted some of his students to see what we were doing. They came wanting to get involved with our moringa project. Prof. Gadzirayi said that our plot of moringa is the largest in Zimbabwe. He also was so surprised to see the condition of our moringa. He said it was the best that he had seen.

During their visit, they harvested some leaves for experiments, but we received word that they were not usable. I was certain this would happen.

I had even suggested that they would need refrigeration to successfully transport the moringa. It has a very brief shelf life once it is harvested.

Professor Ngoni Cherinda is employed by the Harare Institute of Technology. He also visited the mission with three of his students. One of the things they were interested in was the drying of moringa. They had been building dryers for the fruit and vegetable industry for several years. They were interested in building dryers for moringa. I had hoped to make a visit to their workshop to see what they were doing and how it might work for the moringa. This did not work out. Moringa must be handled very differently than fruits or vegetables.

At HCOC, we learned that moringa must be harvested and processed immediately. Once the leaves are picked, they quickly wilt. A field worker brings harvested moringa from the field, and it is passed inside through a window to the wash sinks just under the window. The branches of leaves are washed twice in adjoining sinks and then placed in a third sink to drain. Women are lined on both sides of stainless-steel tables, stripping the leaves and putting them on plastic racks that slide into the dryer. If there is no electricity that day, as often happens, the trays of leaves are placed on bakery racks, and the leaves must air dry. This is not ideal but all that can be done when no electricity is available.

When the women report for work, they go into a dressing room where they shower and change into a clean uniform. A solar water heater is on a stand just outside the shower room. This provides warm water for the showers. They cross the hallway and step into a foot bath and then into clogs that remain in the work zone. This is to reduce the risk of any contamination.

Moringa

ALBERT AND BEAUTY JOIN THE TEAM

Put on then, as God's chosen ones, holy and beloved, compassionate hearts, kindness, humility, meekness, and patience.

Colossians 3:12 (ESV)

Mr. and Mrs. Bondeponde had full-time jobs. Yet they were happily filling in wherever needed when we returned to the U.S. Ralph and I could see the stress they were under at certain times. Soon after Mr. Bondeponde was able to get land donated to the Orphan Care Program off the school property, Ralph decided that we needed someone to be on-site full-time to direct the Orphan Program. That was too much to expect of Mr. Bondeponde. Since no one had a car, he would have had to walk to the new site to check on things happening there. The distance was not far, but to walk there and back each day would have consumed a lot of his time.

We felt the need to leave Mr. Bondeponde as headmaster of the school. He had done an excellent job in getting the school operating as a school should operate. When the mission moved to the new site, Albert Mukondwa was hired as director of the mission. Beauty, his wife, is a registered nurse, and she took over the medical care of the children. You will recall that Ralph and I had met Albert and Beauty during our first trip to Zimbabwe in 1997. This decision freed Mr. and Mrs. Bondeponde to concentrate on the educational aspect of the mission.

I have mentioned Albert previously. He and Beauty were both stationed at the government clinic located in the township not far from the school when we first met them. Eventually, they were transferred to Mutoko, a location about fifty miles east of Murewa. Beauty was hired as a nurse at the hospital in Mutoko; Albert oversaw environmental issues in that district. Ralph and I had kept in touch with Albert and his family over the years. We tried to always visit them when we were in the country. At one point, Albert served on the Board of Directors of the mission. The board was made up of professional people in Harare. Albert and Mr. Bondeponde both served on the board as well. This required them to travel by bus to Harare to attend the meetings.

When the twenty-five acres were granted to the mission, it was fenced with security fencing. In the beginning, there were no buildings and no water. Our first project was to get ground broken for a place for Albert Mukondwa and his family to live. While the house was under construction, wells had to be drilled. Finding water at this new site was critical. It was necessary to bring electricity to the site to pump the water. This was a challenge, and the electricity proved to be unreliable. We had to have water on-site twenty-four seven.

Over time, we put in solar pumps and panels. While expensive, it was the only way to have reliable power. All our water is now pumped by solar power. It is pumped into 20,000-liter tanks. This provides adequate water until the following day, when the pumps will again operate. The buildings that were electrified are now all operated on solar power.

Albert and Beauty were hired to organize the orphan care effort in 2007. While Albert directed the Orphan Program, Beauty, a registered nurse, managed the health of all the children, not just orphans. That relieved me of some of the work I had been doing. We kept Florence, our nurse aide, to help Beauty. Albert and his family resided at the school while a new house was built at the site that had been given for HCOC to expand. They lived in the house that Ralph and I had occupied. It was tight quarters for his family, but it was the only housing available.

Beauty was a wonderful addition to our staff. She is such a loving, caring person, and the children loved her. Beauty had to walk long distances to check on sick children. With her knowledge and care, these children, especially the orphans, began to thrive.

As time went on, a vehicle was purchased for HCOC. Beauty perfected her driving skills and was able to drive and check on more children who were ill. The van allows her to transport children who are ill in a closed vehicle. She has been a blessed asset to the program. Over time, it has been necessary to expand the number of vehicles. Hauling supplies from Murewa and/or Harare requires reliable vehicles.

RETHATCHING RONDAVELS

Even youths shall faint and be weary, and young men shall fall exhausted; but they who wait for the Lord shall renew their strength.

Isaiah 40:30–31 (ESV)

Initially, Mr. Bondeponde was not only the headmaster at the school, but he was also overseeing the work going on to benefit orphans. His hands were more than full, and we feared the demands on his attention would only increase. The school was growing, and he was so terribly busy being headmaster. Ralph and I decided that he needed some help. We felt he had way too much to do to do a good job in both situations.

As stated in the previous chapter, in 2008, Albert Mukondwa, formerly an environmental health technician at the government clinic, was hired to handle the orphan efforts, thus giving Mr. Bondeponde a break from wearing two hats and being on call twenty-four seven. In addition, Beauty Mukondwa, Albert's wife, was hired as a full-time nurse at our first aid station. She would care for the sick or injured children. Florence, the nurse aide, remained on staff to assist Beauty in her work. This allowed for there to be someone always at the station in the event an emergency called the nurse away.

One of the first things that Albert did when he assumed the new position was to assess the living conditions of the orphans. He found many children living in dilapidated housing. When we arrived, there was a big effort underway to repair and re-roof the rondavels the children were living in. Pictured above is only one of many situations that needed attention. Albert had gone around the community soliciting helpers. The effort brought out many people to assist in the work. Housing for orphans was upgraded as well as housing for elderly members of the community.

This was a totally new concept to the local people. You will remember that I indicated elsewhere that, traditionally, families were concerned only about their immediate needs. Helping one's neighbor was not part of their culture. This was because caring for one's own family was difficult by itself. Caring for extended family members was a burden. Often, there was a lack of enough food for the extra mouths to be fed in their own family. Children who were left to fend for themselves often had to scavenge for anything to eat.

We encountered many situations where I am certain that whatever food was available, the adults ate, and the children got nothing. More than once, we had sick children brought to us, and they obviously were starving to death, and yet the parents looked reasonably healthy. Encounters like this took an emotional toll on us. More than once, young children were taken to the hospital in Murewa in serious condition, only to pass away a few days later at the hospital.

William, fifteen years old, and his brother live alone. William's brother was out collecting firewood, so I didn't get to meet him. We delivered a few food supplies to them and checked on what foods they had in stock.

The boys, with the help of a local man who has volunteered his time, are trying to improve their living conditions. (This was obviously happening as the result of us talking at every opportunity about working together for the benefit of all.) A new roof was in progress for the boys' rondavel. Albert suggested that we help by supplying a window and a door since they have neither. If the items are not available in Murewa, the purchase will have to wait until someone goes to Harare.

These boys are missing out on the relationship between father and sons. It is difficult for us to bridge that gap. I am grateful that a local man has stepped up to help the boys. Prior to our arrival, this would never have happened. People only helped immediate family, and sometimes, they didn't even do that. That is really the answer to many of the problems in this area. Working together to help each other has been a new concept for the local people. However, leading by example has helped.

We were informed that in the distant past, such situations would have been handled differently. However, the customs have changed since the government moved people off their land for the white farmers. The communal lands are marginal for farming. The local people are just trying to survive. Some are succeeding better than others.

TRAINING SECONDARY GIRLS TO SEW

Train up a child in the way he should go; even when he is old he will not depart from it.

Proverbs 22:6 (ESV)

One year after the S. E. W. women were doing well on their own, I began training three orphan girls to sew. By this time, the women had been moved out of the classroom they had been occupying. The school was growing, and additional classroom space was needed. The sewing women had been moved from the old classroom to one of the offices that had just been completed at the end of the new preschool building. It was way too small for the group, but it was the only space available at that point. The women moved some of the machines out on the sidewalk in front of the room during the day. That gave them more room to work. In 2008, a building was constructed specifically for the sewing co-op and the knitting co-op that had recently been formed. It was located next to the library/office building that was erected in our second year in Zimbabwe.

Three girls who had completed secondary school came to me asking me to teach them to sew. Eventually, my plan was that they would become part of the sewing co-op. I was looking forward to a time when they could take over the co-op. It amazed me how quickly they learned to manage the sewing machine. I found it much easier to teach them than to teach the women I began with in 1999. Some of the women I began with have quit, and others still don't do very well. A couple of the women have passed away. I suggested to some of the women that they find something else to do to make money. I couldn't afford for them to mess up expensive material anymore. I felt some of these women were the cause of some of the machines always needing repair.

Training these young girls might be the beginning of a skills training center for the orphans who complete their "O" levels satisfactorily. I began with only three girls, and observed to see how it would work out and where it might lead.

These girls, who completed their secondary education, had come wanting to sew. I have my hands full trying to give them a crash course in so little time. However, two of them caught on rapidly and were constructing uniforms with a bit of help. These girls are all orphans.

I was so pleased with the girls learning to sew. They exhibited real promise. Word got out, and this caused the original women to work harder. They felt challenged to measure up to what the young girls could do. The girl who started the previous day completed her secondary education the prior year. She had lost both of her parents and was living alone and caring for two younger children. The bit of money she can earn will certainly help her care for the younger children. All the girls have similar stories.

Mr. Bondeponde came by a couple of weeks later to pay the women for the uniforms that had been made. I was anxious to see the reaction of the girls who had begun to sew very recently. The expression on their faces was priceless. They had only begun and so had made only a few uniforms, but they were delighted to be paid for what they had done.

COMMUNITY WELL REPAIR

I can do all things through him who strengthens me.

Philippians 4:13 (ESV)

One evening, Ralph was notified that two community wells were not functioning, and people had no water. So, on Thursday morning, he headed off to see what would be needed to make them operable. One of the wells he repaired with spare parts that were stored here at HCOC. The second well they pulled apart on Thursday afternoon. Ralph discovered that the pipe was buried in a lot of mud. He determined that the well should be blown out, but he didn't have the necessary equipment.

It was dark when he returned for supper. Early Friday morning, he headed back to finish the job. The crew that gathered removed a section or two of the pipe and reassembled the pump. The well was back in operation, and many people were very happy.

This was only the beginning of repairing wells. Over a period of several weeks, Ralph spent most of his days supervising pump repair of community wells. Note that I said Ralph supervised the pump repair. He felt that if the local men had experience, in the future they could come to Nyamashato to get the equipment and do the repair on their own. He and the local workers wouldn't return home until it was too dark to see what they were doing.

Ralph and I are truly blessed to have many supportive friends. We have been enabled to pay school fees for several bright and deserving students attending boarding schools to expand their education. Funds have been provided for irrigation at the new moringa plot. The same donor has sent money so that Albert may begin a small poultry project to generate income for HCOC.

And now, we have been blessed with a sizeable donation from another donor that will allow Ralph to repair numerous wells in the community. Community wells are not our responsibility and yet they are essential for the health of the community. Our orphans live in the community and use the wells as their source of water. We are working hard to get families in the community to contribute to the repair of the wells. It is not an easy concept for them to accept when they are so accustomed to having government involvement. Their resources are extremely limited. However, at that time, the government was doing nothing. People in the community were using unsafe sources of water. The councilor for Ward 1 scheduled a meeting with the village headmen on Monday. Hopefully, something positive will come from that meeting.

One day, when Ralph was in Murewa to get more repair parts for the wells, he was stopped by some official. They had heard what he was doing. Ralph was told that he was messing with government property. Ralph's reply was that he was providing water for the local people because the wells were not maintained. He asked the official what he was supposed to do. He got no reply.

It was necessary to go to Harare to obtain a large supply of repair parts for the wells. The money sent to us made it possible for Ralph to make these purchases. Mr. Bondeponde followed us to town in the one-and-a-half-ton truck. The truck was full when Ralph completed the purchases. Work will begin tomorrow. Ralph will be supervising a group of villagers and showing them how to repair their wells.

Someone told me they used to watch Ralph drive down the road toward the community clinic. If he saw any men who were not busy, he would stop and say, "We are repairing community wells today. If you are not busy, we sure could use your help." Usually, they would climb in the back of the truck and go with him. His crew was a little different each day. Sometimes, they would be waiting beside the truck when he left the house to go to work. I don't remember how many wells were repaired that year.

On September 11, 2010, there was a surprise birthday party for Ralph's eighty-first birthday. It was attended by teachers, HCOC Executive Committee members, HCOC staff, and some community members. What fun! Ralph was so surprised that he was speechless. That was a first! They went all out with a meal, a birthday cake complete with candles, popcorn, and even a gift. Even the children got involved with the entertainment.

The people gathered gave Ralph a new suitcase. They were afraid that his suitcase was worn out and that he might not come back. That was the last year we traveled to Zimbabwe together. He passed away the following May.

Ralph became ill about three months after our return from the Israel trip in late 2010. He passed away in May of 2011. I carried on the work after Ralph passed. It wasn't ever the same without him, but I felt I could not abandon the children we had been providing for. I went every year through 2018. When COVID-19 hit, it shut down foreign travel. By the time travel resumed, I had reached a point where I didn't feel up to the stress of the journey. I have since turned over the mission to younger people. I am still involved but only in an advisory capacity.

I returned to Zimbabwe in 2011, just three months after Ralph passed. As I was driving to Guzha Primary School, I noticed a group of people gathered at a borehole that had not been repaired last year. The villagers had gathered and were working on their own boreholes. This was a first! I am sure they had taken a lesson from Ralph. In the past, they had always waited for someone to do it for them. There were some parts left over from the work last year that were provided to them. Other parts needed to be purchased for them in Harare. Community members had constructed a fence around the pump to protect it from cattle. A cement basin protects the well from contamination, and they had built a trough leading under the fence to a dug pit lined with cement. The runoff from the pump drains into the pit where the cattle come to drink. The pump is also kept locked and is unlocked only at designated times. The villagers have decided that those who do not contribute to the cost of maintenance cannot have access to the water. Efforts from last year had paid off. The community was finally developing some independence.

AMANDA—A GRANDDAUGHTER'S STORY

And we know that for those who love God all things work together for good, for those who are called according to his purpose.

Romans 8:28 (ESV)

Here are the words of our younger granddaughter, Amanda, after her first trip to Zimbabwe.

I grew up with my grandparents, Ralph and Roberta Pippitt, traveling to and from Zimbabwe. When my sister Ashley was fifteen, my grandparents took her to Zimbabwe. Then, when I was fifteen, I went for nine weeks over summer break. Hearing stories from my grandparents and my sister, I had an idea of what to expect, but I did not expect the impact that it would have on my life. The year was 2010.

It was a long journey to Zimbabwe. We had some airplane trouble getting there and ended up having to have a short night in a hotel in Washington, DC. Once we got to Zimbabwe, we did not get our luggage, but luckily, it arrived the following day. Before heading to the mission, we stocked up on groceries, mostly dry goods, because power was not consistent, and there was no guarantee that the refrigerator would be powered to keep food cold. Driving out to the mission was a long drive; most of it was a bumpy dirt road. I cannot imagine what it is like now. All the children and staff were ecstatic for us to arrive. You could see the relief and joy in their faces as they greeted us.

The house that we lived in had two bedrooms, one bathroom, a living space, and a small kitchen. The bathroom had a sink and a shower; the toilets were pit toilets outside and behind the house. There was running water in the house but no water heater. Instead, there was a tank painted black on the roof of the house. We would take showers in the afternoon after the sun had warmed the water in the tank, but the showers still felt cold.

Within a couple of days of arriving, I acclimated myself to the school by visiting classrooms, the health clinic, and the dining hall for orphans. The classrooms are mostly furnished with items sent from the United States, including desks, chairs, bookshelves, and books. The students were learning from the same textbooks that are no longer current in the U.S. By the time I visited, my grandparents had shipped many forty-foot sea containers of items to Zimbabwe. All the children were eager to learn and well-behaved, at least while I was around. I enjoyed sitting in the classroom with them; I even took a math test in one of the classes.

Occasionally, I would join my grandpa and Albert, the administrator of the mission, to visit the other schools that are supported by HCOC. All the schools are in rough shape. There are broken doors to classrooms, cracked chalkboards, and desks that look like they could collapse at any moment. In many classrooms, there were more children than desks. If the students were small enough, they would share chairs and desks, but that only works until they outgrow the space. There is nothing frivolous about the schools. No posters on the walls, no projectors, not even whiteboards. If the weather was nice, teachers would take classes outside and have students practice writing in the sand.

During lunch, I would head to the dining hall and help where it was needed. Sometimes, I would help serve lunch, clean dishes, or entertain the students. Students ate sadza (ground cornmeal mush) and greens every day; sometimes, there would be meat added to their plates. There was one day I decided to cook lunch for the staff. I made spaghetti with meat sauce and a fruit salad. They seemed to enjoy it, but the following day, they were back to sadza and greens.

After school, there was sports practice. I mostly stayed with the group that played volleyball because I knew more about volleyball than soccer. It was nice to see the students participating in a sport and enjoying themselves. The volleyball team was doing well and went to a regional championship. This looked much different in Zimbabwe. The students walked to and from the event, which was a few kilometers away. Someone gave me a ride to the games, but I walked back with the players. I was always being asked questions about what life was like in the U.S.

It is hard to explain to them the differences, especially at fifteen years old. Looking back now, I would not want to tell them how life is here. We have running water in our homes. We can heat and cool the house depending on the season. We drive everywhere, even if it is just a couple of miles down the road. Power outages are rare, and we normally have power again within a few hours. The list goes on and on.

On days that I did not visit classrooms, I would spend time in the school clinic. Beauty, a registered nurse, and Florence ran the clinic. They would provide care for any student or person in the community that came in. We talked a lot about the diseases that were common and the large number of orphans in the area. Many people suffered from water-borne illnesses and malaria, as well as HIV/AIDS. To prevent waterborne illnesses, my grandparents drilled deep wells. People would walk many kilometers just to get to clean water, then they would have to walk all the way back carrying the water. It was a regular sight to see women and occasionally children carrying large buckets full of water on their heads. It was just another reminder about what we take for granted in the U.S.

The schools provided so much for the orphans. Beyond the lunches that were served, there was a sewing group that made uniforms and knitted sweaters for the children. This group was made up of community members, and they used equipment that was sent over from the U.S. The students were required to be in uniform, so it was important that the sewing group could produce enough for the growing orphans.

I am grateful I got to share my grandparents with the people of Zimbabwe. The work they did starting in 1996 changed the lives of thousands of children and adults. They drilled wells, constructed and repaired buildings, and supported children by providing school fees and uniforms. I am proud of everything they did, and I am happy to see that it is still growing. The people of Zimbabwe needed it then and now.

Amanda—a Granddaughter's Story

CHALLENGES

And Jesus said to him, "'If you can'! All things are possible for one who believes."

Mark 9:23 (ESV)

I traveled again to Zimbabwe a year after Ralph's passing. Three church members joined me on this trip. Albert was waiting at the airport for our arrival. He had brought two pick-up trucks and drivers because he knew we would have lots of luggage. Ralph and I used to always carry the maximum luggage the airlines allowed at that time. Our personal luggage was in a carry-on. We were delivered to the Bed and Breakfast home that Ralph and I had used for many years. Getting a good night's sleep was top of the agenda.

The following day, the plan was for me to fly to S.A. (South Africa) and get the truck Ralph and I had purchased for our own use. We always left it with friends in South Africa when we flew back to the U.S. This allowed us to keep in touch with them. Mr. Penny, one of the board members, took me to the airport while the rest of our team went with Albert. Mr. Penny and I made plans for him to fly to S.A. and drive the truck back with me once the paperwork on my truck was complete so that it could be exported to Zimbabwe. As I was going through security at the airport in Harare, they discovered that I had a lot of cash. So, I had to go to ZIMRA (Zimbabwe Revenue Authority). They were going to take anything over $10,000. I asked how I would get it back. They just smiled at me. I told them that was stealing, and they couldn't do that. Fortunately, cell phones were a thing by then. I was able to call Mr. Penny and he came back to the airport, and I gave the extra money to him in front of ZIMRA officials.

When I arrived in S.A., the truck was being serviced and a windshield replaced. My friend and I shopped for yarn for the knitting co-op. Yarn was not available in Zimbabwe at that time. I found it difficult to locate yarn in S.A. as well. Knitting machines require a special type of yarn.

I had planned to head back to Harare on Saturday. However, Johann, a son of our friends, had just moved into a new house that they had built, and the family was having a housewarming the following day. They insisted that I must stay and attend that event. Johann had stayed with Ralph and me on numerous occasions when he brought a track team to the U.S. for competitions.

Mr. Penny flew to S.A. on Tuesday, and the two of us left Pretoria at 4 a.m. the following morning, hoping to be at the border by 9 a.m. Our goal was to be on the Zimbabwe side by noon. You have heard of the best-laid plans…. Our plans didn't work. We learned we needed an export license to cross the border. When I inquired about that very issue in Pretoria, I was told it wasn't necessary. This requirement went into effect on June 2, and it was now June 10. Weren't we lucky? Fortunately, I knew of a game lodge about thirty kilometers from the border. I couldn't reach them by phone. So, Mr. Penny and I drove there, hoping they had accommodation available. Luck was with us. They had several vacant cabins. Ralph and I had stayed there many times. We ended up being there for three nights.

Finally, the clearance papers from S.A. arrived at six thirty on Saturday morning. It took till 8 to get to the Zimbabwe side of the border crossing. Our papers were checked and rechecked and checked again before we could finally leave S.A. When we arrived on the Zimbabwe side, there were so many buses and people going through that it looked nearly impossible. Mr. Penny called a clearing agent that he knew to see if he could help. He sent one of his men, and we did little but sit and wait. Finally, at three in the afternoon and after many dollars, we were on our way to Harare. Actually, I believe it was record time for the paperwork we had to do. Anyway, we arrived in Harare at about 10 p.m. I will *never* drive on Zimbabwe roads again after dark. What a nightmare!

The new Nissan truck that was purchased had still not arrived in Zimbabwe. South Africa now requires an export license for anyone transporting anything across the border. Nissan indicated in an email to

Albert that it had taken three weeks for them to get the license. Next, we were caught in a backlog of vehicles destined for Zimbabwe. It took another couple of weeks to get the new vehicle. The wait saved between $7,000 and $8,000, so maybe it was worth my time.

The truck that I brought up from South Africa is now registered and licensed in Zimbabwe. Albert purchased insurance, so the truck is legally in Zimbabwe. I still struggle with how complicated such a procedure can be. So much of my time was wasted, not to mention the diesel used running from one office to another, and the office needed was always on the other side of the city.

A SON'S VISIT

The righteous who walks in his integrity—blessed are his children after him!

Proverbs 20:7 (ESV)

Bryce, my youngest son, paid a visit to the mission the year that Ralph passed away. He had very limited time because of his job demands. However, it was great to have him there, even if he only had a few days. He stepped in and fixed things just like his dad, Ralph. As the reader knows by now, electricity is not dependable. So, Bryce connected the generator to the house power, and we were not only able to have refrigeration, but it was also possible to run the washing machine that Ralph and I had previously purchased in South Africa.

When we made a visit to Inyagui, we learned that they were unable to start the generator to pump water. Inyagui did not have electricity, as I have previously mentioned. The garden desperately needed water. Bryce and Jeff worked on the generator and determined that the air filter had not been cleaned. They were finally able to start it by jumping it with the truck battery. Enough water was pumped to last for a few days until a new battery could be purchased.

It was four in the afternoon, and I received a phone call from Albert. Thank goodness cell phones were available by this time. In the early years of the mission, we had no communication once we left Harare to go to the mission. Albert and Godfrey were stranded in Harare. They had gone to town to pick up items necessary for the memorial service that was planned for the following day. They also had a load of food supplies for the feeding center. On their way out of town, they heard a noise and stopped to have a look, only to discover that one of the front wheels was about to come off the truck. Bryce and Jeff left to go pick them up and bring the supplies back that they had purchased.

The poultry project was beginning to expand. A new foul run that would hold many more chickens had just been completed. Chicken wire covered the large window openings in the wall for air circulation. These openings needed to be covered with something to keep the heat in for the baby chicks at night. Bryce purchased rolls of heavy plastic canvas to put on the outside of the poultry runs. The plastic canvas was weighed down with a piece of lumber attached to the bottom. During the day, it was possible to roll it up and tie it in place to provide good ventilation.

There were many projects I would have liked to have had Bryce's help with, but he had to get back to his family and his job. So, his time came to an end far sooner than I would have liked.

A couple of years after Bryce's first visit, he made a second trip to help me carry on some of the work that had been started in previous years. He was immediately put to work on the poultry project. He worked on the woodchipper that arrived on the last shipment we made from the U.S. Our shipment was opened at the border, and things were gone through. That was a first for us. Many things were missing by the time the shipment arrived at the mission. Thankfully, the woodchipper and the rototiller both arrived. However, spare parts for the chipper were missing. I sent information to Bryce, and he brought parts with him from the United States. When Bryce returned from the poultry project, the woodchipper was working properly. Great news! It is used to make bedding for the chickens from the dried corn stalks.

Bryce's short trips were busy ones. There were always things that needed attention, and he had the expertise to see that everything was working properly. I would love to have had him with me all the time. Like father like son!

PASTOR ERIC'S VISIT

Give instruction to a wise man, and he will be still wiser; teach a righteous man, and he will increase in learning.

Proverbs 9:9 (ESV)

Pastor Eric, from New Hope Presbyterian Church in Castle Rock, Colorado, traveled with me one year to witness all the things he had heard about over many years. It was a long trip. The staff had gathered to greet us when we arrived at HCOC.

The morning after our arrival, Beauty, our nurse, picked us up for a tour of the primary schools in the catchment area. She was checking on the orphans enrolled at Inyagu and Guzha. Inyagui was the first stop on the tour. The work that had taken place since a year ago was evident. All the buildings had a fresh coat of paint. The grounds were neat and tidy. Broken windowpanes had been replaced. The children were obviously enjoying the playground set that Ralph had helped erect on his final trip to HCOC. It was a busy place.

Beauty was busy checking on orphans while Eric and I toured the school. Beauty was following up on some of the orphans enrolled and collecting documents needed from the children. It was necessary to do this because of the large number of children trying to take advantage of the help being provided to orphans. The organization was stretched very thin. It was difficult to turn children away when the need was so obvious. However, our resources could do only so much.

When Beauty's work was complete, we proceeded to Guzha, the furthest point in our area of operation. Guzha is a very poor area, and the school is poor as well. We found a class of children meeting in the shade of a tree. Preschoolers met in the library. This had become necessary because some of the classrooms were occupied by secondary students.

Nyamashato Secondary School is the only secondary school for all of Ward 1. Secondary students from this end of Ward 1, in the past, walked a very long distance, of at least ten-plus miles, to attend Nyamashato Secondary School. This was a serious handicap for regular attendance. The parents had decided to build their own secondary school to reduce the distance the children needed to walk. While the school was under construction, the secondary students were using classroom space at Guzha Primary School. This meant that the primary classes had to meet under a tree. It wasn't an ideal situation, but that was their solution.

Pastor Eric had the opportunity to see the location of the well that was drilled at Guzha in 2011. There were few sources of safe water in this area. I relayed the story of this well and explained that the driller had given me a scare when I stopped to check on his progress. He felt that it was going to be a dry hole. I was devastated. However, when he started to pull the drill out of the hole, the water broke through, and water came gushing out. There was a geyser of water. The force of the water broke several sections of casing as the driller attempted to line the hole. It was necessary to contact Harare and have a heavier casing brought out. When the heavier casing was delivered, the driller was able to complete the job. A solar pump and solar panels were installed, along with a security fence and an electric fence as well.

The community came together to dig a trench for water lines to the school grounds, where a 20,000-liter tank was installed on a stand. This provided gravity-fed water for the staff and children at the school. Such a celebration I have never witnessed before in my life when the first water was collected at the faucet. There was singing and dancing by all who witnessed the water at the tap.

The water made it possible for the school to have a garden. They were able to provide vegetables for the kitchen that prepared meals for the orphans. Water is a necessity for human existence. Finding clean water in that part of the world is sometimes difficult to accomplish.

One day, Albert drove Eric and me to visit some orphan boys. We were told the boys had been living like animals until word was sent to HCOC to investigate the matter. Both parents are deceased. With a $1,000 donation from one ZMP church, $1,000 from Rotary, and $600 from ELMA, HCOC was able to construct a toilet/bathing structure as

262   Hope for Zimbabwe Orphans

well as a two-room house. The labor to build these structures was done by the environmental health technician from Madamombe Clinic at no cost to HCOC, except for the materials. This was a special gift from a local community member. This is just one of the many sad stories about orphans who are left with no resources that we encountered over the many years we spent in Zimbabwe.

Fast-forward five years, and those same two boys are living in the house that was built for them, but now they are sixteen years old. They were in secondary school and doing well. A little help made a huge difference in their lives.

On the last day of Eric's visit, we made a final visit to the home of the orphan that Eric had helped to reconstruct a rondavel for. Albert, the orphan, would now have safe housing. We found that a new door frame had been installed, the walls had been plastered with cement inside and out, and a new thatched roof was in place. Two window frames had been installed for lighting and ventilation. Albert, the boy who lives alone, was busy helping the builder. They were preparing to put a new floor in the rondavel.

Over the years, Albert, the orphan, has made improvements to his home. A little help goes a long way sometimes. Eventually, he was hired to work on the poultry project at the new HCOC site.

Staff at HCOC gathered in front of Albert's office for fifteen minutes of devotion each morning before eight. They take turns leading the devotion. On the last morning of Eric's visit, Eric was asked to lead the devotion. This was a good way to end his brief trip.

ROTARY VISITS WATER PROJECTS

Fear not, for I am with you; be not dismayed, for I am your God;
I will strengthen you, I will help you, I will uphold you with my
righteous right hand.

Isaiah 41:10 (ESV)

The Rotary Club of Harare City paid a visit to the HCOC project. Ralph attended their meetings whenever possible over the many years we worked in Zimbabwe. They had become very supportive of our work when they learned what we were doing. The same club partnered with the Castle Rock Rotary Club a previous year on the well projects here in Zimbabwe. However, only one or two people in the Harare club even knew where HCOC was located. It was a real pleasure to host this club for a tour and lunch here at the site.

Albert briefed the Rotarians on the background of the project before beginning the tour. The tour began at Guzha, the most distant point. They visited the site of the well and had an opportunity to see the tank hoisted into place on the stand in the center of the school property. There will be a water faucet located at the base of the tank where teachers and children will be able to get water. It is also located very near the kitchen that will prepare the food for the feeding center at Guzha. It was the first water that could be sourced on-site at the school.

The Rotarians were very impressed with all that has taken place over the last fifteen years. Thanks for this must go to all the people in Denver and around the world who have contributed generously over the years to this mission.

The mission of Rotary International is to "provide service to others, promote integrity, and advance world understanding, goodwill, and peace through our fellowship of business, professional, and community leaders." Those contributors have made all the improvements possible. I believe many in this community have forgotten what it was like in 1996. Schools were already condemned when Ralph and I made our first visit. Renovation of classrooms was of top priority, along with safe water.

The Rotarians that were visiting saw the trucks begin to arrive in the afternoon with equipment and supplies for the wells. There were four workmen, and they remained on location until the pumps and equipment were installed and everything was working properly. Everyone was so excited, especially at Guzha where they have never had water nearby. They can hardly fathom having 10,000 liters of water available twenty-four seven. Yesterday, people watched as the workmen assembled the steelwork for the stand and then watched as they put it in place using their pickup truck to help tilt it upright.

The workmen who will install the solar panels at Guzha are scheduled to arrive in the coming week. It will be exciting to see the first water pumped with solar power. While the work at Guzha was taking place, other workmen were assembling a stand for a 10,000-liter tank at the poultry project at HCOC. Water to fill that tank will be piped from the main tanks at the front of the HCOC property to the poultry project. The trench has been dug, and the pipe is in place. The connections will be made as soon as the tanks and stands are in place.

The Rotarians paid a visit to the HCOC poultry project and witnessed the automatic water to the poultry building being prepared.

After the tour of the entire project, the group assembled in the feeding center, where they were served a fried chicken dinner. The dinner was prepared by Jeff, who was visiting the mission and helping with the expansion of the water projects. The Rotary group returned to Harare after their tour of the various schools to witness the numerous projects that were taking place.

POULTRY

How often would I have gathered your children together as a hen gathers her brood under her wings.

Luke 13:34 (ESV)

In 2006, HCOC was granted twenty-five acres of land by the provincial government specifically for the development of the Orphan Care Program. The property was fenced with an electric fence, and a guard's building was constructed at the entrance. This was necessary to keep out the local livestock that roamed at will. The post is staffed twenty-four-seven, and all persons entering or leaving are monitored and recorded.

Once the fencing was completed, we decided it would be good to get an income-generating project started. The plan from the very beginning had always been for the local community to be involved in the development and care of the program. This is extremely important for the success of any Christian ministry in a third-world country because local "buy-in" by the indigenous people is key.

Having a poultry project on the property was an idea that evolved because it is something the local people are familiar with. Most rural families have a few hens around their property. It would be an effective way to teach the mission to be self-sufficient. It would be necessary to locate the project at the furthest point from the entrance to the new property (far from the housing area). Initially, two poultry buildings were constructed. One building was divided into two compartments. These were to house baby chicks. The plan was to purchase seventy-five chicks that were one day old and get them started. When they were two to three weeks old, another group of seventy-five chicks would be purchased for the second compartment. This was the beginning of the project for raising poultry with an aim to sell the chickens for food at local markets, as well as in the big city. The staff had their difficulties. Initially, they thought it was not necessary to purchase medicine to put in the water for the chickens to ward off disease. I cautioned them about what would happen. Eventually, that caught up with them, and overnight, they lost the entire lot. Lesson learned!

Gradually, the poultry program expanded. Another poultry run was constructed to house 1,000 chicks at one time. It was constructed so that it could be divided into smaller compartments that would house smaller batches of chicks.

As the poultry project grew, water consumption was outpacing their ability to keep water hauled. It was obvious we had to provide a water source at the site. A trench was dug from the storage tanks at the front of the property to the poultry project. A 10,000-liter tank was put on a stand near the first poultry building that had been constructed. This provided water on-site for the chickens. The water was piped into the poultry run to automatic poultry waterers.

The broiler chickens were sold, either whole or by the piece, locally to individual families. The feeding program for the orphans used the chickens in the orphans' diet. Most of the chickens were sold to processors in Harare. They would come at night and pick up the entire flock. Traveling with the chickens at night reduced the loss in transit when the temperatures were extremely hot.

When a batch of chickens was sold, the poultry runs had to be scrubbed with disinfectant to prevent any possibility of losing a new batch of chicks. It was necessary for the run to stand empty for a week or so to air completely. There was not a great deal of profit earned per chicken. Profit is derived from the volume of chickens raised. It was felt that it was necessary for the local people to understand they must contribute to the care of the orphans in their own community, and this was one way to accomplish that goal.

We worked hard to get ZESA (the power company in Zimbabwe) to bring power to the school initially and then to the HCOC site once the land had been granted. The local people were unaware of the inconsistent availability of electricity. Initially, the power was reasonably consistent. The length of time when the power was off was short. As time went on, power became more sporadic. Times without power became a big issue for the entire project, not just the poultry project. As a special note, when Ralph and I first traveled to Zimbabwe, there was no power in this rural area except at the government clinic. A few years later, Ralph contacted the power company and got them to put in power lines to the new HCOC site. This required driving to a remote site to pick up the electric company workers—what a feat! The power company had no form of transportation.

The project caught the attention of USADF (United States Agricultural Development Foundation) located in Harare. USADF sent representatives to see what was happening at the site. The representatives liked what they saw and began to fund additional expansion. USADF funded more poultry runs and electric lights in the poultry runs. Infra-red lights were provided for heat for baby chicks during the cooler weather. Eavestroughs were attached to the edges of the roof to catch the run-off when it rained. This water was channeled to a catch basin and used for irrigation. An incinerator was donated to dispose of the poultry waste. This was a big help in keeping down the fly population.

USADF also provided a walk-in sharp freezer for the chickens as soon as they had been dressed but before transport to butcheries. Unfortunately, USADF did not realize the electricity was off more than it was on. During the rainy season, there was no power at all, so the freezer could not be used. HCOC tried operating the sharp freezers with a generator, but the closest source of diesel fuel was Murewa—twenty miles away. The round trip to Murewa for fuel would take a minimum of two-plus hours, and in the rainy season, it could be much longer. This only added to the expenses.

We had visitors one day from LEAD, the company contracted by USADF to monitor projects that they have funded. The gentlemen spent most of the day here, first checking out the poultry project before sitting down to review the books. They were very impressed with what they saw at the poultry project. In fact, they commented on the fact the production had exceeded their estimated goal.

They next spent time checking the books and the system of accounting. There were only some minor changes that they recommended. This involved a new accounting system required by USADF. Charles and Godfrey, who were employed in the finance department at HCOC,

Poultry 269

had received some training. Yesterday, they learned in more detail how to make the system work for them. When I visited with Charles one morning, he felt that their time, while very intense, had been extremely helpful. He has a better handle on how to move forward. Future audits will be much simpler. I am excited to see things evolving, and the future looks promising.

Finally, a new transformer was installed at the new site. USADF has supported the poultry project at HCOC for the past few years by expanding the infrastructure. They provided the poultry project not only with a walk-in sharp freezer and waste disposal but also with a grinding mill. Several new poultry runs were constructed to accommodate 5,000 chickens in each run at one time. The expansion of the project now has the capacity to raise more than 20,000 chickens at one time.

This self-sufficiency is a hallmark of this well-run organization operating within a very poorly-run country. So, as Jesus said in the book of Luke, a hen gathers its chicks and takes care of them, so too, Renewed Hope Charitable Foundation and Zimbabwe Mission Partnership have been taking care of orphans in a similar way—with loving care. What a great picture to visualize the poultry project!

U.S. VISITORS

A man's steps are from the Lord; how then can anyone understand his way.

Proverbs 20:24 (ESV)

Visitors from the U.S. were a rare experience. One year, three board members from the U.S. came to see what was taking place at the mission. They had heard many of our stories. When we finally arrived at the mission, there was no electricity, as was often the case. Thank goodness for our gas lights. Everyone was anxious to get some rest. It had been a long, difficult trip.

Our house was small and seemed much smaller when we had visitors. One of such visitors, a man named Todd, ended up sleeping on the living room floor on an air mattress that ended up not holding air. Poor Todd. We had no patching material. The two ladies, Carol and Deanna, shared the only other room; it served not only as a bedroom but as a storeroom. Everyone was anxious to help, and things worked out well.

Carol was a nurse and so was interested in meeting Beauty, our nurse for the children. I know a visit to Murewa with children who needed to see the doctor was an experience like nothing she had seen before. She had the opportunity to tour the hospital and see how things are done in a third-world country.

Deanna was interested in visiting some of the orphans and seeing their living conditions. They spent most of their day visiting sick orphans and orphans who lived alone with no adult supervision. This gave the visitors an opportunity to see how the rural people live. This was the first of many trips for Deanna. The children captured her heart.

The community members have been busy for several days shelling the maize at HCOC. This work is all done by the women, and it is done by hand. Albert said they had the best crop they have ever had this year. Albert estimated that they would have seven tons of shelled maize.

There was a huge pile of cobs for composting. The compost that they have made is making a huge difference in the garden. The vegetable crops look wonderful. Albert has been keeping me supplied with head lettuce from the garden.

Todd had the opportunity to visit the hospital in Murewa when he joined Albert as he took Mr. Scott to see the doctor. Mr. Scott was our driver and was a huge help to Albert, our manager. Mr. Scott had not been feeling well and had made numerous trips to the doctor in Murewa. His condition was not improving. The doctor said that he needed an ultrasound because the X-rays showed something, but they needed further information. Albert drove him more than fifty kilometers to Musami Hospital for the scan. They had the machine, but their operator had quit. So, Mr. Scott was taken back to the hospital, and plans were made to take Mr. Scott to Marondera to the provincial hospital on Monday the 6th.

On Monday, when Albert arrived at the provincial hospital, he received the same information that he had received from Musami Hospital. They have an ultrasound machine but no operator. So, Albert decided on his own to go to Harare, and he got the ultrasound done at an emergency center. Then, he transported Mr. Scott back to Murewa Hospital. The doctor called Tuesday to say that the tests had shown a growth in his abdomen near the spleen that is fourteen centimeters in diameter. Albert is conferring with the doctor today. I am certain that surgery will be necessary. Whether they will do it in Murewa or send him to Harare depends on what the doctor advises.

Everyone is very concerned about Mr. Scott. For more than one year, he has volunteered his time at HCOC as a driver. He is here early each day. Mr. Scott is the one who hauled river sand from the river for cement mixing or took food supplies to the other feeding centers. It is Mr. Scott who hauled the water for mixing cement or hauled supplies from Harare. He even drove children to the hospital for check-ups. There has been an increased load on Albert for the past three weeks without him.

Todd was interested in things that Ralph was doing but he spent some of his time with the children. The secondary boys seemed to gravitate toward Todd and had many questions for him. Todd developed quite a following.

For the visitors, the week included seeing the site of the new expansion where trenches were being dug for water lines, future buildings were being sited and staked, a tank stand was being built for the water storage tanks, and the managers' new house was part of the tour.

Deanna and Carol visited the Murewa Hospital when some orphans were taken for check-ups. That proved to be a real eye-opener. Our visitors spent most of one day visiting the homes of sick orphans and orphans who live alone with no adult supervision. Not only did they witness how rural people live, but they were able to see the children in their homes. This trip took them over some rough terrain, and they got to see a lot of the area. All had an opportunity to visit the local government clinic. When they arrived, a man had been brought in who had been gored by a bull. The nurses stitched up the wound, and he hobbled out to the waiting oxcart to be taken home.

The visitors saw a lot during their short visit. It is an impactful experience to witness how people in other parts of the world must live.

Vickie, a dear friend and long-time supporter of the mission in Zimbabwe, traveled with me on my trip in 2013. She was interested in seeing what had been happening at the mission over the many years.

One day, I found Vickie in the garden picking tomatoes. We were able to enjoy fresh tomatoes, lettuce, and onions from the garden that supplied vegetables to the kitchens that prepared meals for the orphans. The drip irrigation that was installed recently has made a huge difference in the abundance to be found in the garden.

Vickie and I walked to the secondary school to pay a visit. We were very impressed to see the changes that have taken place. Students were in the classrooms with a teacher present. Students were busy doing assignments. It was a drastic change from the past and one long overdue. We spent time with Morris, the science teacher. He has authored four science textbooks; these texts have been adopted by the government for secondary schools in all of Zimbabwe. He showed us that there was no science equipment or chemicals for experiments in their laboratory. How can this talented teacher properly teach with no equipment or supplies?

U.S. Visitors

How lucky can we get to have such a teacher at our school in a remote area of Zimbabwe? I hope we can keep him, but I am sure he will look for a place with better accommodation and science equipment.

Tom, a member of one of the supporting churches, has traveled to Zimbabwe on several occasions. His focus has been on the Nyamashato Secondary School and particularly on the Science Department. Piped water into the science building is just one of the needs. Gas for the Bunsen burners can be supplied by bottled gas. That is another expense the school will have to struggle to find funds to cover the cost.

Bill and Joyce Imig traveled to Zimbabwe with me on the last trip I was able to take to the mission. Bill is a Rotary member in Denver and had worked diligently to raise funds for an electric dryer for the moringa. The dryer was scheduled to arrive about the time that we made the trip. He and Joyce were present to see the dryer delivered to the processing building that was nearing completion. Unfortunately, their trip was short, and they were not present to see the dryer operating. Bill did have the opportunity to attend a Rotary meeting with Albert. The club Albert is a member of is the club that Ralph attended when he was in Zimbabwe.

ORGANIZING THE COMMUNITY

When he saw the crowds, he had compassion for them, because they
were harassed and helpless, like sheep without a shepherd.

Matthew 9:36 (ESV)

Soon after my arrival back in Zimbabwe, Albert scheduled a meeting
with a group from the community, including the village headmen, orphan
caregivers, all school headmasters and their SDC (School Development
Committees), church leaders of all the faiths represented in the community, local police, and HCOC Executive Committee. About fifty people
turned out. The meeting was for the purpose of discussing the plight of
the orphans that lived among them. When I was asked to speak to the
group, I shared with the group Matthew 25:31–40. There was a short
discussion about how Jesus might view the ignoring of the orphans by
this community. It was decided that seeing was believing. So, a field trip
was quickly organized. Albert arranged for transportation to take all to
visit some child-headed households.

Most of the people knew each other but the group fell silent when
visiting the homes of orphans living on their own. One home that was
visited was a young boy and a blind grandmother. They had no food and
yet people lived within sight of this homestead. Some of the visitors were
stunned, and others had tears in their eyes. How can they live so close
and not know what is happening next door? I overheard one person say,
"I thought I was poor!" The blind grandmother voiced the issues they
faced, and everyone listened.

After the visit, we returned to HCOC, where lunch was served.
Chicken, of course, was the main item on the menu. When the people had
finished eating, Albert broke the people up into small groups to discuss

some of the issues they had witnessed. They were to return to the main group for a time to share what they had discussed in their small group.

Just a few of the suggestions:

One group decided that the churches should take up offerings and pool their money to purchase things needed by the child-headed households. The items would be shared with all the child-headed families, not just the ones they visited. (This would have never happened in the past. This is not something they would think of doing. I see this society as one where every man is for himself.) In all fairness, I must say that I have been told by some of the older people that this was not always the case. But this attitude has developed over the years when life has become extremely difficult. Every man for himself is the current rule. It has become a survival society.

In discussing this with Albert after the meeting, he explained this would not have been necessary in the past. Village headmen and families always took care of those within the family. However, this has all changed due to the increased mobilization of society. Families do not live close by as in the past. I encountered families where the father passed away and left a wife and children. In at least one instance, the mother disappeared, leaving several small children to fend for themselves. I really had a difficult time wrapping my head around this.

Many people are moving to the city, looking for a better life. In some cases, if they have funding, they are even leaving the country. Another contributing factor was the onset of HIV. Parents die at an earlier age, leaving young children to survive on their own. Extended families may not live close by as in the past. If they do live nearby, they are focused on the survival of their own family. Families are also reluctant to take in a member of a family that is known to have AIDS.

Some members of the group suggested tilling the fields for child-headed households or each family in the village contributing a cup of fertilizer or seed, etc. They even suggested working with the children to help them with the weeding of their fields. It was a very positive meeting. A follow-up meeting was scheduled for August 31.

After the initial meeting, churches in the community began working together to help the orphans in this area. They arranged for the kickoff on Thursday, September 6. To accommodate a large crowd, the group decided to hold the event at the Anglican Church in the township.

One church member had already assumed the responsibility of helping orphans in his village get birth certificates. This was a huge step in the right direction. Albert took the gentleman to Murewa with all the documentation he had gathered to date. Albert had arranged an appointment with the Registrar's Office to meet with this individual on behalf of these orphans.

Up to now, extended families have been unwilling to allow these children access to their birth certificates. It is not uncommon for extended families to treat these children as non-existent, especially if the parents died of AIDS. The children are treated as slaves and not even allowed to go to school. Extended families fear these children as though they were evil spirits. Even HCOC has been unable to obtain the birth certificates from relatives for the documentation required to register an orphan. These orphans, without birth certificates, are non-persons. They can't get a job or a driver's license, take their O-level exam (exam taken at the end of secondary school), or even vote when old enough. For this individual to use his influence in his community has been a huge step in the right direction. When one person takes a bold step, others often follow. I pray that this is the first step for greater things to come.

The gathering of the church community was held on Thursday, September 6. The turnout was beyond expectation. The theme for the day was Matthew 25:31–46. It was such a fitting theme for the mission of the day. In Zimbabwe, when there is a church function, everyone dresses in their church uniform. It was easy to identify the various churches represented. However, everyone was unified in the purpose of the day. This was the kickoff of churches getting involved in their respective villages and helping orphans and anyone in need.

On Friday, a provincial meeting was held in Murewa on malaria prevention. When Albert arrived, he was surprised to see that the meeting had copied the theme from the day before, which was, "R U a Sheep or a Goat?"

He was delayed coming home. People who had not known about the gathering at the Madamombe township, where the Anglican Church was located, wanted to be updated on what had taken place. Albert spent a long time answering all the many questions the community had. They were hearing so much about the gathering from those who had attended the meeting at Madamombe township. Some were even proposing that the business community in Murewa sponsor a fundraiser dinner for the benefit of HCOC. This sounds promising. I am hopeful that they will continue to support the project.

That fundraiser took place after our return to the U.S. I don't recall how much money was raised.

GIRLS WITH A DREAM

This God—his way is perfect; the word of the Lord proves true; he is a shield for all those who take refuge in him.

Psalm 18:30 (ESV)

In 2008, there were two girls who spent a lot of time visiting with me. They were completing their primary education and would be going to secondary school at the beginning of the new school year. Tracey liked to write poetry and brought me her notebook so that I could see some of her work. I was very impressed. Petronella often came with Tracey when she came to see me. Petronella was very shy and had little to say. She was a tiny little girl, so petite for her age.

After some time, I learned that they wanted to go to a boarding school, not the local secondary school. We had never considered such a thing. We had no idea about the cost that would be involved.

Mr. Bondeponde was able to guide Ralph and me in the decision-making process. He felt that they were both capable of handling advanced education. Mr. B recommended that Nyahuni Boarding School, located a distance outside Murewa, would be the best place to send them. He told us that it was one of the best boarding schools in the country. Ralph and I finally decided that we could pay their fees, but the mothers would have to purchase the uniforms and provide for other expenses. At this point in time, the exchange rate of U.S. dollars was still very good. A few U.S. dollars would go a long way. We paid their tuition.

At the end of the first term, I received an invitation to attend the award ceremony. Both girls received recognition for numerous things. I was so proud of their successes. At this point, we were playing it one term at a time. They had to excel for us to continue to fund their education. Mr. Bondeponde was a big help by checking in with the girls from time to time. He would report to us on their progress. If I happened to be in the country at awards time, I was always invited to attend the awards event.

Soon after these two girls went to boarding school, it was reported that school attendance began to improve at the local secondary school, and some students took their studies more seriously. Small study groups developed at the secondary school in Ward 1. Lots of time has passed since we sent Tracey and Petronella off to study for their secondary education. Petronella graduated several years ago from a university in Chinhoyi with a bachelor's degree in food processing. Several students have graduated from other universities with various degrees, some of which are in accounting. One student has completed an accounting degree and is employed by Chegutu, a local school not far from Nyamashato.

Petronella apparently has not been able to find a job. I have recently learned that she has come to HCOC and is volunteering her time to work with the garden workers. She indicated she needs to pay back the cost of her education in some way. Her goal is to teach them what she learned at the university about agriculture as it applies to vegetable gardens. They have a large field of cabbages about ready to go to market. This has the potential of raising some funds to keep the garden expanding. It supplies vegetables for the feeding program in addition to having produce to sell.

Many of the children who have been supported for advanced education have graduated or are getting near their time to graduate. Some have found employment, and others are still looking for a job. They are optimistic people, and they don't give up easily. Petronella is an example of this spirit. HCOC is very proud of her support of the orphan program.

STREET CHILDREN

I am not strong enough to dig, and I am ashamed to beg.

Luke 16:3 (ESV)

Not only are there children in the rural area living on their own, but there are also many forgotten children in Harare. Frequently, when Ralph and I were in town, it would be necessary to make a stop at Farm and City, a large hardware and farm store in the center of the city. We encountered many children at stoplights in this area as well as in other high-traffic areas in the city. They would be begging for whatever one would give them. The moment the stop lights turn red, the children would run from the boulevards into the street and go from car to car, begging for coins. Often, some remain between the lanes of traffic even after the stop lights turn green. It is a miracle they are not struck and killed by the density of the traffic.

One child I recall was often seen in this area, as well as other heavy-traffic areas in the city. He always had a blind woman in tow. The woman could be identified by a black felt hat she wore. It is difficult to know whether the woman was the mother or a granny. My best guess is that she was a granny. The child was small and, I assume, very young, but it is often difficult to estimate age by size; so many children are starving, and growth is stunted.

When I questioned people at City Presbyterian Church in Harare about the children begging, I was told that the children, if put in a home where they can be looked after and fed, only about 40 percent remain. The rest of the children would run away and return to the streets. This is based on our experiences in the early years of our trips to Zimbabwe. I would guess it is even more pronounced now.

I recall an experience Ralph and I had one of the early years in Zimbabwe. We arrived early in the city. I don't recall the reason for parking in a high-rise parking structure. We were going in different directions. As I descended the stairs to the street, I noticed a small boy begging for food. He came out from under the stairs. The child was barefooted and wore only a pair of filthy shorts. His skin looked purple, even though he was a black child. It was winter in Zimbabwe. I was wearing a jacket and was hurrying to get inside a building.

What was I to do? I knew I was not to give the child money, and I didn't have any food with me. I had been warned never to give them money. If I did give money, the word would spread, and I would not be safe in the city from that point forward.

Another common sight is mothers, blind or crippled, with very small children and even infants sitting on the sidewalk, begging. It is financially impossible to help all and yet is a person being the priest or the Levite when they pass these people by? This question always troubled me.

The high-density suburbs were initially located a short distance from the business district of Harare. However, by 2018, the last year I was able to travel to Zimbabwe, the beggars and peddlers had moved into the business district of Harare. It was difficult to be able to enter a bank or department store, let alone some of the up-scale hotels. Walking on the sidewalks in that area was not safe. Now, many of the department stores have moved out of the business district or have closed altogether. I have no idea what the banks have done. Even government buildings have been abandoned, and offices have moved to the outskirts of the city.

ORPHANS LIVING ALONE

Fear not, for I am with you; be not dismayed, for I am your God;
I will strengthen you, I will help you, I will uphold you with my
righteous right hand.

Isaiah 41:10 (ESV)

Bill, a visitor, and I joined Albert when he delivered food to an orphan
living several kilometers from the school. The child was not at home, so
I didn't have a chance to visit with the child, who was twelve years old. I
did talk with the grandmother through Albert. The grandmother is blind
and can barely walk. The grandmother said that a granddaughter was out
collecting firewood. This is a case of a child living with a grandparent,
but the grandparent is dependent on the child.

We need safe houses for children such as these. I worked hard to
get an orphan home started with funds donated at the time of Ralph's
passing. The property was surveyed, and a house was pegged. The roads
inside the property were staked at the same time. The house was begun
before I left that year. When I returned the following year, the house was
complete, except for a few finishing touches. Water was piped into the
house, and the bathrooms were functional.

We were ready to house orphans that were being abused where they
were living. Then, we learned the government had strict requirements.
Many of the requirements would not be of direct benefit to the orphans
and seemed totally unnecessary. The financial expenses would have been
on HCOC. It was impossible to meet all of their demands. We had to
leave the children in their existing living situation instead of putting them
in clean, safe accommodations.

Later in the week, before our visitors left to return to Colorado,
we visited some child-headed households. One stop was made at the

home of two boys who were living alone. We checked to see what food supplies they had and left items they needed. The boys, with the help of a local man, were trying to improve their living conditions. A new roof on their rondavel was under construction. Albert suggested that we help by supplying a window and a door since they have neither. We took care of that issue.

Note that I mentioned a local man was helping the two boys who lived at this location. I want to point out that in the past, this would never have happened. Helping anyone outside the immediate family was unheard of. Our message was finally getting through to the community. We began to see people in the community stepping up to help the orphans.

When Susan, a ZMP board member, paid a visit one year, she was anxious to visit a child-headed household. During her stay, Albert drove her to visit Innocent, a child living alone. He was only fifteen years old and lived in a one-room structure. It was in a serious state of decline and in danger of crumbling away. When asked about any problems he had, he said that the house leaked when it rained, and he wanted space so his young sister could live with him. He got lonely living alone. My heart goes out to these children. Despite everything, his room was neat and as clean as possible under the circumstances. There was a tomato plant growing by the door, and he had a hen and baby chicks in a confined area. Innocent told us that when he needs money for school fees or food, he sells a chicken when they get big enough.

The boy reported to Albert, not long after our visit, that when he returned from school, he found that the hen and all the baby chicks, except one, had been stolen. This broke my heart. I can't understand this, and then I think of those in the community who are hungry and have no way of providing for their family. Perhaps it causes people to take drastic steps.

There was a new toilet building on-site. Some of the neighbors had gotten together and built the structure. HCOC had provided the materials. Construction had paused because they were waiting for the delivery of cement. Some people were learning to help one another. This was an encouraging sign.

When I returned the following year, a new two-room house had been built with the help of neighbors. It was nearing completion. HCOC provided the roofing materials. Innocent was so excited to finally have a sound structure. He was looking forward to his young sister joining him. When we arrived, Innocent was washing up the dishes from feeding the people working on his new house. He seemed so very happy.

Rodders is one of two boys who live alone. William, the older brother, was not at home when we paid a visit. Rodders had lunch ready and was waiting for William to return. We were pleased to find mosquito netting hanging in the place where they sleep at night.

HCOC keeps a supply of netting on hand to provide for children who have a need for such. When asked what the greatest challenges were, he explained that while they were at school one day, someone broke in and stole the battery out of their solar light. Now, they use small bunches of grass that they light. *How safe is that?* I struggle when I think of people stealing from an orphan that has so little. Life in Zimbabwe is not easy at best. For these children, it is a real struggle to just survive. I need to add that we are working in just one Ward. It is only a drop in the bucket of the children in need in all of Zimbabwe. *So much need!*

People have challenged us in the past. They wonder, with the need here in our own country, why do we find it necessary to go halfway around the world to work in Zimbabwe? There is only one answer. God called us to go!

RELIGIOUS TRAINING FOR THE CHILDREN

Train up a child in the way he should go; even when he is old he will
not depart from it.

Proverbs 22:6 (ESV)

During Susan's visit, we had the opportunity to visit the Methodist
church on the Nyamashato School grounds. The church was packed; I
couldn't recall ever seeing so many children in attendance. It was truly
a welcome sight. Later, it was explained that the credit was given to the
pastors who visit each school on a weekly basis. They told us that there
were many children attending all the churches in the area. The pastors
for the local churches had gotten together and came to us proposing to
donate their time in meeting with the orphans. We felt blessed.

During a service at the Methodist church on the school property,
much time was devoted to all that Ralph had done for the church, the
schools, and the community. The church observed that it was just three
years ago that Ralph had passed away. The people will never forget him.
Two of the three pastors came to meet with Parker, Susie, and me. Parker
is a retired pastor. He and Susie had come to visit the mission. The local
pastors are working together with Rev. Gumunyu to develop the spiritual
education of the children in Ward 1. They plan to break the children
into groups according to age, and each pastor will work with one of the
groups, doing activities that are age appropriate. I was pleased to see the
progress made since I was here last year. The pastors are asking for no
compensation, only help with fuel for transportation.

I felt we were finally set for religious training for the children who chose
to attend the sessions held by the pastors. However, it seemed not to be
consistent. Fuel for transportation was an issue, or a vehicle would break
down. I was not comfortable with the sporadic lessons for the children.

Finally, in 2017, a local individual was brought to my attention. He had taken numerous Bible classes at a university. He was a member of the local community. Albert brought Stewart Marufu to meet me. During our initial meeting, Stewart had come prepared with his Bible and his resume. Susan had traveled with me and was involved with the interview we had with Stewart. When I requested to see his Bible, he opened it and handed it to me. His Bible was well-worn, with notations written everywhere. It was obvious that his Bible was well-loved and frequently used. After that initial visit, Stewart and I had many long visits about the future of the children. This friendship allowed me to know Stewart well and his Christian beliefs.

Stewart was hired to be the religious leader of the mission. A motorbike was purchased for his use in traveling to the various schools in Ward 1. He meets the children at each school on a rotating basis. All the children enrolled at each school attend his meetings, not just the orphans. It has made an enormous difference in the behavior of the children. When visitors from the U.S. visit HCOC, they frequently accompany Stewart on his motorbike and that is always a highlight of their time at HCOC. As visitors ride to the various schools on the back of Stewart's motorbike, the children they pass on the dirt roads will wave and greet them as they go by. During the opening lessons that Stewart gives at each of the schools, the children are reminded they are loved by God and their lives matter. In addition, the children are encouraged to treat each other kindly and to show their respect for their teachers.

The teachers frequently comment on improved behavior in specific children. In fact, one of the headmasters made a point of telling a U.S. visitor that the impact of Stewart's lessons has been significant. Stewart has been a true blessing. He has been a loyal friend to the U.S. visitors and is a champion for the HCOC orphans and the community he serves.

Stewart travels throughout the catchment area of HCOC by motorbike. He travels to the individual homes of the children, especially orphans. They participate in their very own Bible lesson taught by Stewart. Susan was able to accompany Stewart on one of these trips.

There is a story I'd like to share about an orphan served by HCOC that further illustrates the impact that Stewart has on the orphans at HCOC. I'll call the child Frank, who is one of nineteen children currently being raised by his grandmother, who they call Gogo in Zimbabwe. Prior to coming to HCOC, Frank and his siblings were homeless in Harare. They were living on the streets of Harare. The conditions the children lived under were unimaginable. The children were reunited with their Gogo during COVID-19. Somehow, they all found their way to the rural area and were living and attending school in Ward 1, the location of HCOC. Stewart traveled to their home, where the children participated in their very own Bible lesson taught by Stewart.

While Stewart was delivering his lesson to Frank and his siblings, I noticed that a small boy retrieved a ball. Then, at the end of the lesson, Stewart asked questions about the lesson (i.e., name a famous man from the Bible). He would ask the question and then toss the ball to a child to answer. The children were excellent at answering his questions and paid attention to what he was saying because they knew he might throw the ball to them. I am sure these visits by Stewart were highlights for the children. Frank followed along diligently with Stewart and actively participated in this lesson. He was eager to learn and tried very hard. HCOC was involved in helping this family build a new structure that became their home.

On another occasion, Stewart was with a group of children at Inyagui when we visited. They had just finished their breakfast. They, along with the rest of the student body and teachers, gathered in the assembly area for a time of worship. I was pleased to see how quickly they responded to Stewart's questions after Stewart delivered a brief message. Stewart originally met with only the orphans. However, the rest of the children felt they were missing out on something. So, now, all the children and even the staff attend his sessions. He has been such a blessing to the mission in Zimbabwe.

Small red Bibles were given to the children that were present. Stewart explained to the children to always carry the Bibles in their pockets. Whenever they had a need or felt discouraged, they were to take out the little Bible and look for a scripture that spoke to their needs. The Bibles had been donated by a friend in Colorado and shipped to Zimbabwe.

In addition to ministering to the children at the schools in Ward 1, Stewart is actively involved in our joint prayer time held on the last Saturday of each month. We are now able to meet by way of Zoom.

This is such a blessing. Board members here who are unable to travel to Zimbabwe can see and interact with Stewart, whom they hear individuals talk about.

Stewart prays earnestly on behalf of the U.S. prayer requests, as well as prayer needs at HCOC. He frequently provides inspiring thoughts and comforting scriptures when his U.S. friends encounter a personal setback or tragedy. He is an inspiration to all, and his impact on orphan lives has been profound.

NEW CLINIC

The Lord sustains him on his sickbed; in his illness you restore him to full health.

Psalm 41:3 (ESV)

In 2018, the clinic for HCOC continued to operate out of the small rooms at the school. This was necessary because there was no facility at the new HCOC site to care for ill children. On my last trip to Zimbabwe, the ZMP received a grant to go toward a new clinic at the HCOC site. This would finally relieve some of the congestion at Nyamashato Primary School, where this project had begun. It also meant that Beauty would not have to walk a distance to go to work at the clinic.

The ground for the clinic was broken in late May 2018. Just digging the trenches for the foundation took many weeks. I was anxious but could see that the work was difficult. I felt for the workmen doing the work. In our country, when a building is started, machinery is brought in to do the digging. This is not true in a third-world country, especially in a remote area where the mission is located. Once the footings are dug, an inspector must come to approve the work before they can proceed with pouring cement. This, sometimes, took a while to get someone there. Usually, Albert would have to drive to Murewa to transport the individual to the site. Another trip would be necessary to take the individual back to Murewa.

The digging of footings continued and went on and on. Albert recommended to the builder that they bring in more help to do the digging. That sped up the process a great deal, but it should have begun sooner. Some workers assemble rebar that goes in the footings before the cement is poured. This step needed to be inspected by the building department before they were given the go-ahead to pour the cement footings for the new structure.

Pouring footings is another slow process. There are no cement trucks that drive up and dump their load where needed. The cement is mixed by hand and then shoveled into the trench that has been dug. This is a lot of back-breaking work and a slow process. It took many days to complete this stage. At the end of each day, the workers had to let the cement run out so that the following day, the workers would have a place to overlap the pour for the new day.

The footings were completed and backfilled before I left Zimbabwe in 2018. From that point, the project steadily moved forward. The facility was finally completed and opened for business. This was years after the footings were dug. Part of the delay was COVID-19 and the shutdown of all work for about two years. Death still happens, and as I mentioned elsewhere, all work stops when there is a funeral in the area.

Beauty no longer needs to walk to Nyamashato to the first aid station there. She is only a short walk from her house to the clinic on HCOC property. It has been necessary to hire additional nurses to handle the number of patients that come to the new clinic. Beauty is often not at the clinic. It is necessary for her to visit the neighboring schools in order to check on the children who may need her attention.

EPILOGUE

I haven't written all the stories that I could have told. There were just too many stories. This book happened because so many people told me that I needed to write a book. I had no idea where to begin or how to go about this. I didn't consider myself to be an author and I still don't. My friend Kathy had just published a book, and I asked her to write my story. We spent many hours together, but I wasn't very much help. I had much difficulty talking about our years in Africa. Finally, I decided that it was my story, and only I could really tell it.

Kathy has continued to be very supportive and has made many suggestions as she has read what I have written. Without her, this would have turned out very differently. I am eternally grateful for her support.

Susan, a dear friend, has been supportive behind the scenes as well. She has been encouraging and has read much of the book and offered suggestions along the way. I would have given up many times if it had not been for her encouraging words.

So, you have just completed reading my story. It is about how my husband and I filled our retirement years by doing mission work that was never on our bucket list. We had planned to build our retirement home and then travel the world while we were physically able. We traveled many thousands of miles, and we had the privilege of seeing many things but not in the way we had envisioned.

God had a different plan! Now that I have had time to reflect on what we did, I would not change it. I would like to add that we never worked harder in our lives, not even when we were building our retirement home. We learned so much and touched the lives of so many children. Seeing the children succeed without families was our reward. Many of the children would not have survived without our intervention or even received an education. Some have even graduated from various universities. One is presently a professor at a university in Zimbabwe.

We were not planning on doing mission work when we left on that first trip to Zimbabwe. Our plan was to help on the first trip and perhaps, if needed, to go back one more year if there were other issues that needed attention. After two years, we saw the extent of the need, and there was no way to not go back. So, our original plans were put on hold. God knew!

We were not fundraisers, but money came in when we needed it. In other words, God provided. Our friends were big supporters, and I am humbled by their generosity. Ralph had always been a very generous person. I am sad to report that most of our big supporters have passed away, and so has Ralph. A pastor friend, who initially worked diligently to help raise funds, has passed on as well.

Now, it is necessary to pass the torch to younger people. Much work remains, and I can no longer travel. I can only imagine what amazing things lay ahead for the people who have committed their time to this work.

Susan has traveled several times to the mission in Zimbabwe. Two of those trips were with me when I was still traveling there. She has been very encouraging and has proofread much of what I have written. Her suggestions have been spot-on. I appreciate her input and the time she devoted to this project.

As I look back at all the stories and the ways in which people's lives were changed, I am humbled to know that God used my husband Ralph and me in this incredible mission journey. When I think of the alternative (first) plan I realize how much *better* was God's plan for our lives. That is probably the theme of this book. I am adding some scriptures to close my thoughts about our creator, God, and how He wants to use us.

Jeremiah 29:11 (ESV), "For I know the plans I have for you, declares the Lord, plans for welfare and not for evil, to give you a future and a hope."

Proverbs 19:21 (ESV), "Many are the plans in the mind of a man, but it is the purpose of the Lord that will stand."

Proverbs 3:5–6 (ESV), "Trust in the LORD with all your heart, and do not lean on your own understanding. In all your ways acknowledge him, and he will make straight your paths."

When God asked Moses to lead His people from captivity in Egypt, Moses said, "Not me—I cannot speak very well," so God gave him the words to say. In fact, God gave him the entire story of the first five books of the Bible way up on Mount Sinai. How amazing is that? God can use each of us if we listen to our hearts and the Holy Spirit that dwells in us. I hope you can see the "strands of God's work" in our lives in this book.

To God be the glory!

AFTERWORD

Would you consider making a tax-deductible donation to Renewed Hope Charitable Foundation (RHCF)? We are struggling to continue to meet the needs of children. Many of these children have no one to be their advocate. Without our intervention, some of these children will perish. Children were perishing years ago when we first began this mission. With your help, this tragedy will not be repeated. I deeply appreciate your support.

To God be the glory!

—Roberta Pippitt

Donations can be mailed to:
RHCF—PO Box 1476—Castle Rock, Colorado—80104.

Or, scan the barcode below, and you will be taken directly to our website (renewed-hope.org), where you can make your tax-exempt donation.

SCAN ME

Printed in the USA
CPSIA information can be obtained
at www.ICGtesting.com
CBHW051953121124
17306CB00002B/2